True Tilc

Arthur Quiller-Couch

Alpha Editions

This edition published in 2024

ISBN : 9789362097842

Design and Setting By
Alpha Editions
www.alphaedis.com
Email - info@alphaedis.com

As per information held with us this book is in Public Domain.
This book is a reproduction of an important historical work. Alpha Editions uses the best technology to reproduce historical work in the same manner it was first published to preserve its original nature. Any marks or number seen are left intentionally to preserve its true form.

Contents

CHAPTER I ....- 1 -
CHAPTER II ....- 8 -
CHAPTER III ....- 17 -
CHAPTER IV ....- 27 -
CHAPTER V ....- 33 -
CHAPTER VI ....- 40 -
CHAPTER VII. ....- 45 -
CHAPTER VIII. ....- 52 -
CHAPTER IX. ....- 59 -
CHAPTER X. ....- 68 -
CHAPTER XI. ....- 74 -
CHAPTER XII. ....- 83 -
CHAPTER XIII. ....- 91 -
CHAPTER XIV. ....- 98 -
CHAPTER XV. ....- 107 -
CHAPTER XVI. ....- 117 -
CHAPTER XVII. ....- 126 -
CHAPTER XVIII. ....- 134 -
CHAPTER XIX. ....- 143 -
CHAPTER XX. ....- 157 -
CHAPTER XXI. ....- 167 -
CHAPTER XXII. ....- 175 -
CHAPTER XXIII. ....- 186 -
CHAPTER XXIV. ....- 193 -
CHAPTER XXV. ....- 204 -
CHAPTER XXVI. ....- 214 -
EPILOGUE ....- 220 -

CHAPTER I

AT THE SIGN OF THE GOOD SAMARITAN

"That it may please Thee to preserve all that travel by land or by water . . . all sick persons, and young children."—THE LITANY.

"I love my love with a H'aitch, because he's 'andsome—"

Tilda turned over on her right side—she could do so now without pain—and lifting herself a little, eyed the occupant of the next bed. The other six beds in the ward were empty.

"I 'ate 'im, because—look 'ere, I don't believe you're listenin'?"

The figure in the next bed stirred feebly; the figure of a woman, straight and gaunt under the hospital bedclothes. A tress of her hair had come uncoiled and looped itself across the pillow—reddish auburn hair, streaked with grey. She had been brought in, three nights ago, drenched, bedraggled, chattering in a high fever; a case of acute pneumonia. Her delirium had kept Tilda—who was preternaturally sharp for her nine years—awake and curious during the better part of two night-watches. Thereafter, for a day and a night and half a day, the patient had lain somnolent, breathing hard, at intervals feebly conscious. In one of these intervals her eyes had wandered and found the child; and since then had painfully sought her a dozen times, and found her again and rested on her.

Tilda, meeting that look, had done her best. The code of the show-folk, to whom she belonged, ruled that persons in trouble were to be helped. Moreover, the long whitewashed ward, with its seven oblong windows set high in the wall—the smell of it, the solitude, the silence—bored her inexpressibly. She had lain here three weeks with a hurt thigh-bone bruised, but luckily not splintered, by the kick of a performing pony.

The ward reeked of yellow soap and iodoform. She would have exchanged these odours at the price of her soul—but souls are not vendible, and besides she did not know she possessed one—for the familiar redolences of naphtha and horse-dung and trodden turf. These were far away: they had quite forsaken her, or at best floated idly across her dreams. What held her to fortitude had been the drone and intermittent hoot of a steam-organ many streets away. It belonged to a roundabout, and regularly tuned up towards evening; so distant that Tilda could not distinguish one tune from another; only the thud of its bass mingled with the buzz of a fly on the window and with the hard breathing of the sick woman.

Sick persons must be amused: and Tilda, after trying the patient unsuccessfully with a few jokes from the *repertoire* of her own favourite clown, had fallen back upon "I love my love"—about the only game known to her that dispensed with physical exertion.

"Sleepin', are you? . . . Well, I'll chance it and go on. I 'ate 'im because he's 'aughty—or 'igh-born, if you like—"

The figure beneath the bedclothes did not stir. Tilda lifted herself an inch higher on the elbow; lifted her voice too as she went on:

"And I'll take 'im to—'OLMNESS—"

She had been watching, expecting some effect. But it scared her when, after a moment, the woman raised herself slowly, steadily, until half-erect from the waist. A ray of the afternoon sun fell slantwise from one of the high windows, and, crossed by it, her eyes blazed like lamps in their sockets.

"—And feed 'im on 'am!" concluded Tilda hurriedly, slipping down within her bedclothes and drawing them tight about her. For the apparition was stretching out a hand. The hand drew nearer.

"It's—it's a name came into my 'ead," quavered the child.

"Who . . . told . . . you?" The fingers of the hand had hooked themselves like a bird's claw.

"Told me yerself. I 'eard you, night before last, when you was talkin' wild. . . . If you try to do me any 'arm, I'll call the Sister."

"Holmness?"

"*You* said it. Strike me dead if you didn'!" Tilda fetched a grip on herself; but the hand, its fingers closing on air, drew back and dropped, as though cut off from the galvanising current. She had even presence of mind to note that the other hand—the hand on which the body propped itself, still half-erect, wore a plain ring of gold. "You talked a lot about 'Olmness—and Arthur. 'Oo's Arthur?"

But the patient had fallen back, and lay breathing hard. When she spoke again all the vibration had gone out of her voice.

"Tell them . . . Arthur . . . fetch Arthur . . . ." The words tailed off into a whisper. Still the lips moved as though speech fluttered upon them; but no speech came.

"You just tell me where he is, and maybe we'll fetch 'im," said Tilda encouragingly.

The eyes, which had been fixed on the child's, and with just that look you may note in a dog's eyes when he waits for his master's word, wandered to the table by the bedside, and grew troubled, distressful.

"Which of 'em?" asked Tilda, touching the medicine bottles and glasses there one by one.

But the patient seemed to shake her head, though with a motion scarcely perceptible.

She could talk no more.

Tilda lay back thinking.

"Sister!" she said, twenty minutes later, when the Second Nurse entered the ward. The Second Nurse had charge just now, the matron being away on her August holiday.

"Well, dear?"

"She wants something." Tilda nodded towards the next bed.

"To be sure she does, and I'm going to give it to her." The Second Nurse, composed in all her movements, bent over the medicine table.

"Garn!" retorted Tilda. "It's easy seen you wasn' brought up along with animals. Look at the eyes of her."

"Well?" The Second Nurse, after a long look at the patient, turned to Tilda again.

"You mind my tellin' you about Black Sultan?"

"Of course I do. He was the one with the bearing rein and the white martingale. Miss Montagu rode him."

"Right-O!" Tilda nodded. "Well, they used to come on next turn to mine, which was the Zambra Fambly, as before the Crowned 'eads—only there wasn' no fambly about it, nor yet no 'eads. Me bein' 'andy an' dressed up, with frizzy 'air, they stood me on a tub with a 'oop, makin' believe 'twas for Miss Montagu to jump through; but of course she didn', reely. When she came round to me she'd only smile and touch me playful under the chin; and that made the sixpenny seats say, "Ow womanly!' or, 'Only think! able to ride like that and so fond of children!' Matter of fact, she 'ad none; and her 'usband, Mike O'Halloran, used to beat her for it sometimes, when he'd had a drop of What-killed-Aunty. He was an Irishman."

"You didn't start to tell me about Mr. O'Halloran."

"No. He wasn' your sort at all; and besides, he's dead. But about Black Sultan—Miss Montagu used to rest 'im, 'alf-way in his turn, while the clown they called Bimbo—but his real name was Ernest Stanley—as't a riddle about a policeman and a red 'errin' in a newspaper. She always rested alongside o' me; and I always stood in the same place, right over a ring-bolt where they made fast one of the stays for the trapeze; and regular as Black Sultan rested, he'd up with his off hind foot and rub the pastern-bone, very soft, on the ring-bolt. So one day I unscrewed an' sneaked it, jus' to see what he'd do. When he felt for it an' missed it, he gave me a look. That's all. An' that's what's the matter with '*er*."

"But what can she be missing?" asked the Second Nurse. "She had nothing about her but an old purse, and nothing in the purse but a penny-ha'penny."

"It don't sound much, but we might try it."

"Nonsense!" said the Second Nurse; but later in the evening she brought the purse, and set it on the table where the patient's eyes might rest on it. For aught she could detect, they expressed no thanks, gave no flicker of recognition. But the child had been watching them too, and was quicker—by one-fifth of a second, perhaps.

It was half-past eight, and the sister turned low the single gas-jet. She would retire now to her own room, change her dress for the night-watching, and return in about twenty minutes. The door had no sooner closed upon her than Tilda stretched out a hand. The sick woman watched, panting feebly, making no sign. The purse—a cheap thing, stamped with forget-me-nots, and much worn at the edges where the papier-mache showed through its sham leather—contained a penny and a halfpenny; these, and in an inner stamp-pocket a scrap of paper, folded small, and greasy with handling.

Still peering across in the dim light, Tilda undid the broken folds and scrambled up to her knees on the bed. It cost her a twinge of pain, but only by standing upright on the bed's edge could she reach the gas-bracket to turn the flame higher. This meant pain sharper and more prolonged, yet she managed it, and, with that, clenched her teeth hard to keep down a cry. The child could swear, on occasion, like a trooper; but this was a fancy accomplishment. Just now, when an oath would have come naturally to a man, she felt only a choking in the throat, and swallowed it down with a sob.

On the paper were four lines, written in pencil in a cramped hand; and, alas! though Tilda could read print, she had next to no acquaintance with handwriting.

The words were a blur to her. She stared at them; but what she saw was the gaze of the sick woman, upturned to her from the bed. The scrap of paper hid it, and yet she saw. She must act quickly.

She gave a reassuring nod, turned the gas-jet low, and slid down into bed with the paper clenched in her hand. But as her head touched the pillow she heard a rustling noise, and craned up her neck again. The patient had rolled over on her left side, facing her, fighting for breath.

"Yes, yes," Tilda lied hardily. "To-morrow—Arthur—they shall send for him to-morrow."

"Four," said the sick woman. The word was quite distinct. Another word followed which Tilda could not catch.

"Four o'clock, or may be earlier," she promised.

"L—l—lozenges," the tongue babbled.

Tilda glanced towards the medicine table.

"Diamonds," said the voice with momentary firmness; "four diamonds . . . on his coat . . . his father's . . . his . . . ."

"Four diamonds, yes?" the child repeated.

"Ned did them . . . he told me . . . told me . . . ." But here the voice wavered and trailed off into babble, meaningless as a year-old infant's. Tilda listened hard for a minute, two minutes, then dropped her head back on her pillow as the door-handle rattled. It was the Second Nurse returning for night duty.

Early next morning the doctor came—a thin young man with a stoop, and a crop of sandy hair that stood upright from his forehead. Tilda detested him.

He and the Second Nurse talked apart for quite a long while, and paid no attention to the child, who lay shamming a doze, but with her ears open.

She heard the doctor say—

"She? Oh, move her to the far end of the ward."

The Second Nurse muttered something, and he went on—

"She is well, practically. All she wants now is someone to keep an eye on her, make her lie up for a couple of hours every day, and box her ears if she won't."

"That's me," thought Tilda. "I'm to be moved out of the way because t'other's going to die; and if she's going to die, there's no time to be lost."

She stirred, lifted her head, and piped—

"Doctor!"

"Hullo, imp! I thought you were sleeping."

"So I was. I sleep 'eaps better now." She drew her hurt leg up and down in the bed. "Doctor, I 'd be all right, certain sure, if you let me out for arf-an-hour. Sister let me sit out for ever so long yestiday, an' while she was dustin' out the men's ward I practised walkin'—all the lenth of the room an' back."

"When I told you never, on any account!" the Sister scolded.

"If I'd only the loan of a crutch!" pleaded Tilda; "an' it couldn' do me no 'arm in this weather."

"Pining for liberty, hey?" said the doctor. (She saw what was passing through his mind, and despised him for it.) "Well, suppose, now, we let you out for just half an hour?"

Tilda clapped her palms together, and her eyes shone. To herself she said: "Kiddin' of me, that's what they are. Want to get me out of the way while they shift the beddin'. Lemme get back my clothes, that's all, an' I'll teach him about pinin' for liberty."

"But," said the doctor severely, lifting a finger, "you're to keep to the pavement mind—just outside, where it's nice and shady. Only so far as the next turning and back; no crossing anywhere or getting in the way of traffic, and only for half an hour. The chimes from St. Barnabas will tell you, if you can't read the clock."

She had learnt to read the time before she was five years old, and had a mind to tell him, but checked herself and merely nodded her head.

"Half an hour, and the pavement only. Is that understood?"

"Honest!"

It annoyed her—when, an hour later, she began to dress for the adventure—to find herself weaker than she had at all supposed. Although she forbore to mention it to the Second Nurse, there was an irresponsible funny feeling in her legs. They seemed to belong to her but by fits and starts. But the clothes were hers: the merino skirt a deal too short for her—she had grown almost an inch in her bed-lying— the chip hat, more badly crushed than ever, a scandal of a hat, but still hers. The dear, dear clothes! She held them in both hands and nuzzled into them, inhaling her lost self in the new-old scent of liberty.

When at length her hat was donned, the notion took her to stand by the sick woman's bed to show herself.

Consciousness had drained away deep into the sick woman's eyes. It wavered there darkly, submerged, half-suspended, as you may see the weed waver in a dim seapool. Did a bubble, a gleam, float up from the depths? At any rate, the child nodded bravely.

"Goin' to fetch 'im, don't you fret!"

CHAPTER II

HOW TRUE TILDA CAME TO DOLOROUS GARD

"Dauntless the slug-horn to my lips I set. And blew 'Childe Roland to the Dark Tower came.'" BROWNING.

Fifty years before, the Hospital of the Good Samaritan had been the pet "charity" of a residential suburb. Factories and slums had since crowded in upon it, ousting the residents and creeping like a tide over the sites of their gardens and villas. The street kept its ancient width, and a few smoke-blackened trees—lilacs, laburnums, limes, and one copper-beech—still dignified the purlieus. Time, ruthless upon these amenities, had spared, and even enlarged, the hospital.

It stood on the shaded side of the street. Nevertheless, the sunshine, reflected from the facade of mean houses across the way, dazzled Tilda as she crossed the threshold of the great doorway and hopped down the steps. There were five steps, and on the lowest she paused, leaning a moment on her crutch before taking the final plunge into liberty.

Then, while she stood blinking, of a sudden a yellowish brown body bounded at her out of the sun-dazzle, pushed her tottering, danced back, and leapt at her again, springing to lick her face, and uttering sharp, inarticulate noises from a throat bursting with bliss.

"'Dolph! O 'Dolph!"

Tilda sank on the lowest step and stretched out both arms. The dog, rushing between them, fairly bowled her backwards; lit in her lap and twisted his body round ecstatically, thrusting, nuzzling at her bosom, her neck, her face—devouring her with love. In her weakness she caught him around the chest, close behind the forelegs, and hugged him to her. So for a quarter of a minute the two rocked together and struggled.

"'Dolph! O good dog! . . . Did Bill send yer?"

'Dolph, recoiling, shook his neck-ruff and prepared for another spring; but Tilda pushed him back and stood up. "Take me along to him," she commanded, and lifted her face impudently to the clock-face of St. Barnabas above the mean roofs. "Barnabas, are yer? Then give my compliments to the doctor, you Barnabas, an' tell 'im to cheese it." 'Dolph—short for Godolphus—pricked both ears and studied the sky-line. Perceiving nothing there—not even a swallow to be chased—he barked twice (the humbug!) for sign that he understood thoroughly, and at once fell to new capers by way of changing the subject. Tilda became severe. "Look here, Godolphus," she explained, "this is biz-strict biz. You may wag your silly Irish tail, but that don't take *me* in. Understand? . . . Well, the first thing you 'ave to do is take me to Bill."

Godolphus was dashed; hurt, it may be, in his feelings. Being dumb, he could not plead that for three weeks daily he had kept watch on the hospital door; that, hungry, he had missed his meals for faith, which is the substance of things unseen; that, a few hours ago, having to choose between half-gods assured and whole gods upon trust—an almost desperate trust—he had staked against the odds. Or, it may be, he forgot all this, and only considered what lay ahead for the child. At any rate, his tail, as he led the way, wagged at a sensibly lower angle.

"Bill can read any kind of 'andwriting," said Tilda, half to herself and half to the dog. "What's more, and whatever's the matter, Bill 'elps."

So she promised herself. It did not strike her that 'Dolph—who in an ordinary way should have been bounding ahead and anon bounding back to gyrate on his hind legs and encourage her—preferred to trot ahead some thirty or forty yards and wait for her to overtake him; nor that, when she came up, he avoided her eyes, pretending that here a doorstep, there a grating or water-main absorbed his curiosity. Once or twice, indeed, before trotting off again, he left these objects of interest to run around Tilda's heels and rub against her crutch. But she was busy with her own plans.

So through a zig-zag of four or five dingy streets they came to one she recognised as that leading into the Plain, or open space where the show-people encamped. At its far end 'Dolph halted. His tail still wagged, but his look was sidelong, furtive, uneasy.

Tilda, coming up with him, stood still for a moment, stared, and caught her breath with a little gasp of dismay.

The Plain was empty.

Circus and menagerie, swing-boats, roundabouts, shooting-galleries—all were gone. The whole area lay trampled and bare, with puddles where the steam-engines had stood, and in the puddles bedabbled relics of paper brushes, confetti bags, scraps torn from feminine flounces, twisted leaden tubes of "ladies' tormentors" cast away and half-trodden into the mire; the whole an unscavenged desolation. Her folk—the show-folk—had deserted her and vanished, and she had not a penny in her pocket. It cost Tilda all her pluck to keep what she called a tight upper lip. She uttered no cry, but seated herself on the nearest doorstep— apparently with deliberation, actually not heeding, still less caring, to whom the doorstep belonged.

"Oh, 'Dolph!" she murmured.

To her credit, in the act of appealing to him, she understood the dog's heroism, and again stretched forth her arms. He had been waiting for this—sprang at her, and again was caught and hugged. Again the two forlorn ones rocked in an embrace.

Brief ecstasy! The door behind them was constructed in two portions, of which the upper stood wide, the lower deceptively on the latch. Against this, as she struggled with Godolphus's ardour, Tilda gave a backward lurch. It yielded, flew open, and child and dog together rolled in across the threshold, while a shop-bell jangled madly above them.

"Get out of this—you and your nasty cur!"

Tilda picked up herself and her crutch, and stood eyeing the shopwoman, who, summoned by the bell, had come rushing from an inner room, and in no sweet temper. From the woman she glanced around the shop— a dairy-shop with a marble-topped counter, and upon the counter a pair of scales and a large yellow block of margarine.

"It was a naccident," said Tilda firmly and with composure. "And my dog isn' a nasty cur; it only shows your ignorance. Be quiet, 'Dolph!"

She had to turn and shake her crutch at Godolphus, who, perceiving his mistress's line of action, at once, in his impulsive Irish way, barked defiance at the shopwoman.

But the shopwoman's eyes rested on the crutch, and the sight of it appeared to mollify her.

"My gracious! I do believe you 're the child was hurt at Maggs's Circus and taken to hospital."

Tilda nodded.

"Did you see me?"

"Carried by on a stretcher—and your face the colour of *that*."
The woman pointed to the marble counter-top.

"I was a serious case," said Tilda impressively. "The people at the Good Samaritan couldn' remember admittin' the likes of it. There were complications."

"You don't say!"

"But what's become of Maggs's?"

"Maggs's left a week ago come Tuesday. I know, because they used to buy their milk of me. They were the first a'most, and the last was the Menagerie and Gavel's Roundabouts. *They* packed up last night. It must be a wearin' life," commented the shopwoman. "But for my part I like the shows, and so I tell Damper—that's my 'usband. They put a bit of colour into the place while they last, besides bein' free-'anded with their money. Light come light go, I reckon; but anyway, it's different from cows. So you suffered from complications, did you?"

"Internal," Tilda assured her in a voice as hollow as she could make it. "I must have spit up a quart of blood, first an' last. An' the medicine I 'ad to take! You wouldn' think it, but the colour was pale 'eliotrope."

"I wonder," said Mrs. Damper sympathetically—"I wonder it stayed in the stomach."

"It didn'."

"Wouldn' you fancy a glass o' milk, now?"

"It's very kind of you." Tilda put on her best manners. "And 'ere's 'ealth!" she added before sipping, when the milk was handed to her.

"And the dog—wouldn' '*e* like something?"

"Well, since you mention it—but it's givin' you a 'eap of trouble. If you 'ave such a thing as a bun, it don't matter 'ow stale."

"I can do better 'n that." Mrs. Damper dived into the inner room, and re-emerged with a plateful of scraps. "There's always waste with children," she explained, "and I got five. You can't think the load off one's shoulders when they're packed to school at nine o'clock. And that, I dessay," she wound up lucidly, "is what softened me t'ards you. Do you go to school, now?"

"Never did," answered Tilda, taking the plate and laying it before Godolphus, who fell-to voraciously.

"I 'd like to tell that to the attendance officer," said Mrs. Damper in a wistful tone. "But p'r'aps it might get you into trouble?"

"You 're welcome."

"He do give me a lot of worry; and it don't make things easier Damper's threatenin' to knock his 'ead off if ever he catches the man darkenin' our door. Never been to school, aven't you? I 'd like to tell 'im, and that, if there's a law, it ought to be the same for all. But all my children are 'ealthy, and that's one consolation."

"'Ealth's the first thing in life," agreed Tilda. "So they've all cleared out?—the shows, I mean."

"Every one—exceptin' the Theayter."

"Mortimer's?" Tilda limped to the open door. "But I don't see him, neither."

"Mortimer's is up the spout. First of all, there was trouble with the lodgings; and on top of that, last Monday, Mr. Hucks put the bailiffs in. This mornin' he sent half a dozen men, and they took the show to pieces and carried it off to Hucks's yard, where I hear he means to sell it by public auction."

"Who's Mr. Hucks?"

"He's the man that farms the Plain here—farms it *out*, I mean," Mrs. Damper explained. "He leases the ground from the Corporation and lets it out for what he can make, and that's a pretty penny. Terrible close-fisted man is Mr. Hucks."

"Oh!" said Tilda, enlightened. "When you talked of farmin', you made me wonder . . .So they're all gone? And Wolverhampton-way, I reckon. That was to be the next move."

"I've often seen myself travellin' in a caravan," said Mrs. Damper dreamily. "Here to-day an' gone to-morrow, and only to stretch out your hand whether 'tis hairpins or a fryin'-pan; though I should never get over travellin' on Sundays." Here, while her eyes rested on the child, of a sudden she came out of her reverie with a sharp exclamation. "Lord's sake! You ain't goin' to tell me they've left you in 'ospital, stranded!"

"That's about it," said Tilda bravely, albeit with a wry little twist of her mouth.

"But what'll you do?"

"Oh, I dunno . . . We'll get along some'ow—eh, 'Dolph? Fact is, I got a job to do, an' no time to lose worryin'. You just read *that*."

Tilda produced and handed her scrap of paper to Mrs. Damper, who took it, unfolded it, and perused the writing slowly.

"Goin' there?" she inquired at length.

"That depends." Tilda was not to be taken off her guard. "I want you to read what it says."

"Yes, to be sure—I forgot what you said about havin' no schoolin'. Well, it says: 'Arthur Miles, surname Chandon, b. Kingsand, May 1st, 1888. Rev. Dr. Purdie J. Glasson, Holy Innocents' Orphanage, Bursfield, near Birmingham '—leastways, I can't read the last line clear, the paper bein' frayed; but it's bound to be what I've said."

"Why?"

"Why, because that's the address. Holy Innocents, down by the canal— I know it, o' course, *and* Dr. Glasson. Damper supplied 'em with milk for over six months, an' trouble enough we had to get our money."

"How far is it?"

"Matter of half a mile, I should say—close by the canal. You cross it there by the iron bridge. The tram'll take you down for a penny, only you must mind and get out this side of the bridge, because once you're on the other side it's tuppence. Haven't got a penny? Well,"—Mrs. Damper dived a hand into her till—"I'll give you one. Bein' a mother, I can't bear to see children in trouble."

"Thank you," said Tilda. "It'll come in 'andy; but I ain't in no trouble just yet."

"I 'spose," Mrs. Damper ventured after a pause, "you don't feel like tellin' me what your business might be down at the orphanage? Not that I'm curious.

"I can't." This was perfectly true, for she herself did not know. "You see," she added with a fine air of mystery, "there's others mixed up in this."

Mrs. Damper sighed.

"Well, I mustn' detain you . . . This Arthur Miles Chandon—he's not a friend of yours by any chance?"

"He's a—sort of connection," said Tilda. "You know 'im, p'r'aps?"

"Dear me, no!"

"Oh,"—the child, without intending it, achieved a fine irony— "I thought you seemed interested. Well, so long! and thank you again— there's a tram stoppin' at the corner! Come along, 'Dolph!"

She was not—she had said it truthfully—by any means in trouble just yet. On the contrary, after long deprivation she was tasting life again, and finding it good. The streets of this Bursfield suburb were far from suggestive of the New Jerusalem—a City of which, by the way, Tilda had neither read nor heard. They were, in fact, mean and squalid, begrimed with smoke and imperfectly scavenged. But they were, at least, populous, and to Tilda the faces in the tram and on the pavements wore, each and all, a friendly—almost an angelic—glow. The tram-car rolled along like a celestial chariot trailing clouds of glory, and 'Dolph, running beside it and threading his way in and out between the legs of the passers-by, was a hound of heaven in a coat effluent of gold. Weariness would come, but as yet her body felt no weariness, buoyed upon a spirit a-tiptoe for all adventure.

The tram reached the iron bridge and drew up. She descended, asked the conductor to direct her to Holy Innocents, and was answered with a jerk of the thumb.

It stood, in fact, just beyond the bridge, with a high brick wall that turned off the street at right angles and overhung the towpath of the canal. Although in architecture wholly dissimilar, the building put her in mind of the Hospital of the Good Samaritan, and her spirits sank for a moment. Its facade looked upon the street over a strip of garden crowded with dingy laurels. It contained a depressingly large number of windows, and it seemed to her that they were at once bare and dirty. Also, and simultaneously, it occurred to her that she had no notion what step to take next, nor how, if she rang the bell, to explain herself. She temporised therefore; whistled to 'Dolph, and turned aside down the steps leading to the towpath. She would con the lie of the land before laying siege—the strength of the castle before summoning the defence.

The castle was patently strong—strong enough to excuse any disheartenment. Scarcely a window pierced its narrow butt-end, four stories high, under which the steps wound. It ended just where they met the towpath, and from its angle sprang a brick wall dead-blank, at least twelve feet high, which ran for eighty or ninety yards along the straight line of the path. Across the canal a row of unkempt cottage gardens sloped to the water, the most of them fenced from the brink of it with decayed palings, a few with elder bushes and barbed wire to fill up the gaps, while at least two ended in moraines of old meat tins and shards of crockery. And between these containing banks wound the canal, shallow and waveless, with noisome weeds trailing on its surface afloat amid soot and iridescent patches or pools of tar. In the cottage gardens not a soul was at work, nor, by their appearance, had a soul worked in them for years past. The canal, too, was deserted, save for one long monkey-boat, black as Charon's barge, that lay moored to a post on the towpath, some seventy-odd yards up stream, near where the wall of the Orphanage ended. Beyond this, and over a line of ragged thorns, the bulk of a red-brick Brewery—its roof crowned with a sky-sign—closed the view.

The monkey-boat lay with her stem down-stream, and her after-part—her habitable quarters—covered by a black tarpaulin. A solitary man was at work shovelling coal out of her middle hold into a large metal bucket. As Tilda hobbled towards him he hoisted the full bucket on his shoulders, staggered across the towpath with it, and shot its contents into a manhole under the brick wall. Tilda drew near and came to a halt, watching him.

"Afternoon," said the man, beginning to shovel again.

"Afternoon," responded Tilda.

He was a young man—she could detect this beneath his mask of coal dust. He wore a sack over his shoulders, and a black sou'wester hat with a hind-flap that fell low over his neck. But she liked the look in his eyes, though the rims of them were red and the brows caked with grit. She liked his voice, too. It sounded friendly.

"Is this the Orph'nige? What they call 'Oly Innercents?" she asked.

"That's so," the young coalheaver answered. "Want to get in?"

"I do an' I don't," said Tilda.

"Then take my advice an' don't."

He resumed his shovelling, and Tilda watched him for a while.

"Nice dorg," said he, breaking off and throwing an affable nod towards Godolphus who, having attracted no attention by flinging himself on the grass with a lolling tongue and every appearance of fatigue, was now filling up the time in quest of a flea. "No breed, but he has points. Where did you pick him up?"

"He belongs to a show."

"Crystal Pallus?"

"And," pursued Tilda, "I was wonderin' if you'd look after him while I step inside?"

She threw back her head, and the man whistled.

"You're a trustin' one, I must say!"

"You'd never be mean enough to make off with 'im, an' I won't believe it of you," spoke up Tilda boldly.

"Eh? I wasn' talkin of the dorg," he explained. "I was meanin' the Orph'nage. By all accounts 'tisn' so easy to get in—an' 'tis a sight harder to get out."

"I've *got* to get in," urged Tilda desperately.

"I've a message for someone inside. His name's Arthur Miles Chandon."

The young coalheaver shook his head.

"I don't know 'im," he said. "I'm new to this job, an' they don't talk to me through the coal-'ole. But you seem a well-plucked one, and what with your crutch—How did you come by it?"

"Kick of a pony."

"Seems to me you've been a good deal mixed up with animals, for your age. What about your pa and ma?"

"Never 'ad none, I thank Gord."

"Eh?" The young man laid down his shovel, lifted the flap of his sou'wester, and scratched the back of his head slowly. "Let me get the hang o' *that*, now."

"I've seen fathers and mothers," said the sage child, nodding at him; "and them as likes 'em is welcome to 'em."

"Gor-a-mussy!" half-groaned the young man. "If you talk like that, they'll take you in, right enough; but as to your gettin' out—"

"I'll get out, one way or 'nother—you see!" Tilda promised. "All you 'ave to do is to take charge o' this crutch an' look after the dog."

"Oh, I'll look after 'im!"

The child shook a forefinger at 'Dolph, forbidding him to follow her. The dog sank on his haunches, wagging a tail that swept the grasses in perplexed protest, and watched her as she retraced her way along the towpath.

Tilda did not once look back. She was horribly frightened; but she had pledged her word now, and it was irredeemable. From the hurrying traffic of the street she took a final breath of courage, and tugged at the iron bell-pull depending beside the Orphanage gate. A bell clanged close within the house, and the sound of it almost made her jump out of her boots.

CHAPTER III

A KIDNAPPING

"_And with that sound the castle all to-brast; so she took him, and they two fared forth hand in hand." "QUEST OF THE GRAIL."

The front door opened, and a slatternly woman in a soiled print dress came shuffling down the flagged pathway to the gate. She wore cloth boots, and Tilda took note that one of them was burst.

"Go away," said the woman, opening the gate just wide enough to thrust out her head. "We don't give nothing to beggars."

"I could 'a told *you* that," retorted Tilda. "But as it 'appens, I ain't one." She pointed to a brass letter-plate beside the wicket—it was pierced with a slit, and bore the legend, *For Voluntary Donations*. "Seems you collect a bit, though. Like it better, I dessay."

"Look here, if you've come with a message, let's 'ave it, an' take yourself off. It's washing-day in the 'ouse, an' I'm busy."

"Ah!" said Tilda politely, "I'm glad I came before you begun. I want"—here she unfolded her scrap of paper and made pretence to read—"I want to see the Reverend Doctor Purdie J. Glasson."

"Then you can't," snapped the woman, and was about to shut the door in her face, but desisted and drew back with a cry as a formidable yellow dog slipped through the opening, past her skirts, and into the garden.

It was 'Dolph, of course. Anxiety for his mistress had been too much for him, and had snapped the bonds of obedience; and knowing full well that he was misbehaving, he had come up furtively, unperceived. But now, having crossed the Rubicon, the rogue must brazen things out— which he did by starting a cat out of one of the dingy laurels, chivvying her some way into the house, and returning to shake himself on the front doorstep and bark in absurd triumph.

"'Dolph! 'Dolph!" called Tilda.

"Belongs to you, does he? Then fetch him out at once! You, and your dogs!"

"I'm fetchin' him fast as I can."

Tilda pushed past her, and advanced sternly to the front doorstep. "'Dolph, come here!" she commanded. 'Dolph barked once again defiantly, then laid himself down on the step in abject contrition, rolling over on his back and lifting all four legs skyward.

Tilda rolled him sideways with a slap, caught him by the scruff of the neck, and began to rate him soundly. But a moment later her grasp relaxed as a door opened within the passage, and at the sound of a footstep she looked up, to see a tall man in black standing over her and towering in the doorway.

"What is the meaning of this noise?" demanded the man in black. He was elderly and bald, with small pig-eyes, grey side-whiskers, and for mouth a hard square slit much like that of the collecting-box by the gate. A long pendulous nose came down over it and almost met an upthrust lower jaw. He wore a clerical suit, with a dingy white neck-tie; the skin about his throat hung in deep folds, and the folds were filled with an unpleasing grey stubble.

"If—if you please, sir, I was comin' with a message, an' he started after a cat. I can't break 'im of it."

"Turn him out," said the man in black. He walked to the gate and held it open while Tilda ejected Godolphus into the street. "I never allow dogs on my premises."

"No, sir."

"Now tell me your message."

"It's about a—a boy, sir," stammered Tilda, and felt a horrible fear creeping over her now that she approached the crisis. "That is, if you're the Reverend Doctor Glasson."

"I am Doctor Glasson. Well?"

"It's about a boy," harked back poor Tilda. "He's called Arthur Miles Surname Chandon—an' he was born at a place called Kingsand, if that's any 'elp—an' there's somebody wants to see 'im most particular."

"Come indoors."

Doctor Glasson said it sharply, at the same time turning right about and leading the way towards the house. Tilda followed, while behind her the excluded 'Dolph yapped and flung himself against the gate. But the gate was lined on the inside with wire-netting, and the garden wall was neither to be leapt nor scaled.

In the porch Dr. Glasson stood aside to let the servant precede them into the house, looked after her until she vanished down the length of a dark passage that smelt potently of soapsuds and cabbage-water, and motioned the child to step within. She obeyed, while her terror and the odours of the house together caught her by the throat. But worse was her dismay when, having closed the front door, the Doctor bolted it and slipped a chain on the bolt.

"The first door to the left, if you please." He stepped past her and pushed it open, and she entered, albeit with quaking knees. The room—a large and high one—was furnished barely and like an office—with a red flock wallpaper, a brown linoleum on the floor, and in the centre of the linoleum a bulky roll-top desk and a Windsor chair. Other Windsor chairs stood in array against the walls, and a couple of rosewood bookcases with glass fronts. There was also by the fireplace an armchair covered with American leather, a rag-work hearth-rug, and a large waste-paper basket stuffed with envelopes and circulars. Over the mantelshelf hung a print in an Oxford frame, with the title *Suffer Little Children to Come unto Me*, and a large stain of damp in the lower left-hand corner. The mantelshelf itself supported a clock, a pair of bronze candlesticks, a movable calendar, a bottle of paste, and a wooden box with *For the Little Ones* painted on it in black letters.

All this the child took in almost at a glance, and notwithstanding that the room was dark. Yet it had two large windows, and they were curtainless. Its gloom came of the thick coating of dirt on their upper panes, and a couple of wire blinds that cut off all light below.

Doctor Glasson had walked straight to his desk, and stood for a few moments with his back to the child, fingering his papers and apparently engaged in thought. By-and-by he picked up a pair of spectacles, turned, and adjusted them slowly whilst he stared down on her.

"Where did you get this information?"

Tilda's first impulse was to show him her scrap of paper, but she thought better of it. She would keep it back while she could, as a possible trump card. Besides, she feared and distrusted this man with the little eyes. Seen through glasses they were worse than ever.

"He's wanted by someone very particular," she repeated.

"By whom? Speak up, child! Who sent you?"

Heaven knows to what invisible spirits the child appealed. They were certainly disreputable ones, as will be seen; but they heard her prayer, and came to her now in her extremity. Hardly knowing what she did, she opened on this man a pair of eyes seraphically innocent, and asked—

"W'y, haven't you seen my aunt?"

"Your aunt?"

"She *promised* to call here at twelve-thirty, an' I was to meet her. But"—here Tilda had to keep a tight hold on her voice—"per'aps I'm early?"

"It's close upon one o'clock," said Doctor Glasson, with a glance towards the mantelshelf. "What is your aunt's name, and her business?"

"She's called Brown—Martha Brown—*Mrs.* Martha Brown, and she keeps a milliner's shop in the Edgeware Road, London," panted Tilda.

"I should have asked, What is her business with me?" Doctor Glasson corrected his question severely.

"I think—I dunno—but I *think*, sir, she might be wantin' to enter me for a orphlan. My pa, sir, was knocked down an' killed by a motor-car. It was in the early days," pursued Tilda, desperate now and aghast at her own invention. The lies seemed to spring to her lips full grown. "Pa was a stableman, sir, at Buckin'am Palace, and often and often I've 'eard 'im tell mother what'd be the end of 'im. He 'd seen it in a dream. And mother, *she* was a stewardess in a Sou'-Western boat that got cut in two last year. Maybe you read of it in the papers?"

Tears by this time filled the child's eyes. She was casting about to invent a last dying speech for her mother, when Doctor Glasson interrupted.

"If your aunt wishes to place you here, it might perhaps be managed, for a consideration. Just now we have no room for-er—non-paying children. But you began by asking for Arthur Miles."

"Surname Chandon."

"Yes—quite so—Chandon." He picked up a pencil and a half-sheet of paper from the desk, and wrote the name. "Born at Kingsand—I think you said Kingsand? Do you happen to know where Kingsand is? In what county, for instance?"

But Tilda had begun to scent danger again, she hardly knew why, and contented herself with shaking her head.

"Someone wants to see him. Who?"

"She's—an invalid," Tilda admitted.

"Not your aunt?"

"She's a—a *friend* of my aunt's."

Doctor Glasson pulled out a watch and compared it with the clock on the mantelshelf. While he did so Tilda stole a look up at his face, and more than ever it seemed to her to resemble a double trap—its slit of a mouth constructed to swallow anything that escaped between nose and chin.

"Your aunt is far from punctual. You are sure she means to call?"

"Sure," answered Tilda still hardily. "'Twelve-thirty' was her last words when she left me at the doctor's—my 'ip bein' 'urt, sir, through tumblin' out of a nomnibus, three weeks ago. But you never can depend on 'er to a few minutes up 'an down. She gets into the streets, watchin' the fashions, an' that carries 'er away. P'r'aps, sir, I 'd better go back into the street and 'ave a look for her."

"I think you had better wait here for her," said Doctor Glasson, shutting his lips with a snap. "There are some picture-books in the drawing-room."

He led the way. The drawing-room lay at the back of the house—an apartment even more profoundly depressing than the one she had left. Its one important piece of furniture was a circular table of rosewood standing in the centre of the carpet under a brass gaselier, of which the burnish had perished in patches; and in the centre of the table stood a round-topped glass case containing a stuffed kestrel, with a stuffed lark prostrate under its talons and bleeding vermilion wax. Around this ornament were disposed, as the Doctor had promised, a number of albums and illustrated books, one of which he chose and placed it in her hands, at the same time bringing forward one of a suite of rosewood chairs ranged with their backs to the walls. He motioned her to be seated.

"You shall be told as soon as ever your aunt arrives."

"Yes, sir," said Tilda feebly. For the moment all the fight had gone out of her.

He stood eyeing her, pulling at his bony finger-joints, and seemed on the point of putting some further question, but turned abruptly and left the room.

As the door closed—thank Heaven, at least, he did not bolt this one also!—a dry sob escaped the child. Why had she told that string of falsehoods? She was trapped now—imprisoned in this horrible house, not to be released until this fictitious aunt arrived, which, of course, would be never. The book on her lap lay open at a coloured lithograph of Mazeppa bound upon his steed and in full flight across the Tartar steppes. She knew the story—was it not Mr. Maggs's most thrilling "equestrian *finale*," and first favourite with the public? At another time she would have examined the picture eagerly. But now it swam before her, unmeaning. She closed the book, threw a glance around the four corners of the room, another at the stuffed kestrel—whose pitiless small eye strangely resembled Doctor Glasson's—and dragged herself to the window.

The lower panes of the window were filled with coloured transparencies representing in series the history of the Prodigal Son. They excluded a great deal of daylight and the whole of the view. Even by standing on tip-toe she could not look over them, and she dared not try to raise the sash.

By-and-by a thought struck her. She went back to her chair, lifted it, carried it to the window and climbed upon it; and this was no small feat or succession of feats, for as yet her thigh pained her, and fear held her half-paralysed.

What she looked upon was an oblong space enclosed by brick walls ten or twelve feet high, and divided by a lower wall—also of brick—into two parallelograms of unequal width. Of these the wider was a gravelled yard, absolutely bare, in extent perhaps an acre; and here, in various knots and groups, were gathered some two dozen children. Alongside of the yard and upon its left—that is to say, as Tilda guessed, between it and the canal—ran a narrower strip of kitchen garden, planted with leeks, cabbages, potatoes, and ending in a kind of shed—part glass-house, part out-house—built in lean-to fashion against the terminal wall, which overtopped it by several feet. The children in the yard could not look into this garden, for the dividing wall reached far above their heads.

Tilda, too, had no eyes for the garden, after a first glance had assured her it was empty. The children engaged all her attention. She had never seen anything like them; and yet they were obviously boys and girls, and in numbers pretty equally divided, What beat her was that they neither ran about nor played at any game, but walked to and fro—to and fro—as though pacing through some form of drill; and yet again they could not be drilling, for their motions were almost inert and quite aimless. Next, to her surprise, she perceived that, on no apparent compulsion, the boys kept with the boys in these separate wandering groups, and the girls with the girls; and further that, when two groups met and passed, no greeting, no nod of recognition, was ever exchanged. At any rate she could detect none. She had heard tell—indeed, it was an article of faith among the show-children with whom she had been brought up—that the sons and daughters of the well-to-do followed weird ways and practised discomfortable habits—attended public worship on Sundays, for instance, walking two and two in stiff raiment. But these children were patently very far from well-to-do. The garments of some hung about them in rags that fell short even of Tilda's easy standard. The spectacle fascinated her. For the moment it chased fear out of her mind. She was only conscious of pity—of pity afflicting and indefinable, far beyond her small understanding, and yet perhaps not wholly unlike that by which the great poet was oppressed as he followed his guide down through the infernal circles and spoke with their inhabitants. The sight did her this good—it drove out for a while, along with fear, all thought of her present situation. She noted that the majority were in twos or threes, but that here and there a child walked solitary, and that the faces of these solitary ones were hard to discern, being bent towards the ground . . .

The door-handle rattled and called her back to terror. She had no time to clamber down from her chair. She was caught.

But it was a woman who entered, the same that had opened the front gate; and she carried a tray with a glass of water on it and a plate of biscuits.

"The Doctor told me as 'ow you might be 'ungry," she explained.

"Thank you," said Tilda. "I—I was lookin' at the view."

For an instant she thought of appealing to this stranger's mercy. The woman's eyes were hard, but not unkind. They scrutinised her closely.

"You take my advice, an' get out o' this quick as you can."

The woman thumped down the tray, and made as if to leave the room with a step decisive as her speech. At the door, however, she hesitated.

"Related to 'im?" she inquired.

"Eh?" Tilda was taken aback. "'Oo's 'im?"

"I 'eard you tell the Doctor you wanted to see 'im."

"An' so I do. But I'm no relation of 'is—on'y a friend."

"I was thinkin' so. Lawful born or come-by-chance, the child's a little gentleman, an' different from the others. Blood al'ays comes out, don't it?"

"I s'pose so."

Tilda, still perched on her chair, glanced out at the children in the yard.

"You won't see 'im out there. He's in the shed at the end o' the kitchen garden, cleanin' the boots. If you've got anything good to tell 'im, an' 'll promise not to be five minutes, I might give you a run there while the Doctor's finishin' his dinner in his study. Fact is," added this strange woman, "the child likes to be alone, an' sometimes I lets 'im slip away there—when he's good, or the Doctor's been extra 'ard with 'im."

"Beats 'im?" asked Tilda, and suddenly, still erect on her chair and looking down on the woman, felt her courage flowing back full and strong. "He's a beast, then."

"You musn' talk like that," said the woman hurriedly, with a glance back at the half-open door. "Hut he's 'ard if you cross 'im—an' the child's pay bein' be'ind—'and—"

"What's your name?" demanded Tilda.

"Sarah 'Uggins."

"Miss or Missis?"

"What's that to you?"

The blood surged into the woman's face, and she eyed the child suspiciously under lowered brows. Tilda slipped down from her chair. She had a sense of standing dangerously on the edge of something evil, forbidden. If only she could scream aloud and rush out—anywhere—into the open air!

"I—I was only wantin' to speak polite," she stammered. "I been impident to yer. But O, Sarah 'Uggins—O, ma'am—'elp me see 'im an' get away, an' I'll bless yer name fur ever and ever! Amen."

"Nip in front o' me," said the woman, "and be quick, then! First turnin' to the right down the stairs, an' don't clatter yer boots."

Tilda obeyed breathlessly, and found herself in a dark stone stairway. It led down steeply to the basement, and here her guide overtook and stepped ahead of her. They passed through two dirty kitchens, through a wash-house littered with damp linen and filled with steam from a copper in the corner, and emerged upon a well-court foetid with sink-water and decaying scraps of vegetables. They had met no one on their way, and it crossed Tilda's mind—but the thought was incredible—that Sarah Huggins served this vast barracks single-handed. A flight of stone steps led up from this area to the railed coping twenty feet aloft, where the sky shone pure and fresh.

"Up there, an' you 're in the garden." Tilda ran, so fast that at the head of the steps she had to clutch at the railing and draw breath.

The garden, too, was deserted. A gravelled path, scarcely four feet wide, ran straight to the end of it, and along this she hurried, not daring to look back, but aware that all the back windows were following her—watching and following her—with horrible curtainless eyes.

The garden, planted for utility, was passably well kept. It contained, in all its parcelled length, not a single flower. At the very end a few currant bushes partially hid the front of the shed and glass-house. They were the one scrap of cover, and when she reached them she had a mind to crouch and hide, if only for a moment, from the staring windows.

Her own eyes, as she passed these bushes, were fastened on the shed. But it seemed that someone else had discovered shelter here; for with a quick, half-guttural cry, like that of a startled animal, a small figure started up, close by her feet, and stood and edged away from her with an arm lifted as if to ward off a blow.

It was a small boy—a boy abominably ragged and with smears of blacking thick on his face, but for all that a good-looking child. Tilda gazed at him, and he gazed back, still without lowering his arm. He was trembling, too.

"Doctor Livingstone, I presume?" said Tilda, lifting the brim of her chip hat and quoting from one of Mr. Maggs's most effective dramatic sketches. But as the boy stared, not taking the allusion, she went on, almost in the same breath, "Is your name Arthur—Arthur Miles?"

It seemed that he did not hear. At any rate he still backed and edged away from her, with eyes distended—she had seen their like in the ring, in beautiful terrified horses, but never in human creatures.

—"Because, if you 're Arthur Miles, I got a message for you."

A tattered book lay on the turf at her feet. She picked it up and held it out to him. For a while he looked at her eyes, and from them to the book, unable to believe. Then, with a noise like a sob, he sprang and snatched it, and hid it with a hug in the breast of his coat.

"I got a message for you," repeated Tilda. "There's someone wants to see you, very bad."

"You go away!" said the boy sullenly. "You don't know. If *he* catches you, there's no chance."

Tilda had time in her distress to be astonished by his voice. It was pure, distinct, with the tone of a sphere not hers. Yet she recognised it. She had heard celestial beings—ladies and gentlemen in Maggs's three-shilling seats—talk in voices like this boy's.

"I've took a 'eap o' trouble to find yer," she said. "An' now I've done it, *all* depends on our gettin' out o' this. Ain't there no way? *Do* try to think a bit!"

The boy shook his head.

"There isn't any way. You let me alone, and clear."

"He can't do worse'n kill us," said Tilda desperately, with a look back at the house. "S'help me, let's try!"

But her spirit quailed.

"He won't kill you. He'll catch you, and keep you here for ever and ever."

"We'll try, all the same."

Tilda shut her teeth and held out a hand—or rather, was beginning to extend it—when a sound arrested her. It came from the door of the glass-house, and as she glanced towards it her heart leapt and stood still.

"'Dolph!"

Yes, it was 'Dolph, dirty, begrimed with coal; 'Dolph fawning towards her, cringing almost on his belly, but wagging his stump of a tail ecstatically. Tilda dashed upon him.

"Oh, 'Dolph!—*how?*"

The dog strangled down a bark, and ran back to the glass-house, but paused in the doorway a moment to make sure that she was following. It was all right. Tilda had caught the boy's hand, and was dragging him along. 'Dolph led them through the glass-house and down a flight of four steps to the broken door of a furnace-room. They pushed after him. Behind the furnace a second doorway opened upon a small coal-cellar, through the ceiling of which, in the right-hand corner, poured a circular ray of light. The ray travelled down a moraine of broken coal, so broad at the base that it covered the whole cellar floor, but narrowing upwards and towards the manhole through which the daylight shone.

Down through the manhole, too—O bliss!—came the sound of a man's whistle.

"*Ph'ut! Phee-ee—uht!* Darn that fool of a dog! *Ph'w*—"

"For the Lord's sake!" called Tilda, pushing the boy up the coal-shute ahead of her and panting painfully as her feet sank and slid in the black pile.

"Eh? . . . Hullo!" A man's face peered down, shutting off the daylight. "Well, in all my born days—"

He reached down a hand.

"The boy first," gasped Tilda, "—and quick!"

CHAPTER IV

IN WHICH CHILDE ARTHUR LOSES ONE MOTHER AND GAINS ANOTHER.

"But and when they came to Easter Gate, Easter Gate stood wide; 'y' are late, y' are late,' the Porter said; 'This morn my Lady died.'"—OLD BALLAD.

"Well, in all my born days!" said the young coalheaver again, as he landed the pair on the canal bank.

He reached down a hand and drew up 'Dolph by the scruff of his neck. The dog shook himself, and stood with his tail still wagging.

"Shut down the hole," Tilda panted, and catching sight of the iron cover, while the young man hesitated she began to drag at it with her own hands.

"Steady on there!" he interposed. "I got five hundred more to deliver."

"You don't deliver another shovelful till we're out o' this," said Tilda positively, stamping the cover in place and standing upon it for safety. "What's more, if anyone comes an' arsks a question, you ha'n't seen us."

"Neither fur nor feather of ye," said the young man, and grinned.

She cast a look at the boy; another up and down the towing-path.

"Got such a thing as a cake o' soap hereabouts? You wouldn', I suppose—" and here she sighed impatiently.

"I 'ave, though. Always keeps a bit in my trouser pocket." He produced it with pride.

Said Tilda, "I don't know yername, but you're more like a Garden Angel than any I've met yet in your walk o' life. Hand it over, an' keep a look-out while I wash this child's face. I *can't* take 'im through the streets in this state." She turned upon the boy. "Here, you just kneel down—so—with your face over the water, an' as near as you can manage." He obeyed in silence. He was still trembling. "That's right, on'y take care you don't overbalance." She knelt beside him, dipped both hands in the water, and began to work the soap into a lather. "What's the 'andiest way to the Good Samaritan?" she asked, speaking over her shoulder.

"Meanin' the 'orspital?"

"Yes." She took the boy's passive face between her hands and soaped it briskly. "The 'andiest way, *an'* the quietest, for choice."

"The 'andiest way," said the young coalheaver, after considering for half a minute, "an' the quietest, is for me to cast off the bow-straps here an' let her drop across stream. You can nip up through the garden yonder—it don't belong to nobody just now. That'll bring you out into a place called Pollard's Row, an' you turn straight off on your right. First turnin' opposite on the right by the 'Royal Oak,' which is a public-'ouse, second turnin' to the left after that, an' you're in Upper Town Street, an' from there to the Good Samaritan it's no more 'n a stone's throw."

Tilda was silent for a few moments whilst she fixed these directions in her mind.

"It do seem," she said graciously while she dried the boy's face with the skirt of her frock, "like as if you 'd dropped 'ere from 'eaven. What we should a-done without you, I can't think."

"You'd best thank that dog o' your'n." The young man bent to cast off his rope. "He broke away from me once, an' I made sure I'd lost 'im. But by-an'-by back he came like a mad thing, an' no need to tell me you was inside there. He was neither to hold nor to bind, an' I do believe if he hadn't thought o' the manhole he'd 'a-broke the wall down, or elst his 'eart."

"When I tell you 'e got me in as well as out—But, good sake, I musn' stand 'ere talkin'! Gimme my crutch, an' shove us across, that's a dear man."

She pushed the boy before her on to the barge. 'Dolph sprang on board at their heels, and the young coalheaver thrust the bows across with his pole. The canal measured but seventeen or eighteen feet from brink to brink, and consequently the boat, which was seventy feet long at least, fell across at a long angle. The garden on the opposite shore was unfenced, or rather, its rotten palings had collapsed with time and the pressure of a rank growth of elder bushes.

"So long, an' th' Lord bless yer!"

Tilda took the boy's hand and jumped ashore.

"Same to you, an' wishin' you luck!" responded the young coalheaver cheerfully. "Look 'ere," he added, "if you get in trouble along o' this, I'm willin' to stand in for my share. Sam Bossom's my name— employ of Hucks, Canal End Basin. If they lag you for this, you just refer 'em to Sam Bossom, employ of Hucks—everyone knows Hucks; an' I'll tell 'em—well, darned if I know what I'll tell 'em, unless that we was all under the influence o' drink."

"You're a white man," responded Tilda, "though you don't look it; but there ain't goin' to be no trouble, not if I can 'elp. If anyone arsks questions, you han't seen us, mind."

"Fur nor feather of ye," he repeated. He watched the pair as they dived through the elder bushes; saw them, still hand in hand, take the path on the left side of the garden, where its party hedge could best screen them from the back windows of the Orphanage; and poled back meditatively.

"Got an 'ead on her shoulders, that child!" On their way up the garden Tilda kept silence. She was busy, in fact, with Sam Bossom's complicated itinerary, repeating it over and over to fix it in her mind. She was fearful, too, lest some inquisitive neighbour, catching sight of them, might stop them and challenge to know their business. The streets once gained, she felt easier—easier indeed with every yard she put between her and that house of horrors. But the streets, too, held their dangers. The bells had rung in the elementary schools; all respectable boys and girls were indoors, deep in the afternoon session, and she had heard of attendance officers, those prowling foes.

At the end of Pollard's Row—a squalid street of tenement houses—she suffered indeed a terrible scare. A benevolent-looking middle-aged lady—a district visitor, in fact—emerging from one of these houses and arrested perhaps at sight of the crutch or of the boy's strange rags, stopped her and asked where she was going.

Tilda fell back on the truth. It was economical.

"To the 'orspital," she answered, "the Good Samaritan."

Then she blundered.

"It's 'ereabouts, ain't it, ma'am?"

"Not very far," replied the lady; "two or three streets only. Shall I show you the way? I have plenty of time."

"Thank you," said Tilda (she was suffering a reaction, and for a moment it dulled the edge of her wits), "but I know the Good Samaritan, an' they know all about me."

"What's the matter?"

"'Ip trouble, ma'am. I been treated for it there these three weeks."

"That is strange," said the lady. "You have been going there for three weeks, and yet you don't know your way?"

"I been a in-patient. I was took there"—she was about to say "on a stretcher," but checked herself in time—"I was took there in the evenin' after dark. Father couldn' take me by day, in his work-time. An' this is my first turn as day-patient, an' that's why my brother 'ere is let off school to see me along," she wound up with a desperate rush of invention.

"You don't live in my district? What's your father's name?"

"No, ma'am. He's called Porter—Sam Porter, an' he works on the coal-barges. But I wouldn' advise you, I reely wouldn', because father's got opinions, an' can't abide visitors. I've 'eard 'im threaten 'em quite vi'lent."

"Poor child!"

"But I won't 'ave you say anything 'gainst father," said Tilda, taking her up quickly, "for 'e's the best father in the world, if 'twasn' fur the drink."

The effect of this masterstroke was that the lady gave her a copper and let her go, wishing her a speedy recovery. The gift, although she took it, did not appear to placate Tilda. She hobbled up the next street with quickened pace, now and then muttering angrily.

"Serves me right!" she broke out at length. "Bill—you don't know Bill, but 'e's the wisest man in the 'ole world, *an'* the kindest, *an'* the bestest. Bill would 'a-slapped my ear if 'e 'd 'eard me jus' now. Near upon gave the show away, I did, an' all through wantin' to 'ear somebody else tell what I knew a'ready. Never let nobody else make sure for you—that's one o' Bill's sayin's. Take warnin' by me, an' don't you ever forget it, Arthur Miles."

The boy had not spoken all the way. He glanced at her timidly, and she saw that he did not understand. Also it was plain that the streets, with their traffic, puzzled him; at the approach of every passer-by he would halt uncertainly, like a puppy not yet way-wise. By-and-by he said—

"But if that's so, you must be my sister."

"I'm not," said Tilda sharply. "What put it into your 'ead?"

"You told the lady—" he began.

"Eh? So I did. But that was all flam." He could make nothing of this. "I was kiddin' of 'er—tellin' what wasn' true," she explained.

He walked forward a few steps with a frown—not disapproving, but painfully thinking this out.

"And about the Hospital—wasn't that true either?"

"Yes," Tilda nodded. "We're goin' to the 'orspital all right. That's why I came to fetch yer. There's someone wants to see yer, ever so bad."

"I know about the Good Samaritan," announced the boy.

Tilda stared.

"I bet yer don't," she contradicted.

"He found a man, a traveller, that some thieves had hurt and left by the road. Going down to Jericho, it was; and he poured oil and wine into his wounds."

"Oh, cheese it!" said Tilda. "Oo's a-kiddin' now? An' see 'ere, Arthur Miles—it don't matter with me, a lie up or down; I'm on'y Tilda. But don't you pick up the 'abit, or else you'll annoy me. I can't tell why ezactly, but it don't *sit* on you."

"Tilda?" The boy caught up her name like an echo. "Tilda what?"

"The Lord knows. Tilda *nothin'*—Tilda o' Maggs's, if you like, an' nobody's child, anyway."

"But that isn't *possible*," he said, after thinking a moment.
"They called me that sometimes, back—back—"

"At the Orph'nige, eh? 'Oo called you that? The Doctor? No," said Tilda hurriedly, as he halted with a shiver, "don't look be'ind; 'e's not anywhere near. An' as for the Good Samaritan, you're wrong about that, too; for *'ere's* the Good Samaritan!"

She pointed at the building, and he stared. He could not comprehend at all, but she had switched him off the current of his deadly fear.

"Now you just wait 'ere by the steps," she commanded, "an' 'Dolph'll wait by you an' see you come to no 'arm. Understand, 'Dolph? I'm goin' inside for a minute—only a minute, mind; but if anybody touches Arthur Miles, you *pin* 'im!"

'Dolph looked up at his mistress, then at the boy. He wagged his tail, not enthusiastically. He would fain have followed her, but he understood, and would obey.

Tilda went up the steps, and up the stairs. On the landing, as chance would have it, she met the Second Nurse coming out from the ward, with a sheet in one hand and a tray of medicines in the other.

"You extremely naughty child!" began the Second Nurse, but not in the shrill tone nor with quite the stern disapproval the child had expected. "When the doctor told you half an hour exactly, and you have been *hours!* What *have* you been doing?"

"Lookin' up the old folks," she answered, and took note first that the medicine bottles were those that had stood on the sick woman's table, and next that the Second Nurse, as she came out, transferred the sheet to her arm and closed the door behind her.

"You must wait here for a moment, now you have come so late. I have had to give you another bed; and now I've to fetch some hot water, but I'll be back in a minute."

"Folks don't make beds up with hot water," thought Tilda.

She watched the nurse down the passage, stepped to the door, and turned the handle softly.

There was no change in the ward except that a tall screen stood by the sick woman's bed. Tilda crept to the screen on tip-toe, and peered around it.

Ten seconds—twenty seconds—passed, and then she drew back and stole out to the landing, closing the door as softly as she had opened it. In the light of the great staircase window her face was pale and serious.

She went down the stairs slowly.

"Seems I made a mistake," she said, speaking as carelessly as she could, but avoiding the boy's eyes. "You wasn' wanted up there, after all."

But he gazed at her, and flung out both arms with a strangling sob.

"You won't take me back! You'll hide me—you won't take me back!"

"Oh, 'ush!" said Tilda. "No, I won't take yer back, an' I'll do my best, but—oh, 'Dolph!"—she brushed the back of her hand across her eyes and turned to the dog with the bravest smile she could contrive— "to think of me bein' a mother, at *my* time o' life!"

CHAPTER V

TEMPORARY EMBARRASSMENTS OF A THESPIAN.

"Sinner that I am," said the Showman, "see how you are destroying and ruining my whole livelihood!"—DON QUIXOTE.

Mr. Sam Bossom, having poled back to the towpath, stepped ashore, made fast his bow moorings, stood and watched the two childish figures as they passed up the last slope of the garden out of sight, and proceeded to deliver his remaining hundredweights of coal—first, however, peering down the manhole and listening, to assure himself that all was quiet below.

"If," said he thoughtfully, "a man was to come an' tell me a story like that, I'd call 'im a liar."

Twice or thrice before finishing his job he paused to listen again, but heard nothing. Still in musing mood, he scraped up the loose coal that lay around the manhole, shovelled it in, re-fixed the cover, and tossed his shovel on board. His next business was to fetch a horse from the stables at the Canal End and tow the boat back to her quarters; and having taken another glance around, he set off and up the towpath at a pretty brisk pace. It would be five o'clock before he finished his work: at six he had an engagement, and it would take him some time to wash and titivate.

Canal End Basin lay hard upon three-quarters of a mile up stream, and about half that distance beyond the bend of the Great Brewery—a malodorous pool packed with narrow barges or monkey-boats—a few loading leisurably, the rest moored in tiers awaiting their cargoes. They belonged to many owners, but their type was well nigh uniform. Each measured seventy feet in length, or a trifle over, with a beam of about seven; each was built with rounded bilges, and would carry from twenty-five to thirty tons of cargo; each provided, aft of its hold or cargo-well, a small cabin for the accommodation of its crew by day; and for five-sixths of its length each was black as a gondola of Venice. Only, where the business part of the boat ended and its cabin began, a painted ribbon of curious pattern ornamented the gunwale, and terminated in two pictured stern-panels.

Wharves and storehouses surrounded the basin, or rather enclosed three sides of it, and looked upon the water across a dead avenue (so to speak) of cranes and bollards; buildings of exceedingly various height and construction, some tiled, others roofed with galvanised iron. Almost every one proclaimed on its front, for the information of the stranger, its owner's name and what he traded in; and the stranger, while making his choice between these announcements, had ample time to contrast their diversity of size and style with the sober uniformity that prevailed afloat.

The store and yard of Mr. Christopher Hucks stood at the head of the basin, within a stone's-throw of the Weigh Dock, and but two doors away from the Canal Company's office. It was approached through folding-doors, in one of which a smaller opening had been cut for pedestrians, and through this, on his way to the stables in the rear, Mr. Sam Bossom entered. He entered and halted, rubbing his eyes with the back of his hand, which, grimed as it was with coal grit, but further inflamed their red rims. In the centre of the yard, which had been empty when he went to work, stood a large yellow caravan; and on the steps of the caravan sat a man—a stranger—peeling potatoes over a bucket.

"Hullo!" said Sam.

The stranger—a long-faced man with a dead complexion, an abundance of dark hair, and a blue chin—nodded gloomily.

"The surprise," he answered, "is mutual. If it comes to *that*, young man, you are not looking your best either; though doubtless, if washed off, it would reveal a countenance not sicklied o'er with the pale cast of thought—thought such as, alas! must be mine—thought which, if acquainted with the poets, you will recognise as lying too deep for tears."

"Governor settin' up in a new line?" asked Sam, slowly contemplating the caravan and a large tarpaulin-covered wagon that stood beside it with shafts resting on the ground.

"If, my friend, you allude to Mr. Christopher Hucks, he is not setting up in any new line, but pursuing a fell career on principles which (I am credibly informed) are habitual to him, and for which I can only hope he will be sorry when he is dead. The food, sir, of Mr. Christopher Hucks is still the bread of destitution; his drink, the tears of widows; and the groans of the temporarily embarrassed supply the music of his unhallowed feast."

"There is a bit o' that about the old man, until you get to know him," assented Sam cheerfully.

"Mr. Christopher Hucks—" began the stranger with slow emphasis, dropping a peeled potato into the bucket and lifting a hand with an open clasp-knife towards heaven.

But here a voice from within the caravan interrupted him.

"Stanislas!"

"My love?"

"I can't find the saucepan."

A lady appeared at the hatch of the doorway above. Her hair hung in disarray over her well-developed shoulders, and recent tears had left their furrows on a painted but not uncomely face.

"I—I—well, to confess the truth, I pawned it, my bud. Dear, every cloud has its silver lining, and meanwhile what shall we say to a simple fry? You have an incomparable knack of frying."

"But where's the dripping?"

Her husband groaned.

"The dripping! The continual dripping! Am I—forgive the bitterness of the question—but am I a stone, love?"

He asked it with a hollow laugh, and at the same time with a glance challenged Sam's approval for his desperate pleasantry.

Sam jerked his thumb to indicate a wooden out-house on the far side of the yard.

"I got a shanty of my own across there, *and* a few fixin's. If the van's anchored here, an' I can set you up with odds-an'-ends such as a saucepan, you're welcome."

"A friend in need, sir, is a friend indeed," said the stranger impressively; and Sam's face brightened, for he had heard the proverb before, and it promised to bring the conversation, which he had found some difficulty in following, down to safe, familiar ground. "Allow me to introduce you—but excuse me, I have not the pleasure of knowing your name—"

"Sam Bossom."

"Delighted! 'Bossom' did you say? B—O—double S—it should have been 'Blossom,' sir, with a slight addition; or, with an equally slight omission—er—'Bosom,' if my Arabella will excuse me. On two hands, Mr. Bossom, you narrowly escape poetry." (Sam looked about him uneasily.) "But, as Browning says, 'The little more and how much it is, the little less and what miles away.' Mine is Mortimer, sir—Stanislas Horatio Mortimer. You have doubtless heard of it?"

"Can't say as I 'ave," Sam confessed.

"Is it possible?" Mr. Mortimer was plainly surprised, not to say hurt. He knit his brows, and for a moment seemed to be pondering darkly. "You hear it, Arabella? But no matter. As I was saying, sir, I desire the pleasure of introducing you to my wife, Mrs. Mortimer, better known to fame, perhaps, as Miss Arabella St. Maur. You see her, Mr. Bossom, as my helpmeet under circumstances which (though temporarily unfavourable) call forth the true woman—naked, in a figurative sense, and unadorned. But her Ophelia, sir, has been favourably, nay enthusiastically, approved by some of the best critics of our day."

This again left Sam gravelled. He had a vague notion that the lady's Ophelia must be some admired part of her anatomy, but contented himself with touching his brow politely and muttering that he was Mrs. Mortimer's to command. The lady, who appeared to be what Sam called to himself a good sort, smiled down on him graciously, and hoped that she and her husband might be favoured with his company at supper.

"It's very kind of *you*, ma'am," responded Sam; "but 'fact is I han't knocked off work yet. 'Must go now and fetch out th' old hoss for a trifle of haulage; an' when I get back I must clean meself an' shift for night-school—me bein' due early there to fetch up leeway. You see," he explained, "bein' on the move wi' the boats most o' my time, I don't get the same chances as the other fellows. So when I hauls ashore, as we call it, I 'ave to make up lost time."

"A student, I declare!" Mr. Mortimer saluted him. Rising from the steps of the caravan, he rubbed a hand down his trouser-leg and extended it. "Permit me to grasp, sir, the horny palm of self-improvement. A scholar in humble life! and—as your delicacy in this small matter of the saucepan sufficiently attests—one of Nature's gentlemen to boot! I prophesy that you will go far, Mr. Bossom. May I inquire what books you thumb?"

"Thumb?" Sam, his hard hand released, stared at it a moment perplexed. "That ain't the *method*, sir; not at our school. But I'm gettin' along, and the book is called Lord Macaulay."

"What? Macaulay's *Essays?*"

"It's called *Lays*, sir—Lord Macaulay's *Lays*. The rest of the class chose it, an' I didn' like to cry off, though I 'd not a-flown so high as a lord myself—not to start with."

"The *Lays of Ancient Rome?* My dear Bossom—my dear Smiles—you'll allow me to dub you Smiles? *On Self Help*, you know. I like to call my friends by these playful sobriquets, and friends we are going to be, you and I. My dear fellow, I used to know 'em by heart—"

  'Lars Porsena of Clusium
    By the nine gods he swore—'

"—Is that the ticket, hey?"

Mr. Mortimer clapped him on the shoulder. "Dang it!" breathed Sam, "how small the world is!"

"Smiles, we must be friends. Even if, for a paltry trifle of seven pounds fifteen and six, I am condemned by your master (whom you will excuse my terming a miscreant) to eke out the dregs of my worthless existence in this infernal yard—no, my loved Arabella, you will pardon me, but as a practical man I insist on facing the worst—even so I have found a congenial spirit, a co-mate and brother in exile, a Friend in my retreat Whom I can whisper: 'Solitude is sweet.' Pursue, my dear Smiles! You are young: hope sits on your helm and irradiates it. For me, my bark is stranded, my fortunes shipwrecked, my career trickles out in the sands. Nevertheless, take the advice of an Elder Brother, and pursue. By the way"—Mr. Mortimer drew from his breast-pocket the stump of a half-consumed cigar—"I regret that I have not its fellow to offer you; but could you oblige me with a match?"

Sam produced a couple of sulphur matches.

"I thank you." Mr. Mortimer lit and inhaled. "A—ah!" he sighed between two luxurious puffs. "Connoisseurs—epicures—tell me a cigar should never be lit twice. But with tobacco of this quality—the last of the box, alas! All its blooming companions—and, between you and me, smuggled." He winked knowingly.

Just then a hooter from the Great Brewery announced five o'clock. Sam groaned. He had engaged himself to the schoolmaster for an hour's private tuition before the Evening Class opened, and Mr. Mortimer's fascinating talk had destroyed his last chance of keeping that engagement. Even if he dropped work straight away, it would take him a good three-quarters of an hour to clean himself and don his best suit.

He was explaining this to Mr. and Mrs. Mortimer when, his eyes resting on the empty shafts of the wagon, a happy thought occurred to him.

"O' course," he began, "—but there, I don't like to suggest it, sir."

"Say on, my friend."

"Well—I was thinkin' that you, may be, bein' accustomed to hosses—"

"My father," put in Mr. Mortimer, "rode to hounds habitually. A *beau ideal*, if I may say so, of the Old English squire. It is in the blood."

"I *know* it's a come-down," Sam owned. "And a shilling at most for overtime—meanin' no offence—"

Mr. Mortimer waved a hand.

"If," said he, "it be a question of my rendering you any small service, I beg, my friend—I command—that all question of pecuniary recompense be left out of the discussion."

Sam, feeling that he had to deal with a noble character, explained that the job was an easy one; merely to lead or ride one of the horses down the hauling-path to where the boat lay, to hitch on the tackle, cast off straps, pull up and ship the two crowbars to which they were made fast, and so take the tiller and steer home. The horse knew his business, and would do the rest.

"And you can't mistake the boat. *Duchess of Teck* is her name, an' she lies about three ropes' lengths this side of the iron bridge, just as you come abreast o' the brick wall that belongs to the Orph'nage."

"Bring forth the steed," commanded Mr. Mortimer. "Nay, I will accompany you to the stables and fetch him."

"*And* the saucepan! Don't forget the saucepan!" Mrs. Mortimer called after them in a sprightly voice as they crossed the yard together.

"Ha, the saucepan!" Within the stable doorway Mr. Mortimer stood still and pressed a hand to his brow. "You cannot think, my dear Smiles, how that obligation weighs on me. The expense of a saucepan—what is it? And yet—" He seemed to ponder. Of a sudden his brow cleared. "—Unless, to be sure—that is to say, if you should happen to have a shilling about you?"

"I got no change but 'arf-a-crown, if that's any use," answered the charmed Sam.

"Nothing smaller? Still," suggested Mr. Mortimer quickly, "I could bring back the change."

"Yes, do."

"It will please Arabella, too. In point of fact, during the whole of our married life I have made it a rule never to absent myself from her side without bringing back some trifling gift. Women—as you will understand one of these days—set a value on these *petits soins*; and somewhere in the neighbourhood of the iron bridge a tinsmith's should not be hard to find... Ah, thanks, my dear fellow—thanks inexpressibly! Absurd of me, of course; but you cannot think what a load you have taken off my mind."

Sam unhitched one of a number of hauling tackles hanging against the wall, and led forth his horse—a sturdy old grey, by name Jubilee. Casting the tackle carelessly on the animal's back, he handed Mr. Mortimer the headstall rope, and left him, to return two minutes later with the saucepan he had promised.

"She must use this one for the time," he explained. "And afterwards yours will come as a surprise."

"It must be so, I suppose," assented Mr. Mortimer, but after a pause, and reluctantly, averting his eyes from the accursed thing.

To spare him, Sam hurried across to deliver it to the lady, who awaited them in the doorway: and thus approaching he became aware that she was making mysterious signals. He glanced behind him. Plainly the signals were not directed at her husband, who had halted to stoop and pass a hand over old Jubilee's near hind pastern, and in a manner almost more than professional. Sam advanced, in some wonder. Mrs. Mortimer reached down a shapely hand for the pan-handle, leaned as she did so, and murmured—

"You will not lend money to Stanislas? He is apt, when the world goes ill with him, to seek distraction, to behave unconventionally. It is not a question of drowning his cares, for the least little drop acting upon his artistic temperament—"

But at this moment her husband, having concluded his inspection of the grey, called out to be given a leg-up, and Sam hurried back to oblige.

"Thank you. Time was, Smiles, when with hand laid lightly on the crupper, I could have vaulted."

Overcome by these reminiscences, Mr. Mortimer let his chin sink, his legs dangle, and rode forward a pace or two in the classical attitude of the Last Survivor from Cabul; but anon looked up with set jaw and resolution in his eye, took a grip with his knees, and challenged—

"Give a man a horse he can ride,
 Give a man a boat he can sail,
 And his something or other—I forget
  the exact expression—
 On sea nor shore shall fail!"

—"Fling wide the gate, Smiles!" He was now the Dashing Cavalier, life-sized. "Take care of yourself, poppet!"

He gave his bridle-rein a shake (so to speak), turned, blew a kiss to his spouse, dug heel and jogged forth chanting—

"*Tirra tirra* by the river
 Sang Sir Lancelot!"

CHAPTER VI.

MR. MORTIMER'S ADVENTURE.

"Old mole! canst work i' the earth so fast?"—HAMLET

All the way along the canal bank Mr. Mortimer continued to carol. Mercurial man! Like all actors he loved applause, but unlike the most of them he was capable of supplying it when the public failed; and this knack of being his own best audience had lifted him, before now, out of quite a number of Sloughs of Despond and carried him forward singing.

He had left care behind him in Mr. Hucks's yard, and so much of noble melancholy as he kept (for the sake of artistic effect) took a tincture from the sunset bronzing the smoke-laden sky and gilding the unlovely waterway. Like the sunset, Mr. Mortimer's mood was serene and golden. His breast, expanding, heaved off all petty constricting worries, "like Samson his green wythes": they fell from him as he rode, and as he rode he chanted—

> "The sun came dazzling thro' the leaves
>   And flamed upon the brazen greaves
>   Of bold Sir Lancelot . . ."

Old Jubilee—if, like John Gilpin's horse, he wondered more and more— was a philosophical beast and knew his business. Abreast of the boat, beside the angle of the Orphanage wall, he halted for his rider to alight, and began to nose for herbage among the nettles. Nor did he betray surprise when Mr. Mortimer, after a glance down the towpath towards the iron bridge and the tram-lights passing there, walked off and left him to browse.

Fifteen minutes passed. The last flush of sunset had died out of the sky, and twilight was deepening rapidly, when Mr. Mortimer came strolling back. Apparently—since he came empty-handed—his search for a saucepan had been unsuccessful. Yet patently the disappointment had not affected his spirits, for at sight of Old Jubilee still cropping in the dusk he stood still and gave utterance to a lively whoop.

The effect of this sobered him. Old Jubilee was not alone. Hurriedly out of the shadow of the Orphanage wall arose a grey-white figure—a woman. It seemed that she had been kneeling there. Now, as Mr. Mortimer advanced, she stood erect, close back against the masonry, waiting for him to pass.

"'S a female," decided Mr. Mortimer, pulling himself together and advancing with a hand over his brow, the better to distinguish the glimmer of her dress. "'S undoubtedly a female. Seems to be looking for something . . ." He approached and lifted his hat. "Command me, madam!"

The woman drew herself yet closer under the shadow.

"Go your way, please!" she answered sharply, with a catch of her breath.

"You mishun'erstand. Allow me iggs—I beg pardon, eggs—plain. Name's Mortimer—Stanislas 'Ratio, of that ilk. A Scotch exshpression." Here he pulled himself together again, and with an air of anxious lucidity laid a precise accent on every syllable. "The name, I flatter myself, should be a guarantee. No reveller, madam, I s'hure you; appearances against me, but no Bacchanal; still lesh—shtill *less* I should iggs—or, if you prefer it, eggs—plain, gay Lothario. Trust me, ma'am—married man, fifteen years' standing—Arabella—tha's my wife— never a moment's 'neasiness—"

> 'Two shouls'—you'll excuse me, souls—' with but a single thought,
> Two hearts that beat ash one.'

"Between you and me, ma'am, we have thoughts of applying for Dunmow flitch. Quaint old custom, Dunmow flitch. Heard of it, I dareshay?"

"I wish you would go about your business."

Mr. Mortimer emitted a tragic laugh.

"I will, madam—I will: if it please you witness to what base uses we may return, Horatio. Allow me first remove mishunderstanding. Preshumed you to be searching for something—hairpin for exshample. Common occurrence with my Arabella. No offensh—merely proffered my shervices . . . The deuce! What's *that*?"

The woman seemed inclined to run, but stood hesitating.

"You heard it? There! close under the wall—"

Mr. Mortimer stepped forward and peered into the shadow. He was standing close above the manhole, and to the confusion of all his senses he saw the cover of the manhole lift itself up; saw the rim of it rise two, three inches, saw and heard it joggle back into its socket.

"For God's sake go away!" breathed the woman.

"Norrabit of it, ma'am. Something wrong here. Citizen's duty, anything wrong—"

Here the cover lifted itself again. Mr. Mortimer deftly slipped three fingers under its rim, and reaching back with his other hand produced from his pocket the second of Sam's two matches.

"Below there!" he hailed sepulchrally, at the same moment striking the match on the tense seat of his trousers and holding it to the aperture. "Nero is an angler in the lake of darkness . . . Eh? . . . Good Lord!"— he drew back and dropped the match—"it's a clergyman!"

He clapped down the cover in haste, sprang to his feet, and lifting his hat, made her the discreetest of bows. He was sober, now, as a judge.

"A thousand pardons, madam! I have seen nothing—believe me, nothing."

He strode in haste to Old Jubilee's headstall and began to back him towards the boat. The woman gazed at him for a moment in mere astonishment, then stepped quickly to his side.

"I didn' know," she stammered. "You don't look nor talk like a bargee."

Here her voice came to a halt, but in the dusk her eyes appeared to question him.

"Few of us are what we seem, ma'am," Mr. Mortimer sighed. "Bargee for the nonce I am, yet gentleman enough to understand a delicate situation. Your secret is safe with me, and so you may tell your—your friend."

"Then you must a-seen them?" she demanded.

"Them?" echoed Mr. Mortimer.

"No," she went on hurriedly, mistaking his hesitation. "They made you promise, an' I don't *want* to know. If I knew, he'd force it out o' me, an' then he 'd cut my heart out."

She glanced over her shoulder, and Mr. Mortimer, interpreting the glance, nodded in the direction of the manhole.

"Meanin' his Reverence?" he asked.

"His name's Glasson. The Orph'nage belongs to him. It's a serious thing for him to lose one o' the children, and he's like a madman about it ever since . . ." She broke off and put out a hand to help him with the haulage tackle. "Where are you taking her?"

"Her? The boat? Oh, back to Hucks's—Christopher Hucks, Anchor Wharf, Canal End Basin. 'Anchor,' you'll observe,—supposed emblem of Hope." He laughed bitterly.

"Yes, yes," she nodded. "And quick—quick as ever you can! Here, let me help—" She caught at one of the two crowbars that served for mooring-posts and tugged at it, using all her strength. "He'll be coming around here," she panted, and paused for a moment to listen. "If he catches me talkin', God knows what'll happen!" She tugged again.

"Steady does it," said Mr. Mortimer; and having helped her to draw the bar up, he laid it in the boat as noiselessly as he could and ran to the second. "There's no one coming," he announced. "But see here, if you're in fear of the man, let me have another go at the manhole. He may be down there yet, and if so I'll give him the scare of his life. Yes, ma'am, the scare of his life. You never saw my Hamlet, ma'am? You never heard me hold parley with my father's ghost? Attend!"

Mr. Mortimer stepped to the manhole and struck thrice upon it with his heel.

"Glasson!" he called, in a voice so hollow that it seemed to rumble down through the bowels of earth. "Glasson, forbear!"

"For God's sake—" The woman dragged at his shoulder as he knelt.

"All is discovered, Glasson! Thy house is on fire, thy orphans are flown. Rake not the cellarage for their bones, but see the newspapers. Already, Glasson, the newsboys run about the streets. It spreads, Glasson; may'st hear them call. Like wildfire it spreads. "Orrible discovery of 'uman remains! A clergyman suspected!'"

Here Mr. Mortimer, warm to his work, let out a laugh so blood-curdling that Old Jubilee bolted the length of his rope.

"The boat!" gasped the woman.

"Eh?"

Mr. Mortimer turned and saw the boat glide by the bank like a shadow; heard the thud of Old Jubilee's hoofs, and sprang in pursuit. The woman ran with him.

But the freshest horse cannot bolt far with a 72-feet monkey-boat dragging on his shoulders, and at the end of fifty yards, the towrope holding, Old Jubilee dropped to a jog-trot. The woman caught her breath as Mr. Mortimer jumped aboard and laid hold of the tiller. But still she ran beside panting.

"You won't tell him?"

Mr. Mortimer waved a hand.

"And—and you'll hide 'em—for he's bound to come askin'—you'll hide 'em if you can—"

Mr. Mortimer heard, but could not answer for the moment, the steerage claiming all his attention. When he turned towards the bank she was no longer there. He looked back over his shoulder. She had come to a dead halt and stood watching, her print gown glimmering in the dusk. And so, as the boat rounded the bend by the Brewery, he lost sight of her.

He passed a hand over his brow.

"Mysterious business," he mused; "devilish mysterious. On the face of it looks as if my friend Smiles, not content with self-help in its ordinary forms, has been helping himself to orphans! Must speak to him about it."

He pondered, gazing up the dim waterway, and by-and-by broke into a chuckle.

He chuckled again twenty minutes later, when, having stabled Old Jubilee, he crossed the yard to sup and to season the meal with a relation of his adventure.

"Such an encounter, my poppet!" he announced, groping his way across to the caravan, where his spouse had lit the lamp and stood in the doorway awaiting him. "Smiles—our ingenuous Smiles—has decoyed, has laid me under suspicion; and of what, d'you think? Stealing orphans!"

"Hush!" answered Mrs. Mortimer. "They 're here."

"They? Who? . . . Not the bailiffs? Arabella, don't tell me it's the bailiffs again!"

Mr. Mortimer drew back as though a snake lay coiled on the caravan steps.

"It's not the bailiffs, Stanislas; it's the orphans."

"But—but, my sweet, there must be some mistake. I—er—actually, of course, I have nothing to do with any orphans whatsoever."

"Oh, yes, you have," his wife assured him composedly. "They are inside here, with a yellow dog."

While Mr. Mortimer yet reeled under this news the door of the courtyard rattled and creaked open in the darkness. A lantern showed in the opening, and the bearer of it, catching sight of the lit caravan, approached with quick, determined strides.

"Can you inform me," asked a high clerical voice, "where I can find Mr. Christopher Hucks?"

The stranger held his lantern high, so that its ray fell on his face, and with that Mr. Mortimer groaned and collapsed upon the lowest step, where mercifully his wife's ample shadow spread an aegis over him.

"Mr. Hucks, sir?" Mrs. Mortimer answered the challenge. "I saw him, not twenty minutes ago, step into his private office there to the left, and by the light in the window he's there yet."

"But who is it?" she asked, as the stranger, swinging his lantern, marched straight up to Mr. Hucks's door.

"Good Lord, it's the man himself—Glasson! And he's come for his orphans."

"He shan't have 'em, then," said Mrs. Mortimer.

CHAPTER VII.

IN WHICH MR. HUCKS TAKES A HAND.

"*A many-sided man.*"—COLERIDGE ON SHAKESPEARE.

Let Mr. Christopher Hucks introduce himself in his own customary way, that is, by presenting his card of business:—

———————— | | | CHRISTOPHER HUCKS | | | | ANCHOR WHARF, CANAL END BASIN, BURSFIELD | | CANAL CARRIER, LIGHTERMAN, FREIGHTER AND WHARFINGER | | BOAT BUILDER, COAL AND GENERAL MERCHANT | | AUCTIONEER, PRACTICAL VALUER, HOUSE AND ESTATE AGENT | | | | ———— ——————- | | | | FIRE, LIFE, ACCIDENT AND PLATE GLASS INSURAMCES EFFECTED | | FIRE AND INCOME TAX CLAIMS PREPARED AND ADJUSTED | | LIVE STOCK INSURED AGAINST DEATH FROM ACCIDENT OR DISEASE | | SERVANTS REGISTRY OFFICE | | | | ————————— | | | | AGENT FOR JOHN TAYLOR AND CO.'S PHOSPHATE AND SOLUBLE BONE | | MANURES | | COPPERAS, CHARCOAL, ETC., FOR SEWAGE AND OTHER PURPOSES | | ACIDS AND ANILINES FOR THE TEXTILE TRADES | | | | ——————— | | | | VALUATIONS FOR PROBATE EMIGRATION AGENT | | PRIVATE ARRANGEMENTS NEGOTIATED WITH CREDITORS | | | | ——————- | | | | N.B.—ALL KINDS OF RIVER AND CANAL CRAFT BUILT OR REPAIRED, | | PURCHASED, SOLD, OR TO LET. NOTE THE ADDRESS | | |

Mr. Hucks, a widower, would have to be content in death with a shorter epitaph. In life his neighbours and acquaintances knew him as the toughest old sinner in Bursfield; and indeed his office hours (from 9 a.m. to 9 p.m. nominally—but he was an early riser) allowed him scant leisure to practice the Christian graces. Yet though many had occasion to curse Mr. Hucks, few could bring themselves to hate him. The rogue was so massive, so juicy.

He stood six feet four inches in his office slippers, and measured fifty-two inches in girth of chest. He habitually smoked the strongest shag tobacco, and imbibed cold rum and water at short intervals from morning to night; but these excesses had neither impaired his complexion, which was ruddy, jovial and almost unwrinkled, nor dimmed the delusive twinkle of his eyes. These, under a pair of grey bushy brows, met the world humorously, while they kept watch on it for unconsidered trifles; but never perhaps so humorously as when their owner, having clutched his prey, turned a deaf ear to appeal. For the rest, Mr. Hucks had turned sixty, but without losing his hair, which in colour and habit resembled a badger's; and although he had lived inland all his life, carried about with him in his dress, his gait, his speech an indefinable suggestion of a nautical past. If you tried to fix it, you found yourself narrowed down to explaining it by the blue jersey he wore in lieu of shirt and waistcoat. (He buttoned his braces over it, and tucked its slack inside the waistband of his trousers.) Or, with luck, you might learn that he habitually slept in a hammock, and corroborate this by observing the towzled state of his back hair. But the suggestion was, in fact, far more subtle, pervasive—almost you might call it an aroma.

The Counting House—so he called the single apartment in which he slung his hammock, wrote up his ledgers, interviewed his customers, and in the intervals cooked his meals on an oil-stove—was, in pact, a store of ample dimensions. To speak precisely, it measured thirty-six feet by fourteen. But Mr. Hucks had reduced its habitable space to some eight feet by six, and by the following process.

Over and above the activities mentioned on his business card, he was a landlord, and owned a considerable amount of cottage property, including a whole block of tenement houses hard by The Plain. Nothing could be simpler than his method of managing this estate. He never spent a penny on upkeep or repairs. On a vacancy he accepted any tenant who chose to apply. He collected his rents weekly and in person, and if the rent were not forthcoming he promptly distrained upon the furniture.

By this process Mr. Hucks kept his Counting House replete, and even crowded, with chattels, some of which are reckoned among the necessaries of life, while others—such as an accordion, a rain-gauge, and a case of stuffed humming-birds—rank rather with its superfluities. Of others again you wondered how on earth they had been taken in Mr. Hucks's drag-net. A carriage umbrella, for example, set you speculating on the vicissitudes of human greatness. When the collection impinged upon Mr. Hucks so that he could not shave without knocking his elbow, he would hold an auction, and effect a partial clearance; and this would happen about once in four years. But this clearance was never more than partial, and the residuum ever consisted in the main of musical instruments. Every man has his own superstitions, and for some reason Mr. Hucks—who had not a note of music in his soul—deemed it unlucky to part with musical instruments, which was the more embarrassing because his most transitory tenants happened to be folk who practised music on the public for a livelihood—German bandsmen, for instance, not so well versed in English law as to be aware that implements of a man's trade stand exempt from seizure in execution. Indeed, the bulk of the exhibits in Mr. Hucks's museum could legally have been recovered from him under writ of replevy. But there they were, and in the midst of them to-night their collector sat and worked at his ledger by the light of a hurricane lamp.

A knock at the door disturbed his calculations.

"Come in!" he called, and Dr. Glasson entered.

"Eh? Good evenin'," said Mr. Hucks, but without heartiness.

He disliked parsons. He looked upon all men as rogues more or less, but held that ministers of religion claimed an unfair advantage on the handicap. In particular this Dr. Glasson rubbed him, as he put it, the wrong way.

"Good evening," said Dr. Glasson. "You will excuse my calling at this late hour."

"Cert'nly. Come to pay for the coals? Fifteen tons best Newcastle at eighteen shillin' makes thirteen ten, and six pounds owin' on the last account—total nineteen ten. Shall I make out the receipt?"

"You don't seriously expect me, Mr. Hucks, to pay for your coals on the same day you deliver them—"

"No," Mr. Hucks agreed, "I didn' *expect* it; but I looked for ye to pay up the last account before I sent any more on credit. I've told Simmonds he was a fool to take your order, and he'll get the sack if it happens again. Fifteen tons, too! But Simmonds has a weak sort of respect for parsons. Sings in the choir somewhere. Well, if you ain't come to pay, you've come for something; to explain, may be, why you go sneakin' around my foreman 'stead of dealin' with me straight an' gettin' 'no' for an answer."

"Your manner is offensive, Mr. Hucks, but for the moment I must overlook it. The fact is, I want information, if you can give it, on an urgent matter. One of my charges is missing."

"Charges?" repeated Mr. Hucks. "Eh? Lost one of your orphans? Well, I haven't found him—or her, if it's a girl. Why don't you go to the police?"

"It is a boy. Naturally I hesitate to apply to the police if the poor child can be recovered without their assistance. Publicity in these matters, as no doubt you can understand—"

Mr. Hucks nodded.

"I understand fast enough."

"The newspapers exaggerate . . . and then the public—even the charitable public—take up some groundless suspicion—"

"Puts two and two together," agreed Mr. Hucks, still nodding, "and then the fat's in the fire. No, I wouldn' have the police poke a nose into the 'Oly Innocents—not if I was you. But how do *I* come into this business?"

"In this way. One of your employees was delivering coal to-day at the Orphanage—"

"Fifteen ton."

"—and I have some reason to believe that the child escaped by way of the coal-cellar. I am not suggesting that he was helped."

"Aren't you? Well, I'm glad to hear you say it, for it did look like you was drivin' at something o' the sort. I don't collect orphans, for my part," said Mr. Hucks with a glance around.

"What I meant to say was that your man—whoever he was—might be able to give some information."

"He might," conceded Mr. Hucks guardedly, "and he mightn't; and then again he might be more able than willin'."

"Must I remind you, Mr. Hucks, that a person who abets or connives at the sort of thing we are discussing is likely to find himself in trouble? or that even a refusal of information may be awkwardly construed?"

"Now see here, Glasson"—Mr. Hucks filled his pipe, and having lit it, leaned both elbows on the table and stared across at his visitor— "don't you ride the high horse with me. A moment ago you weren't suggestin' anything, and you'd best stick to that. As for my man— whoever he was—you can't charge him with stealin' one o' your blessed orphans until you lay hold on the orphan he stole and produce him in court. That's *Habeas Corpus*, or else 'tis *Magna Charter*—I forget which. What's more, you'd never face a court, an' you know it." He cast a curious glance at the Doctor's face, and added, "Sit down."

"I beg your pardon?"

"Sit down. No, not there." But the warning came too late. "Not hurt yourself, I hope?" he asked, as the Doctor rubbed that part of himself which had come into collision with the sharp edge of a concertina. "Clear away that coil of hose and take a seat on the packing-case yonder. That's right; and now let's talk." He puffed for a moment and appeared to muse. "Seems to me, Glasson, you're in the devil of a hurry to catch this child."

"My anxiety is natural, I should hope."

"No it ain't," said Mr. Hucks with brutal candour.

"And that's what's the matter with it. What's more, you come to me. Now," with continued candour, "I ain't what you might call a model

Christian; but likewise you don't reckon me the sort that would help you pick up orphans just for the fun of handin' 'em over to you to starve. So I conclude," Mr. Hucks wound up, "there's money in this somewhere."

Doctor Glasson did not answer for a few seconds. He seemed to be considering. His eyes blinked, and the folds of his lean throat worked as if he swallowed down something.

"I will be frank with you, Mr. Hucks," he said at length. "There may or may not be, as you put it, money in this. I have kept this child for close upon eight years, and during the last two the Orphanage has not received one penny of payment. He was brought to us at the age of two by a seafaring man, who declared positively that the child was not his, that he was legitimate, and that he had relatives in good position. The man would not tell me their names, but gave me his own and his address—a coast-guard station on the East coast. You will pardon my keeping these back until I know that you will help me."

"Go on."

"Sufficiently good terms were offered, and for six years my charges were regularly met without question. Then payment ceased. My demands for an explanation came back through the Dead Letter Office, and when I followed them up by a journey to the address given, it was to learn that my man—a chief boatman in the coast-guard service—had died three months before, leaving no effects beyond a pound or two and the contents of his sea-chest— no will—and, so far as could be traced, no kith or kin. So far, Mr. Hucks, the business does not look promising."

"All right, Glasson. You keep a child for two years on charity, and then get into a sweat on losing him. I trust your scent, and am not disheartened— yet."

"The boy has considerable natural refinement."

"You didn't keep him for *that*?"

"It has often suggested to me that his parentage was out of the ordinary— that he probably has relatives at least—er—well-to-do. But the main point is that he did not escape to-day of his own accord. He was kidnapped, and in circumstances that convince me there has been a deliberate plot. To my mind it is incredible that these children, without collusion—" But here Doctor Glasson pulled himself up and sat blinking.

"Eh? Was there more than one?" queried Mr. Hucks, sharp as a knife.

"There was a small girl, not one of my charges. She called on me shortly after midday with a story that an aunt of hers, who may or may not exist, but whom she pretended to anticipate, took an interest in this child. While she waited for this aunt's arrival, the—er—matron, Mrs. Huggins, incautiously allowed her access to the kitchen garden, where—without my knowledge and against my rules—the boy happened to be working. The pair of them have disappeared; and, further, I have convinced myself that their exit was made by way of the coal-shaft."

"A small girl, you say? What age?"

"About ten, as nearly as I can guess. A slip of a child, very poorly dressed, and walking with a decided limp."

"I follow you this far," said Mr. Hucks, ruminating. "—Allowin' there's a plot, if 'tis worth folks' while to get hold o' the child, 'tis worth your while to get him back from 'em. But are you sure there's a plot? There it don't seem to me you've made out your case."

Mr. Hucks said it thoughtfully, but his mind was not working with his speech. The coals, as he knew—though he did not propose to tell the Doctor, at any rate just yet—had been delivered by Sam Bossom. Of complicity in any such plot as this Sam was by nature incapable. On the other hand, Sam was just the fellow to help a couple of children out of mere kindness of heart. Mr. Hucks decided to have a talk with Sam before committing himself. He suspected, of course—nay, was certain—that Glasson had kept back something important.

Thus his meditations were running when the Doctor's reply switched the current in a new direction.

"You have not heard the whole of it. As it happens, the man in charge of the coal-boat was not, as I should judge, one of your regular employees—certainly not an ordinary bargeman—but a person whose speech betrayed him as comparatively well educated."

"Eh?" Mr. Hucks sat upright and stared.

"I am not suggesting—"

"No, damme—you 'd better not!" breathed Mr. Hucks.

"Very possibly he had bribed your man with the price of a pot of beer. At all events, there he was, and in charge of the boat."

"You saw him? Spoke to him?"

"To be accurate, he spoke to me—down the coal-shaft, as I was examining it. I judged him to be simulating drunkenness. But his voice was a cultivated one—I should recognise it anywhere; and Mrs. Huggins, who saw and spoke with him, describes him as a long-faced man, of gentlemanly bearing, with a furred collar."

"Good Lord! Mortimer!" ejaculated Mr. Hucks, but inwardly.

"I need hardly point out to you that a bargee in a furred collar—"

"No, you needn't." Mr. Hucks rose from his chair. "See here, Glasson, you've come with a notion that I'm mixed up in this. Well, as it happens, you're wrong. I don't ask you to take my word—I don't care a d—n whether you believe me or not—only you're wrong. What's more, I'll give no promise to help—not to-night, anyway. But I'm goin' to look into this, and to-morrow I'll tell you if we play the hand together. To-morrow at nine-thirty, if that suits? If not, you can go and get the police to help."

"Time may be precious," hesitated Glasson.

"Mine is, anyway," Mr. Hucks retorted. "Let me see you out. No, it's no trouble. I'm goin' to look into this affair right away."

He handed the Doctor his lantern, opened the door for him, and walked with him three parts of the way across the yard. As they passed the caravan door his quick ear noted a strange sound within. It resembled the muffled yap of a dog. But Mr. and Mrs. Mortimer did not keep a dog.

He halted. "There's the gate. Good night," he said, and stood watching while Glasson passed out. Then, swinging on his heel, he strode back to the caravan.

"Mortimer!" he challenged, mounting to the third step and knocking.

"Ha! Who calls?" answered the deep voice of Mr. Mortimer after two seconds' interval.

"Hucks. And I want a word with you."

The door opened a little way . . . and with that someone within the van uttered a cry, as a dark object sprang out over the flap, hurtled past Mr. Hucks, and hurled itself across the court towards the gate.

"'Dolph! 'Dolph!" called an agonised voice—a child's voice.

"The dog's daft!" chimed in Mr. Mortimer.

"'E'll kill 'im!"

As Mr. Hucks recovered his balance and stared in at the caravan doorway, now wide open, from the darkness beyond the gate came a cry and a fierce guttural bark—the two blent together. Silence followed. Then on the silence there broke the sound of a heavy splash.

CHAPTER VIII.

FLIGHT.

"_So all night long and through the dawn the ship cleft her way." — ODYSSEY, ii.

Mr. Hucks ran. Mr. Mortimer ran. As they reached the gate they heard the voice of Doctor Glasson uplifted, gurgling for help.

They spied him at once, for by a lucky chance his lantern—one of the common stable kind, with panes of horn—had fallen from his grasp as he pitched over the edge of the basin. It floated, bobbing on the waves cast up by his struggles and splashings, and by the light of it they quickly reached the spot. But unluckily, though they could see him well enough, they could not reach Doctor Glasson. He clung to the head-rope of a barge moored some nine feet from shore, and it appeared that he was hurt, for his efforts to lift himself up and over the stem of the boat, though persistent, were feeble, and at every effort he groaned. The dog—cause of the mischief—craned forward at him over the water, and barked in indecent triumph.

Mr. Mortimer, who had gone through the form of tearing off his coat, paused as he unbuttoned his waistcoat also, and glanced at Mr. Hucks.

"Can you swim?" he asked. "I—I regret to say it is not one of my accomplishments."

"I ain't goin' to try just yet," Mr. Hucks answered with creditable composure. "They 're bound to fetch help between 'em with the row they 're making. Just hark to the d—d dog."

Sure enough the alarm had been given. A voice at that moment hailed from one of the boats across the water to know what was the matter, and half a dozen porters, canal-men, night watchmen from the warehouses, came running around the head of the basin; but before they could arrive, a man dashed out of the darkness behind the two watchers, tore past them, and sprang for the boat. They heard the thud of his feet as he alit on her short fore-deck, and an instant later, as he leaned over the stem and gripped Dr. Glasson's coat-collar, the light of the bobbing lantern showed them his face. It was Sam Bossom.

He had lifted the Doctor waist-high from the water before the other helpers sprang on board and completed the rescue. The poor man was hauled over the bows and stretched on the fore-deck, where he lay groaning while they brought the boat alongside the quay's edge. By this time a small crowd had gathered, and was being pressed back from the brink and exhorted by a belated policeman.

It appeared as they lifted him ashore that the Doctor, beside the inconvenience of a stomachful of dirty canal water, was suffering considerable pain. In his fright (the dog had not actually bitten him) he had blundered, and struck his knee-cap violently against a bollard close by the water's edge, and staggering under the anguish of it, had lost his footing and collapsed overboard. Then, finding that his fingers could take no hold on the slippery concrete wall of the basin, with his sound leg he had pushed himself out from it and grasped the barge's head-rope. All this, between groans, he managed to explain to the policeman, who, having sent for an ambulance stretcher, called for volunteers to carry him home; for home Dr. Glasson insisted on being taken, putting aside—and with great firmness—the suggestion that he would be better in hospital.

Sam Blossom was among the first to offer his services. But here his master interposed.

"No, no, my lad," said Mr. Hucks genially, "you've behaved pretty creditable already, and now you can give the others a turn. The man's all right, or will be by to-morrow; and as it happens," he added in a lower tone, "I want five minutes' talk with you, and at once."

They watched while the sufferer was hoisted into his stretcher. So the escort started, the policeman walking close behind and the crowd following the policeman.

"Now," said Mr. Hucks as they passed out of sight, "you'll just step into the yard and answer a few questions. You too, sir," he turned to Mr. Mortimer and led the way. "Hullo!"—he let out a kick at Godolphus snuffling at the yard gate, and Godolphus, smitten on the ribs, fled yelping. "Who the devil owns that cur?" demanded Mr. Hucks, pushing the gate open.

"I do," answered a voice just within, close at his elbow. "An' I'll arsk you not to fergit it. Ought to be ashamed o' yerself, kickin' a pore dumb animal like that!"

"Eh?" Mr. Hucks passed down into the darkness. "Sam, fetch a lantern . . . So you 're the young lady I saw just now inside o' the van, and unless I'm mistaken, a nice job you're responsible for."

Tilda nodded. 'Dolph's indiscretion had put her in a desperate fix; but something told her that her best chance with this man was to stand up to him and show fight.

"Is he drowned?" she asked.

"Drowned? Not a bit of it. Only a trifle wet, and a trifle scared— thanks to that poor dumb animal of yours. A trifle hurt, too."

"I'm sorry he wasn't drowned," said Tilda.

"Well, you 're a nice Christian child, I must say. Start with kidnappin', and then down on your luck because you haven't wound up with murder! Where's the boy you stole?"

"In the caravan."

"Fetch him out."

"Shan't!"

"Now look here, missie—"

"I shan't," repeated Tilda. "Oh, Mr. Bossom, you won't let them! They're strong, I know . . . but he's got a knife that he took when Mr. Mortimer's back was turned, and if they try to drag 'im back to that Orph'nige—"

"Stuff and nonsense!" Mr. Hucks interrupted. "Who talked about handin' him back? Not me."

"Then you won't?"

"I'm not sayin' that, neither. Fetch the boy along into my Counting House, You and me must have a talk about this—in fact, I want a word with everybody consarned."

Tilda considered for a moment, and then announced a compromise.

"Tell you what," she said, "I don't mind comin' along with you first— not if you let 'Dolph come too."

"I shan't let him murder *me*, if that's in your mind."

Mr. Hucks grinned.

"You can call the others in if he tries," Tilda answered seriously. "But he won't, not if you be'ave. An' then," she went on, "you can arsk me anything you like, an' I'll answer as truthful as I can."

"Can't I see the boy first?" asked Mr. Hucks, hugely tickled.

"No, you can't!"

"You're hard on me," he sighed. The child amused him, and this suggestion of hers exactly jumped with his wishes. "But no tricks, mind. You others can look after the boy—I make you responsible for him. And now this way, missie, if you'll do me the honour!"

Tilda called to 'Dolph, and the pair followed Mr. Hucks to the Counting House, where, as he turned up the lamp, he told the child to find herself a seat. She did not obey at once; she was watching the dog. But 'Dolph, it appeared, bore Mr. Hucks no malice. He walked around for thirty seconds smelling the furniture, found a rag mat, settled himself down on it, and sat wagging his tail with a motion regular almost as a pendulum's. Tilda, observing it, heaved a small sigh, and perched herself on the packing-case, where she confronted Mr. Hucks fair and square across the table.

"Now you just sit there and answer me," said Mr. Hucks, seating himself and filling a pipe. "First, who's *in* this?"

"Me," answered Tilda. "Me and 'im."

Mr. Hucks laid down his pipe, spread his fingers on the table, and made as if to rise.

"I thought," said he, "you had more sense in you 'n an ord'nary child. Seems you have less, if you start foolin'."

"I can't 'elp 'ow you take it," Tilda answered. "I got to tell you what's true, an' chance the rest. Mr. Sam Bossom, 'e gave us a 'and at the coal-'ole, an' Mr. Mortimer got mixed up in it later on; an' that's all *they* know about it. There's nobody elst, unless you count the pore woman at the orspital, an' *she's* dead."

"That aunt of yours—is *she* dead too?"

Tilda grinned.

"You've been talkin' to Glasson."

"P'r'aps," suggested Mr. Hucks, after a shrewd glance at her, "you'd best tell me the story in your own way."

"That's what I'd like. You see," she began, "I been laid up three weeks in 'orspital—the Good Samaritan, if you know it—along o' bein' kicked by a pony. End o' last week they brought in a woman—dyin' she was, an' in a dreadful state, an' talkin'. I ought to know, 'cos they put her next bed to mine; s'pose they thought she'd be company. All o' one night she never stopped talkin', callin' out for somebody she called Arthur. 'Seemed as she couldn' die easy until she'd seen 'im. Next day—that's yesterday—her mind was clearer, an' I arsked her who Arthur was an' where he lived, if one had a mind to fetch 'im. I got out of her that he was called Arthur Miles Surname Chandon, an' that he lived at 'Oly Innercents. So this mornin', bein' allowed out, I went down to the place an' arsked to see Arthur Miles Surname Chandon. First thing I noticed was they didn' know he was called Chandon, for Glasson took a piece o' paper an' wrote it down. I was afraid of Glasson, an' pitched that yarn about an aunt o' mine, which was all kid. I never 'ad no aunt."

"What's your name, by the way?"

"Tilda."

"Tilda what?"

"That's what they *all* arsks," said Tilda wearily. "I dunno. If a body *can't* do without father an' mother, I'll make up a couple to please you, same as I made up a aunt for Glasson. Maggs's Circus is where I belong to, an' there 'twas Tilda, or 'The Child Acrobat' when they billed me."

"You don't look much like an acrobat," commented Mr. Hucks.

"Don't I? Well, you needn't to take *that* on trust, anyway."

The child stepped down from the packing-case, stretched both arms straight above her, and began to bend the upper part of her body slowly backward, as though to touch her heels with the backs of her fingers, but desisted half-way with a cry of pain. "Ow! It hurts." She stood erect again with tears in her eyes. "But 'Dolph will show you," she added upon a sudden happy thought, and kneeling, stretched out an arm horizontally.

"Hep, 'Dolph!"

The dog, with a bark of intelligence, sprang across her arm, turned on his hind legs, and sprang back again. She crooked her arm so that the tips of her fingers touched her hip, and with another bark he leapt between arm and body as through a hoop.

"He don't properly belong to me," explained Tilda. "He belongs to Bill, that works the engine on Gavel's roundabouts; but he larned his tricks off me. That'll do, 'Dolph; go an' lie down."

"He's a clever dog, and I beg his pardon for kicking him," said Mr. Hucks with a twinkle.

"He's better 'n clever. Why, 'twas 'Dolph that got us out."

"What, from the Orph'nage?"

"Yes." Tilda described how the Doctor had shut her in his drawing-room, how she had escaped to the garden and found the boy there, and how 'Dolph had discovered the coal-shaft for them. "An' then Mr. Bossom 'e 'elped us out an' put us across the canal. That's all the 'and '*e* took in it. An' from the canal I 'urried Arthur Miles up to the Good Samaritan; but when we got there his mother was dead—becos o' course she must a-been his mother. An' so," Tilda wound up, "I turned-to an' adopted 'im, an' we came along 'ere to arsk Mr. Bossom to 'elp us. An' now—if you give 'im up it 'll be a burnin' shame, an' Gawd'll pull your leg for it."

"That's all very well," said Mr. Hucks after a few moments' thought. "That's all very well, missie," he repeated, "but grown-up folks can't take your easy way wi' the law. You're askin' me to aid an' abet, knowin' him to be stolen; an' that's serious. If 'twas a matter between you an' me, now—or even between us an' Sam Bossom. But the devil is, these playactors have mixed themselves up in it, and the Doctor is warm on Mortimer's scent."

"I thought o' that d'reckly he told me. But O, Mr. 'Ucks, I thought on such a neav'nly plan!" Tilda clasped hands over an uplifted knee and gazed on him. Her eyes shone. "They told me you was keepin' them here for debt; but that's nonsense, becos they can't never pay it back till you let 'em make money."

"A fat lot I shall ever get from Mortimer if I let him out o' my sight. You don't know Mr. Mortimer."

"Don't I?" was Tilda's answer. "What d'yer take me for? Why *everybody* knows what Mr. Mortimer's like—everybody in Maggs's, anyway. He's born to borrow, Bill says; though at *Hamlet* or *Seven Nights in a Bar-Room* he beats the band. But as I said to his wife, 'Why shouldn' Mr. 'Ucks keep your caravan against what you owe, an' loan you a barge? He could put a man in charge to look after your takin's, so's you wouldn' get out o' reach till the money was paid: an' you could work the small towns along the canal, where the shows don't almost never reach. You won't want no more'n a tent,' I said, 'an' next to no scenery; an' me an' Arthur Miles could be the *Babes in the Wood* or the *Princes in the Tower* for you, with 'Dolph to fill up the gaps.'"

"Darn *me*," said Mr. Hucks, staring, "if you're not the cleverest for your size!"

"'Eav'nly—that was Mrs. Mortimer's word for it; an' Mr. Mortimer said 'twas the dream of 'is life, to pop—"

"Eh?"

"It began with pop—to pop something Shakespeare in places where they 'adn't 'eard of 'im. But you know 'is way."

Mr. Hucks arose, visibly pondering. 'Dolph, who had been keeping an eye on him, rose also, and 'Dolph's tail worked as if attached to a steam engine.

"There's a cargo, mostly beer, to be fetched up from Stratford," said Mr. Hucks after a pause. "Sam Bossom might take down the *Success to Commerce* for it, and he's as well out o' the way wi' the rest o' you."

Tilda clapped her hands.

"Mind you," he went on, "I'm not includin' any orphan. I got no consarn with one. I haven't so much as seen him."

He paused, with his eyes fixed severely on Tilda's.

She nodded.

"O' course not."

"And if, when you go back to the van and tell the Mortimers, you should leave the door open for a minute, forgetful-like, why that's no affair o' mine."

"I'm a'most certain to forget," owned Tilda. "If you'd been brought up half yer time in a tent—"

"*To* be sure. Now attend to this. I give Sam Bossom instructions to take the boat down to Stratford with three passengers aboard—you and the Mortimers—as a business speckilation; and it may so happen—I don't say it will, mind you—that sooner or later Mortimer'll want to pick up an extry hand to strengthen his company. Well, he knows his own business, and inside o' limits I don't interfere. Still, I'm financin' this voyage, as you might say, and someone must keep me informed. F'r instance, if you should be joined by a party as we'll agree to call William Bennetts, I should want to know how William Bennetts was doin', and what his purfessional plans were; and if you could find out anything more about W. B.—that he was respectably connected, we'll say—why so much the better. Understand?"

"You want Mr. Mortimer to write?" asked Tilda dubiously.

"No, I don't. I want *you* to write—that's to say, if you can."

"I can print letters, same as the play-bills."

"That'll do. You can get one o' the Mortimers to address the envelopes. And now," said Mr. Hucks, "I'd best be off and speak to Sam Bossom to get out the boat. Show-folks," he added thoughtfully, "likes travellin' by night, I'm told. It's cooler."

Two hours later, as the Brewery clock struck eleven, a canal-boat, towed by a glimmering grey horse, glided southward under the shadow of the Orphanage wall. It passed this and the iron bridge, and pursued its way through the dark purlieus of Bursfield towards the open country. Its rate of progression was steady, and a trifle under three miles an hour.

Astride the grey horse sat Mr. Mortimer, consciously romantic. The darkness, the secrecy of the flight—the prospect of recovered liberty—beyond this, the goal! As he rode, Mr. Mortimer murmured beatifically—

"To Stratford! To Stratford-on-Avon!" Sam Bossom stood on the small after-deck and steered. In the cabin Mrs. Mortimer snatched what repose was possible on a narrow side-locker to a person of her proportions; and on the cabin floor at her feet, in a nest of theatrical costumes, the two children slept dreamlessly, tired out, locked in each others arms.

CHAPTER IX.

FREEDOM.

"O, a bargeman's is the life for me, Though there's nothin' to be seen but scener-ee!"—
OLD SONG.

A pale shaft of daylight slanted through the cabin doorway. It touched Tilda's eyelids, and she opened them at once, stared, and relaxed her embrace.

"Awake?" asked Mrs. Mortimer's voice from the shadow above the locker. "Well, I'm glad of that, because I want to get to the stove. Sardines," said Mrs. Mortimer, "you can take out with a fork; but, packed as we are, when one moves the rest must follow suit. Is the boy stirring too?"

"No," answered Tilda, peering down on him. But as she slipped her arm from under his neck, he came out of dreamland with a quick sob and a shudder very pitiful to hear and to feel. "Hush!" she whispered, catching at his hand and holding it firmly. "It's *me*—Tilda; an' you won't go back there never no more."

"I—I thought—" said he, and so with an easier sob lay still.

"O' course you did," Tilda soothed him. "But what's 'appened to the boat, ma'am?"

"We are at anchor. If you want to know why, you had best crawl out and ask Mr. Bossom. He gave the order, and Stanislas has gone ashore to buy provisions. Marketing," said Mrs. Mortimer, "is not my husband's strong point, but we'll hope for the best."

The cabin doorway was low as well as narrow. Looking through it, Tilda now discerned in the gathering daylight the lower half of Sam Bossom's person. He sat with his legs dangling over the break of the stairway, and as the children crawled forth they perceived that he was busy with a small notebook.

"Why are we stoppin' here?" demanded Tilda, with a glance about her.

The boat lay moored against the bank opposite the towpath, where old Jubilee stood with his face deep in a nosebag. He stood almost directly against the rising sun, the effect of which was to edge his outline with gold, while his flank presented the most delicate of lilac shadows. Beyond him stretched a level country intersected with low hedges, all a-dazzle under the morning beams. To the left the land sloped gently upward to a ridge crowned, a mile away, by a straggling line of houses and a single factory chimney. Right astern, over Mr. Bossom's shoulder, rose the clustered chimneys, tall stacks, church spires of the dreadful town, already wreathed in smoke. It seemed to Tilda, although here were meadows and clean waterflags growing by the brink, and a wide sky all around, that yet this ugly smoke hung on their wake and threatened them.

"Why are we stoppin'?" she demanded again, as Sam Bossom, with a hurried if friendly nod, resumed his calculations.

"And four is fifteen, and fifteen is one-an'-three," said he. "Which," he added, looking up as one who would stand no contradiction, "is the 'alf of two-an'-six . . . You'll excuse me, missy, but business first an' pleasure afterwards. We're stoppin' here for the day."

"For the day?" echoed Tilda, with a dismayed look astern. "An' we've on'y come this far!"

"Pretty good goin', *I* should call it," Mr. Bossom assured her cheerfully. "Six locks we've passed while you was asleep, not countin' the stop-lock. But maybe you 're not used to travel by canal?"

"I thank the Lord, no; or I'd never 'ave put Mr. 'Ucks up to it. Why, I'd *walk* it quicker, crutch an' all."

"What'd you call a reas'nable price for eggs, now—at this time o' year?" asked Mr. Bossom, abstractedly sucking the stump of a pencil and frowning at his notebook. But of a sudden her words seemed to strike him, and he looked up round-eyed.

"You ain't tellin' me *you* put this in 'Ucks's mind?"

"'Course I did," owned Tilda proudly.

"An' got me sent to Stratford-on-Avon!" Mr. Bossom added. "Me that stood your friend when *you* was in a tight place!"

"No, I didn'. It was 'Ucks that mentioned Stratford—said you'd find a cargo of beer there, which sounded all right: an' Mortimer jumped at it soon as ever he 'eard the name. Mortimer said it was the dream of his youth an' the perspiration of his something else—I can't tell the ezact words; but when he talked like that, how was I to guess there was anything wrong with the place?"

"There ain't anything wrong wi' the *place*, that I know by," Mr. Bossom admitted.

"But I remember another thing he said, because it sounded to me even funnier. He said, 'Sweet swan of Avon upon the banks of Thames, that did so please Eliza and our James.' Now what did he mean by that?"

Mr. Bossom considered and shook his head.

"Some bank-'oliday couple, I reckon; friends of his, maybe. But about that swan—Mortimer must 'a-been talkin' through his hat. Why to get to the

Thames that bird'd have to go up the Stratford-on-Avon to Kingswood cut, down the Warwick an' Birmingham to Budbrooke—with a trifle o' twenty-one locks at Hatton to be worked or walked round; cross by the Warwick an' Napton—another twenty-two locks; an' all the way down the Oxford Canal, which from Napton is fifty miles good."

"She'd be an old bird before she got there, at our pace," Tilda agreed. "But, o' course, Mr. Bossom, if we want to get to Stratford quick, an' you don't, you'll make the pace what you like an' never mind us."

"Who said I didn' want to get to Stratford?" he asked almost fiercely, and broke off with a groan.

"Oh, it's 'ard!—it's 'ard! . . . And me sittin' here calcilatin' eggs an' milk domestic-like and thinkin' what bliss . . . But you don't understand. O' course you don't. Why should you?"

Tilda placed her hands behind her back, eyed him for half-a-minute, and sagely nodded.

"Well, I never!" she said. "Oh, my goodness gracious mercy me!"

"I can't think what you 're referrin' to," stammered Mr. Bossom.

"So we're in love, are we?"

He cast a guilty look around.

"There's Mortimer, comin' down the path, an' only two fields away."

"And it's a long story, is it? Well, I'll let you off this time," said Tilda. "But listen to this, an' don't you fergit it. If along o' your dawdlin' they lay hands on Arthur Miles here, I'll never fergive you— no, never."

"You leave that to me, missie. And as for dawdlin', why if you understood about canals you 'd know there's times when dawdlin' makes the best speed. Now just you bear in mind the number o' things I've got to think of. First, we'll say, there's you an' the boy. Well, who's goin' to look for you here, aboard an innercent boat laid here between locks an' waitin' till the full of her cargo comes down to Tizzer's Green wharf or Ibbetson's? Next"—he checked off the items on his fingers—"there's the Mortimers. In duty to 'Ucks, I got to choose Mortimer a pitch where he'll draw a 'ouse. Bein' new to this job, I'd like your opinion; but where, thinks I, 'll he likelier draw a 'ouse than at Tizzer's Green yonder?—two thousand op'ratives, an' I doubt if the place has ever seen a travellin' theayter since it started to grow. Anyway, Mortimer has been pushin' inquiries: an' that makes Secondly. Thirdly, I don't know much about play-actors, but Mortimer tells me he gets goin' at seven-thirty an' holds 'em spellbound till something after ten; which means that by the time we've carted back the scenery *an'* shipped *an'* stowed it, *an'* got the tarpaulins on, *an'* harnessed up, we shan't get much change out o' midnight. Don't lose your patience now, because we haven't come to the end of it yet—not by a long way. By midnight, say, we get started an' haul up to Knowlsey top lock, which is a matter of three miles. What do we find there?"

"Dunno," said Tilda wearily. "A brass band per'aps, an' a nillumynated address, congratylatin' yer."

Sam ignored this sarcasm.

"We find, likely as not, a dozen boats hauled up for the night, blockin' the fairway, an' all the crews ashore at the 'Ring o' Bells' or the 'Lone Woman,' where they doss an' where the stablin' is. Not a chance for us to get through before mornin'; an' then in a crowd with everybody wantin' to know what Sam Bossom's doin' with two children aboard. Whereas," he concluded, "if we time ourselves to reach Knowlsey by seven in the mornin', they'll all have locked through an' left the coast clear."

Said Tilda, still contemptuous—

"I 'd like to turn Bill loose on this navigation o' yours, as you call it."

"Oo's Bill?"

"He works the engine on Gavel's roundabouts; an' he's the best an' the cleverest man in the world."

"Unappre'shated, I spose?"

"Why if you 'ad Bill aboard this boat, in less'n a workin' day he'd 'ave her fixed up with boiler an' engine complete, an' be drivin' her like a train."

Mr. Bossom grinned.

"I'd like to see 'im twenty minutes later, just to congratilate 'im. You see, missie, a boat can't go faster than the water travels past 'er—which is rhyme, though I made it myself, an' likewise reason. Can she, now?"

"I s'pose not," Tilda admitted doubtfully.

"Well now, if your friend Bill started to drive th' old *Success to Commerce* like a train, first he'd be surprised an' disappointed to see her heavin' a two-foot wave ahead of her—maybe more, maybe less—along both banks; an' next it might annoy 'im a bit when these two waves fell together an' raised a weight o' water full on her bows, whereby she 'd travel like a slug, an' the 'arder he drove the more she wouldn' go; let be that she'd give 'im no time to cuss, even when I arsked 'im perlitely what it felt like to steer a monkey by the tail. Next *an'* last, if he should 'appen to find room for a look astern at the banks, it might vex 'im—bein' the best o' men as well as the cleverest—to notice that he 'adn't left no banks, to speak of. Not that 'twould matter to 'im pers'nally—'avin' no further use for 'em."

Tilda, confounded by this close reasoning, was about to retreat with dignity under the admission that, after all, canal-work gave no scope to a genius such as Bill's, when 'Dolph came barking to announce the near approach of Mr. Mortimer.

Mr. Mortimer, approaching with a gait modelled upon Henry Irving's, was clearly in radiant mood. Almost he vaulted the stile between the field and the canal bank. Alighting, he hailed the boat in nautical language—

"Ahoy, Smiles! What cheer, my hearty?"

"Gettin' along nicely, sir," reported Mr. Bossom. "Nicely, but peckish. The same to you, I 'ope."

"Good," was the answer. "Speak to the mariners: fall to't yarely, or we run ourselves aground. Bestir, bestir!"

Tilda, who for the last minute or so had been unconsciously holding Arthur Miles by the hand, was astonished of a sudden to find it trembling in hers.

"You mustn' mind what Mr. Mortimer says," she assured the child encouragingly—"it's on'y his way."

Mr. Mortimer stepped jauntily across the gang-plank, declaiming with so much of gesture as a heavy market-basket permitted—

"The pirates of Parga, who dwell by the waves,
 And teach the pale Franks what it is to be slaves,
 Shall leave by the beach, Smiles, the long galley and oar—"

"I have done it, Smiles. In the words of the old-time classical geometer, I have found it; and as he remarked on another occasion (I believe subsequently), 'Give me where to stand, and I will move the Universe.' His precise words, if I recall the original Greek, were *Dos Pou Sto*—and the critical ear will detect a manly—er—self-reliance in the terse monosyllables. In these days," pursued Mr. Mortimer, setting down the market-basket, unbuttoning his furred overcoat, extracting a green and yellow bandanna from his breastpocket and mopping his heated brow, "in these days we have lost that self-confidence. We are weary, disillusioned. We have ceased to expect gold at the rainbow's foot. Speaking without disrespect to the poet Shelley"—here he lifted his hat and replaced it—"a new Peneus does *not* roll his fountains against the morning star, whatever that precise—er—operation may have been. But let us honour the aspiration, Smiles, though the chill monitor within forbid us to endorse it. 'A loftier Argo'"—Mr. Mortimer indicated the *Success to Commerce* with a sweep of the hand—

"A loftier Argo cleaves the main
  Fraught with a later prize;
Another Orpheus—you'll excuse the comparison—sings again,
  And loves, and weeps—and dies."

"Stanislas, you have not forgotten the eggs, I hope?" interposed the voice of Mrs. Mortimer from the cabin.

"I have not, my bud. Moreover, as I was just explaining to our friend, I have secured a *Pou Sto*—a hall, my chick—or perhaps it might be defined more precisely as a—er—loft. It served formerly—or, as the poets would say, whilom—as a barracks for the Salvation Army; in more recent times as a store for—er—superphosphates. But it is commodious, and possesses a side-chamber which will serve us admirably for a green-room when the proprietor—an affable person by the name of Tench— has removed the onions at present drying on the floor; which he has engaged to do."

"Are you tellin' me," inquired Sam, "that you've been and 'ired the room?"

"At the derisory charge of four-and-six for the night. As a business man, I believe in striking while the iron is hot. Indeed, while we are on the subject, I may mention that I have ordered the bills. *Professor and Madame St. Maw*— my Arabella will, I know, forgive my reverting to the name under which she won her maiden laurels—it cost me a pang, my dear Smiles, to reflect that the fame to be won here, the honour of having popularised HIM, here on the confines of his native Arden, will never be associated with the name of Mortimer. *Sic vos non vobis*, as the Mantuan has poignantly observed. But for the sake of the children— and, by the way, how do my bantlings find themselves this morning? Tol-lollish, I trust?—for the sake of the children it was necessary, as we used to say with the Pytchley, to obscure 'the scent. Talking of scent, Smiles, it might be advisable—what with the superphosphates and the onions—to take some counteracting steps, which your ingenuity may be able to suggest. The superphosphates especially are— er—potent. And, by one of those coincidences we meet, perhaps, oftener than we note, Mr. Tench's initial is 'S'—standing for Samuel."

Mr. Mortimer extracted an egg from his basket and rubbed it with his bandanna thoughtfully before passing it down to his wife.

"So you've been an' ordered the bills too?" murmured Mr. Bossom. "And what will the bills run to?—if, as the treasurer, I may make so bold."

"To the sum of five shillings precisely, which will, of course, be hypothecated as a first charge upon our takings, and which I ask you, my dear Smiles, as treasurer to debit to that account in due form, here and now." It would have been hard to conceive any manner more impressively business-like than Mr. Mortimer's as he made this demand. "You will excuse my putting it so plainly,

Smiles, but I may venture a guess that in the matter of conducting a theatrical tour you are, comparatively speaking, a tiro?"

"I've got to account to 'Ucks, if that's what you mean," Sam assented.

"The bill, Smiles, is the theatrical agent's first thought; the beginning which is notoriously half the battle. For three-inch lettering—and to that I restricted myself—five shillings can only be called dirt cheap. Listen—"

PROFESSOR AND MADAME ST. MAUR, OF THE LEADING LONDON THEATRES

PART I.—WITH VOICE AND LUTE, A POT-POURRI PART II.—AN HOUR WITH THE BEST DRAMATISTS

THE WHOLE TO CONCLUDE WITH THAT SIDE-SPLITTING DUOLOGUE ENTITLED,

'COURTSHIP IN THE RAIN'

PASSION WITH REFINEMENT AND MIRTH WITHOUT VULGARITY

Reserved Seats, One Shilling. Unreserved, Sixpence. Gallery (limited), Threepence only

DOORS OPEN AT 7.30; TO COMMENCE AT 8. CARRIAGES AT HALF-PAST TEN

"Why carriages?" asked Mr. Bossom.

"It's the usual thing," answered Mr. Mortimer.

"You bet it isn't, at Tizzer's Green. Well, the first job is breakfast, an' after breakfast we'll get Old Jubilee round by the footbridge an' make shift to borrow a cart down at Ibbetson's, for the scenery. You didn' forget the bacon?"

Mr. Mortimer unwrapped a parcel of greasy paper and exhibited six slices.

"A Baconian—O, Shakespeare, forgive!" He said this in a highly jocular manner, and accompanied it with a wink at Tilda, who did not understand the allusion. But again she felt the child's hand thrill and tremble, and turned about, eyeing him curiously. Her movement drew upon him the Mortimerian flow, ever ebullient and ever by trifles easily deflected.

"Yes, Arthur Miles—if I may trouble you to pass it down to the cook's galley—thank you; these eggs too—be careful of them—Yes, we are bound for Stratford-on-Avon, Shakespeare's birthplace!" Again he lifted and replaced his hat. "Enviable boy! What would young Stanislas Mortimer not have given at your age to set eyes on that Mecca! Yet, perchance, he may claim that he comes, though late, as no unworthy votary. A Passionate Pilgrim, shall we say? Believe me, it is in the light of a pilgrimage that I regard this—er—jaunt. Shall we dedicate it to youth, and name it Childe Arthur's Pilgrimage?"

By this time smoke was issuing in a steady stream from the stove-pipe above the cabin-top, and presently from within came the hiss and fragrance of bacon frying. Sam Bossom had stepped ashore, and called to the children to help in collecting sticks and build a fire for the tea-kettle. Tilda, used though she was to nomad life, had never known so delightful a picnic. Only her eyes wandered back apprehensively, now and then, to the smoke of the great town. As for Arthur Miles—Childe Arthur, as Mr. Mortimer henceforth insisted on their calling him—he had apparently cast away all dread of pursuit. Once, inhaling the smell of the wood fire, he even laughed aloud—a strange laugh, and at its close uncannily like a sob. Tilda, watching him quietly, observed that he trembled too—trembled all over—from time to time. She observed, too, that this happened when he looked up from the fire and the kettle; but also that in looking up he never once looked back, that his eyes always wandered along the still waterway and to the horizon ahead. This puzzled her completely.

Breakfast followed, and was delightful, though not unaccompanied by terrors. A barge hove in sight, wending downwards from Bursfield, and the children hid. It passed them, and after ten minutes came a couple from the same direction, with two horses hauling at the first, and the second (which Sam called a butty-boat) towed astern. Each boat had a steersman, and the steersman called to Sam and asked for news of his young woman; whereupon Sam called back, offering to punch their heads for twopence. But it was all very good-natured. They passed on laughing, and the children re-emerged. The sun shone; the smoke of the embers floated against it, across the boat, on the gentlest of breezes; the food was coarse, but they were hungry; the water motionless, but Mr. Mortimer's talk seemed to put a current into it, calling them southward and to high adventures—southward where no smoke was, and the swallows skimmed over the scented water-meads. Even the gaudily-painted cups and saucers, which Mr. Mortimer produced from a gaudily-painted cupboard, made part of the romance. Tilda had never seen the like. They were decorated round the rims with bands of red and green and yellow; the very egg-cups were similarly banded; and portraits of the late Queen Victoria and the Prince Consort decorated the cupboard's two panels.

Breakfast over, she helped Mr. Mortimer to wash up, and while she helped was conscious of a new and uncomfortable feeling, of which she could make no account with herself. It was not the stuffiness of the cabin that oppressed her; nor the dread of pursuit; nor anxiety for Arthur Miles, lest he should run off and fall into mischief. By stooping a little she could keep him in view, for he had settled himself on the after-deck, and was playing with 'Dolph—or, rather, was feeling 'Dolph's ears and paws in a wondering fashion, as one to whom even a dog was something new and marvellous; and 'Dolph, stretched on his side in the sunshine, was undergoing the inspection with great complaisance. No; the cause of her restlessness was yet to seek.

She went out and sat upon the cabin step for awhile, deep in thought, her eyes fixed on Sam Bossom, who, just beyond the cabin roof, was stooping over the well and untying its tarpaulins. By and by she sprang to her feet and walked forward to him.

"Mr. Bossom," she said with decision, "I know what's the matter with me."

"Then," answered Sam, "you 're luckier than most people."

"I want a wash."

"Do you, now? Well, as to that, o' course you're the best judge; but I 'adn't noticed it."

"You wouldn't, 'ardly," said Tilda, "seein' as I 'ad one on'y yestiddy. But that's the worst of 'orspitals. They get you inside, an' a'most before you know where you are, they've set up a 'abit. I dessay it'll wear off, all right; but oh, Mr. Bossom—"

"Would you mind callin' me Sam? It's more ushual."

"Oh, Mr. Sam, this mornin' I'm feelin' it all over. If I got a pailful out o' the canal, now?"

"I wouldn' recommend it—not 'ereabouts." Sam, eyeing her with his head cocked slightly aside, spoke gently as one coaxing a victim of the drink habit. "But, as it 'appens, a furlong this side of Ibbetson's you'll find the very place. Take Arthur Miles along with you. He'll be thankful for it, later on—an' I'll loan you a cake o' soap."

CHAPTER X.

THE FOUR DIAMONDS.

"Where the hazel bank is steepest,
Where the shadow falls the deepest,
Where the clustering nuts fall free,
That's the way for Billy and me."—JAMES HOGG.

The spot was a hollow between two grassy meadows, where a brook came winding with a gentle fall, under coverts of hazel, willow and alder, to feed the canal. It was a quite diminutive brook, and its inflow, by the wharf known as Ibbetson's, troubled the stagnant canal water for a very short distance. But it availed, a mile above, to turn a mill, and— a marvel in this country of factories—it had escaped pollution. Below the mill-dam it hurried down a pretty steep declivity, dodging its channel from side to side, but always undercutting the bank on one side, while on the other it left miniature creeks or shoals and spits where the minnows played and the water-flies dried their wings on the warm pebbles; always, save that twice or thrice before finding its outlet it paused below one of these pebbly spits to widen and deepen itself into a pool where it was odds that the sun, slanting through the bushes, showed a brown trout lurking.

By such a pool—but they had scared away the trout—our two children were busy. Tilda, her ablutions over, had handed the cake of soap to Arthur Miles, scrambled out on the deeper side, and ensconced herself in the fork of an overhanging hazel-mote; where, having reached for a cluster of nuts and cracked them, she sat and munched, with petticoat dripping and bare legs dangling over the pool.

"Be sure you don't fergit be'ind the ears," she admonished the boy. "You may think you're on'y a small boy an' nobody's goin' to search yer corners; but back at the Good Samaritan there was a tex' nailed up— *Thou Gawd seest me*; and Sister said 'E was most partic'lar just in the little places you wouldn't think."

By her orders the boy had stripped off shirt and stockings, and stood now almost knee-deep in the water, lathering his hair and face and neck and shoulders with vigour. Tilda observed that his skin was delicately fair and white. She had never seen a more beautiful boy. But he was slender, and would need mothering.

"You're comin' to it nicely," she called down to him. "It feels funny to start with, but in the end you'll a'most get to like it."

"I *do* like it."

She considered for a while.

"If that's so," she said, "you 'd better strip all over an' 'ave done with it. I was bringin' you to it gradual."

"But—"

"Oh, *that's* all right. I knows my manners. Be quick as you can, so's not to catch cold, an' I'll take a stroll up the bank an' give a call if anyone's comin'."

She scrambled back to firm ground and set off for a saunter up stream, pausing here to reach for a nut, there to pluck a ripe blackberry, and again to examine a tangle of bryony, or the deep-red fruit of the honey-suckle; for almost all her waking life had been spent in towns among crowds, and these things were new and strange to her. She met no one on her way until, where the stream twisted between a double fold of green pasture slopes, she came to the mill—a tall rickety building, with a tiled roof that time had darkened and greened with lichens, and a tall wheel turning slowly in a splash of water, and bright water dancing over a weir below. In the doorway leaned a middle-aged man, powdered all over with white, even to the eyelids. He caught sight of her, and she was afraid he would be angry, and warn her off for trespassing; but he nodded and called out something in a friendly manner— "Good day," perhaps. She could not hear the words for the hum of the weir and the roaring of the machinery within the building.

It was time to retrace her steps, and she went back leisurably, peering for trout and plucking on the way a trail of the bryony, berried with orange and scarlet and yellow and palest green, to exhibit to Arthur Miles. She found him seated on the near bank, close beside her hazel-mote. He did not hear her barefooted approach, being absorbed in the movements of a wagtail that had come down to the pebbly spit for its bath; and Tilda started scolding forthwith. For he sat there naked to the waist, with his shirt spread to dry on the grass. He had given it a thorough soaping, and washed it and wrung it out: his stockings too.

"You'll catch yer death!" threatened Tilda.

But he was not shivering—so blandly fell the sun's rays, and so gently played the breeze.

"I can't make you out," she confessed. "First when I came on yer—an' that was on'y yestiddy—you was like a thing afraid o' yer own shadder. An' now you don't appear to mind nothin'—not even the chance o' bein' found an' took back."

The boy drew a long breath.

"You're shakin' with cold, though. There! What did I tell yer?" But a moment later she owned herself mistaken. He was not cold at all.

"It's all so—so good," he murmured, more to himself than to her.

"What's good?"

He reached out for the trail of bryony in her lap and fingered it wonderingly, without speaking for a while. Then, lifting his hand, he laid it for a moment against her upper arm—the lightest touch—no more.

"You," he said. "You—and everything."

"Of all the queer boys—" she began, and broke off with a catch of the breath. "Hulloa!"

The boy looked up to see her eyes fixed, round and wide, on his naked shoulder.

"What's that mark you got there?" she demanded.

"This?" He put up a hand to a pattern of four diamonds joined in a horizontal line. "I don't know. I've wondered sometimes—"

"But you must 'ave come by it some'ow. Can't you remember?"

He shook his head.

"It has been there always. And yet I couldn't have been born with it."

"'Course yer couldn'," she agreed

The mark was pencilled in thin lines of red a little below the right shoulder, across the width of the deltoid muscle, and in figures about half an inch tall. "'Course yer couldn'," she repeated. "That's tattooin', if ever there was tattooin'; an', what's more," she went on, nodding her head with great positiveness, "I know who done it, leastways I know part of 'is name . . . Don't stare, now; lemme *think* . . . Yes, it's plain as plain. 'Four di'monds,' she said; an' di'monds they are, same as on a pack o' cards—me all the time thinkin' of them as the ladies wear on their fingers. But 'on his coat,' she said; nothin' about yer shoulder."

"'She'? Who was 'she'?" asked the boy. "Never you mind," said Tilda hurriedly. "But him as done it was called Ned. Now try to think if you ever came across a party as was called Ned?"

"There was a boy called Ned at Holy Innocents; but he died in the time we all had sore throats—and, besides, he was the youngest of us. I don't remember any other."

"Any sailor-man, then? It's mostly sailors that know about tattooin'."

"Oh, yes," he answered promptly, to her surprise. "There were lots of sailors—five or six, I think. They had long glasses, and used to watch the sea. And one played music on a thing that went *so*."

He brought his hands together, drew them wide, and brought them together again—the palms open.

"That would be a concertina," nodded Tilda, "or elst an accordion. Now try to think, becos' all this is very important . . . Where was this place? and what like was it?"

He considered for a while, frowning to help his memory.

"There was a line of white houses, and one had red flowers in the window . . . and a pole, with flags on it . . . and ships passing . . . and from the houses a path went down to the sea. I remember quite well what it was like down there . . . with waves coming in, but not reaching to us, and sand where I played, and rocks, and pools full of shells and brown flowers. There were shells, too, on the rocks, with live things inside—though they never moved. I don't think I knew their name; but I know it now. They were called 'scammels.'"

"I've ate limpets," said Tilda; "limpets an' whelks. But I never 'eard o' scammels. An' you don't remember the name o' this place?"

"It must have been the Island," said the boy slowly.

"Wot Island? Island's a sort o' place, but no place in partic'lar."

"I don't know . . . It must have been the Island, though."

"Now listen. Did you ever 'appen to 'ear tell of 'Olmness?"

She asked it eagerly, watching his face. But it gave no answer to her hopes. His eyes were dreamy. The word, if it struck at all on his hearing, struck dully.

"I don't see that the name matters," he said after a long pause, "so long as it's the Island. We 're going there, and we shall find out all about it when we get to Stratford."

"Shall we?" asked Tilda, considerably astonished. "But *why*, in the world?"

"Because . . . Didn't you hear Mr. Mortimer say that Shakespeare was born there?"

"I did," said Tilda. "'Ow's that goin' to 'elp us?"

"I don't know," the boy confessed, dragging a book from his pocket. It was a ragged copy of the "Globe" Shakespeare, lacking its covers and smeared with dirt and blacking. "But he knows all about the Island."

"So *that*," said Tilda, "is what 'urt me in the night! It made my ribs all sore. I fergot the book, an' thought you must be sufferin' from some kind o' growth; but didn't like to arsk till I knew yer better— deformed folks bein' mostly touchy about it. When you stripped jus' now, an' nothin' the matter, it puzzled me more'n ever. 'Ere—show me where 'e tells about it," she demanded, taking the volume and opening it on her lap.

"It's all at the beginning, and he calls it *The Tempest* . . . But it will take you ever so long to find out. There was a ship wrecked, with a wicked duke on board, and he thought his son was drowned, but really it was all brought about by magic . . . In the book it's mostly names and speeches, and you only pick up here and there what the Island was like."

"But what makes you sure it's *your* Island?"

"You wait till we get to Stratford and ask him," said the boy, nodding, bright and confident.

"Arsk'oo? Shakespeare? Sakes alive, child! Don't yer know 'e's been dead these 'undreds o' years?"

"Has he?" His face fell, but after a moment grew cheerful again. "But that needn't matter. There must be heaps of people left to tell us about it."

Tilda closed the book. She had learnt a little, but had been disappointed in more. She felt desperately sorry for the child with this craze in his head about an Island. She had a suspicion that the memories he related were all mixed up with fictions from the play. As she put it to herself, "'E don't mean to kid, but 'e can't 'elp 'isself." But there was one question she had omitted and must yet ask.

"You said, jus' now, you used to play by the sea, somewheres beneath that line o' white houses you was tellin' of. Well, you couldn' a-got down there on your own, at that age—could yer, now? W'ich means you must a-been carried."

"I suppose so."

"No supposin' about it. You *must* a-been. Wot's more, you talked about the waves comin' in an' not reachin'—'us,' you said. 'Oo was it with yer? Think now! Man or woman?"

"A woman," he answered after a pause, knitting his brows.

"Wot like?"

Then happened something for which—so quiet his words had been—Tilda was in no wise prepared. He turned his eyes on her, and they were as the eyes of a child born blind; blank, yet they sought; tortured, yet dry of tears. His head was tilted back, and a little sideways. So may you see an infant's as he nuzzles to his mother's breast. The two hands seemed to grope for a moment, then fell limp at his side.

"Oh, 'ush!" besought Tilda, though in fact he had uttered no sound. "'Ush, an' put on your shirt, an' come 'ome! We'll get Mrs. Mortimer to dry it off by the stove."

She helped him on with it, took him by the hand, and led him back unresisting.

They reached the canal bank in time to see Sam Bossom leading Old Jubilee down the towpath, on his way to borrow a cart at Ibbetson's. And 'Dolph— whom Tilda had left with strict orders to remain on board— no sooner caught sight of the children than he leapt ashore and came cringing.

The dog appeared to be in mortal terror; a terror at which the children no longer wondered as they drew near the boat. Terrible sounds issued from the cabin—cries of a woman imploring mercy, fierce guttural oaths of a man determined to grant none.

"Good Lord!" exclaimed Tilda, gripping Arthur Miles more tightly by the hand and hurrying him into a run. "Whatever's taken the couple?"

She paused at the gangway and listened, peering forward.

"Oh, banish me, my lord, but kill me not!" wailed the voice of Mrs. Mortimer.

"Down, base one!" shouted her husband's.

"Kill me to-morrow; let me live to-night!"

"Nay, if you strive—a little more stress, dear, on 'to-night,' if I may suggest— Nay, if you strive—!"

"Shall we take it again, Stanislas? You used to take the pillow at 'Kill me not.'"

"I believe I did, my bud. We are rusty—a trifle rusty—the both of us."

"Kill me to-morrow; let me live—" entreated Mrs. Mortimer.

"What's all this, you two?" demanded Tilda, springing down the cabin steps and hurling herself between them.

"Hullo! Come in!" answered Mr. Mortimer genially. "This? Well, I hope it is an intellectual treat. I have always looked upon Mrs. Mortimer's Desdemona as such, even at rehearsal."

CHAPTER XI.

THE "STRATFORD-ON-AVON"

"*Day after day, day after day We stuck.*"—COLERIDGE, Rime of the Ancient Mariner

"Well, and 'ow did the performance go off?"

When Tilda awoke at seven o'clock next morning, the *Success to Commerce* had made three good miles in the cool of the dawn, and come to anchor again (so to speak) outside the gates of Knowsley top lock, where, as Sam Bossom explained later, the canal began to drop from its summit level. Six locks, set pretty close together, here formed a stairway for its descent, and Sam would hear no word of breakfast until they had navigated the whole flight.

The work was laborious, and cost him the best part of an hour. For he had to open and shut each pair of gates single-handed, using a large iron key to lift and close the sluices; and, moreover, Mr. Mortimer, though he did his best, was inexpert at guiding the boat into the lock-chamber and handling her when there. A dozen times Sam had to call to him to haul closer down towards the bottom gates and avoid fouling his rudder.

The children watched the whole operation from shore, now and then lending their small weight to push open the long gate-beams. 'Dolph, too, watched from shore; suspiciously at first, afterwards with a studied air of boredom, which he relieved by affecting, whenever the heel of a stern-post squeaked in its quoin, to mistake it for a rat—an excuse for aimless snuffling, whining and barking. And Mrs. Mortimer looked on from the well by the cabin door, saucepan in hand, prepared to cook at the shortest notice. It was fascinating to see her, at first in the almost brimming lock, majestically erect (she was a regal figure) challenging the horizon with a gaze at once proud, prescient of martyrdom, and prepared; and then, as Sam opened the sluices, to watch her descend, inch by inch, into the dark lock-chamber. Each time this happened Mr. Mortimer exhorted her—"Courage, my heart's best!"—and she made answer each time, "Nay, Stanislas, I have no terrors."

Mr. Mortimer, at the fifth lock, left Old Jubilee and walked around to remark to Tilda that on the boards some such apparatus—"if it could be contrived at moderate expense"—would be remarkably effective in the drowning scene of *The Colleen Bawn*; or, in the legitimate drama, for the descent of Faustus into hell; "or, by means of a gauze transparency, the death of Ophelia might be indicated. I mention Ophelia because it was in that part my Arabella won what—if the expression may be used without impropriety—I will term her spurs. I am given to understand, however," added Mr. Mortimer, "that the apparatus requires a considerable reservoir, and a reservoir of any size is only compatible with fixity of tenure. An Ishmael—a wanderer upon the face of the earth—buffeted this way and that by the chill blast of man's ingratitude, more keenly toothed (as our divine Shakespeare observed) than winter's actual storm—but this by the way; it is not mine to anticipate more stable fortune, but rather to say with Lear—"

"'Blow, winds, and crack your cheeks!'"

"I merely drop the suggestion—and I pass on."

He folded his arms and passed on. That is to say, he strode off in a hurry at a summons from Sam to stand by and pole the boat clear as the lower lock-gates were opened.

Somehow Tilda divined that Mr. and Mrs. Mortimer were in high spirits this morning, and it was with reasonable confidence that, after they had moored below locks and breakfasted, she sought Sam—who had withdrawn to the bows with his account book—and inquired how the performance had gone off.

"There was a small misunderstandin' at the close," he answered, looking up and pausing to moisten the lead of his pencil, "owin' to what the bills said about carriages at ten-thirty. Which the people at Tizzer's Green took it that carriages was to be part of the show, an' everyone to be taken 'ome like a lord. There was a man in the gallery, which is otherwise back seats at threppence, got up an' said he'd a-come on that contrack, an' no other. Mortimer made 'im a speech, and when that wouldn' do I copped 'im on the back o' the neck."

"An' after that, I s'pose, there was a free fight?"

"No," said Sam; "you 'd be surprised how quiet 'e took it. 'E was unconscious."

She eyed him thoughtfully.

"It don't seem like you, neither," she said, "to strike a man so 'ard, first blow."

"You're right, there; it *ain't* like me, an' I felt sorry for the fella'. But I 'ad to relieve my feelin's."

"What was the matter with yer feelin's?"

"'Arrowed—fairly 'arrowed." Sam shot an uneasy glance aft towards the cabin top where Mr. and Mrs. Mortimer sat amicably side by side, he conning a part while she mended a broken string on her guitar. Beyond them, stretched on the after deck with 'Dolph for company, Arthur Miles leaned over the gunwale, apparently studying the boat's reflection in the water. "Between you an' me," Sam confessed, "I can't get no grip on play-actors; an'

I'm sorry I ever took up with 'em." He consulted his accounts. "He cleared three pound twelve an' nine las' night—but 'ow? That Mortimer carried on something 'ateful. There was 'is wife—you wouldn' think it in ordinary life, but, dressed up, she goes to your 'eart; an' she wore, first an' last, more dresses than you could count. First of all she 'it a little tambourine, an' said she was a gipsy maid. 'I'm a narch little gipsy,' she said, 'an' I never gets tipsy'—"

"Why *should* she?"

"'But I laugh an' play,' she said, 'the whole o' the day, such a nartless life is mine, ha, ha!' which wasn' none of it true, except about the drink, but you could see she only done it to make 'erself pleasant. An' then she told us ow' when they rang a bell somebody was goin' to put Mortimer to death, an' 'ow she stopped that by climbin' up to the bell and 'angin' on to the clapper. Then in came Mortimer an' sang a song with 'er—as well 'e might—about 'is true love 'avin' 'is 'eart an' 'is 'avin' 'ers, an' everyone clappin' an' stampin' an' ancorein' in the best of tempers. Well, an' what does the man do after an interval o' five minutes, but dress hisself up in black an' call 'er names for 'avin' married his uncle? This was too much for the back seats, an' some o' them told 'im to go 'ome an' boil 'is 'ead. But it 'ad no effect; for he only got worse, till he ended up by blackin' 'is face an' smotherin' 'er with a pillow for something quite different. After that he got better, an' they ended up by playin' a thing that made everybody laugh. I didn' 'ear it, but took a walk outside to blow off steam, an' only came back just as the fuss began about the carriages. Fact is, missy, I can't abear to see a woman used abuseful."

"That's because you 're in love," said Tilda. "But, if you'll listen to me, women ain't always what you take 'em for."

"Ain't they?" he queried. "I'd be sorry to believe that; though 'twould be 'elpful, I don't mind tellin' you."

"I've known cases—that is, if you *want* to be cured—"

"I do, an' I don't," he groaned. But it was clear that in the main he did not; for he changed the subject hastily. "See 'ere, would you mind takin' 'old o' the book an' checkin' while I counts out the money. Total takin's—four, three, three—less 'ire of 'all, four-an'-six—"

"I can read figures an' print," owned Tilda, "but 'andwriting's too much for me; an' yours, I dare say, isn' none o' the best."

"I've improved it a lot at the night school. But what is it puzzlin' you?" he asked, looking up as he counted.

She held out the book, but not as he had handed it. The light breeze had blown over two or three of its leaves, covering the page of accounts.

"Oh, *that?*" he stammered, and a blush spread to his ears. "I didn' mean you to see—"

"What is it?"

"Well—it's potery, if you must know. Leastways it's meant to be potery. I make it sometimes."

"Why?"

"To relieve my feelin's."

"'Pears to me your feelin's want a deal o' relievin', one way an' another. Read me some."

"You're sure you won't laugh?"

"Bless the man! 'Ow can I tell till I've 'eard it? Is it meant to be funny?"

"No."

"Well, then, I'm not likely to laugh. It don't come easy to me, any'ow: I seen too many clowns."

She handed him the book. He chose a poem, conquered his diffidence, and began—

"Stratford-on-Avon, Stratford-on-Avon—
 My heart is full of woe:
 Formerly, once upon a time
 It was not ever so."

"The love that then I faltered
 I now am forced to stifle;
 For the case is completely altered
 And I wish I had a rifle."

"I wish I was wrecked
 Like Robinson Crusoe,
 But you cannot expect
 A canal-boat to do so."

"Perhaps I ought to explain, though?" he suggested, breaking off.

"If you don't mind."

"You see I got a brother—a nelder brother, an' by name 'Enery; an' last year he went for a miner in South Africa, at a place that I can't neither spell nor pronounce till it winds up with 'bosh.' So we'll call it Bosh."

"Right-o! But why did he go for that miner? To relieve 'is feelin's?"

"You don't understand. He went out *as* a miner, havin' been a pit-hand at the Blackstone Colliery, north o' Bursfield. Well, one week-end— about a month before he started—he took a noliday an' went a trip with me to Stratford aboard this very boat. Which for six months past I'd 'ad a neye upon a girl in Stratford. She was a General—"

"Salvation Army?"

"—A Cook-general, in a very respectable 'ouse'old—a publican's, at the 'Four Alls' by Binton Bridges. Me bein' shy—as you may 'ave noticed— I 'adn't, as you might say, put it to 'er; an' likewise until the matter was settled I didn' like to tell 'Enery. But I interjuced 'im—the same bein' 'er Sunday out; an' afterwards, when he called 'er a monstrous fine girl, I felt as 'appy as if he'd given me ten shillin'. Which only proves," Sam commented bitterly, "what I say in the next verse—"

"I'd rather be in prison
 Than in this earthly dwellin',
 Where nothin' is but it isn'—
 An there ain't no means of tellin'!"

"—Which when, the night before he started, he comes to me an' says that he an' Mary 'ave made a match of it, an' would I mind keepin' an eye on 'er an' writin' regular to say 'ow she was gettin' on, it fair knocked me out."

"You never told 'im?"

"I didn' like to. To start with 'e was always my fav'rite brother, an' I couldn' bear his startin' in low spirits an' South Africa such a distance off; beside which, I told mysel', the girl must surely know 'er own mind. So now you know," concluded Sam, "what I means by the nex' verse—"

"Stratford-on-Avon, Stratford-on-Avon—
 My true love she is false;
 I 'd rather not go to Stratford-on-Avon
 If I could go anywheres else."

"But you promised to keep an eye on her."

"'Enery 'ears from me regilar," said Sam evasively.

"If you don't pay 'er no visits," Tilda insisted, "the more you write the more you must be tellin' lies; an' that's not fair to 'Enery."

Sam considered this for a while, and ended by drawing a folded scrap of paper from his trouser-pocket.

"I don't tell no more than can't be 'elped, missie. You just list'n to this."

He read:—

Dear Brother 'Enery,—This comes opin' to find you well as it leaves me at Stratford. M. sends her love, an' you will be pleased to 'ear she grows beautifuller every day an' in character likewise. It do seem to me this world is a better place for containin' of her; an' a man ought to be 'appy, dear 'Enery, when you can call 'er mine—"

"That don't seem right to me some'ow," commented Tilda.

Sam scratched his head.

"What's wrong with it?"

"'Pears to me it ought to be 'yours'—'When you can call her yours.'"

"I don't like that neither, not altogether. S'pose we scratch it out an' say, 'A man ought to be 'appy when 'e can call 'er 'isn'? That what schoolmaster calls the third person."

"There didn' ought to be no third person about it," said Tilda severely; "on'y 'Enery an' 'er. Well, go on."

"I can't. That's so far as I've written up to the present. It's a rough copy, you understand; an' at Stratford I allow to write it out fair an' post it."

Tilda took a turn at considering.

"The further I go on this v'yage," she announced,—"w'ich, per'aps, 'twould be truthfuller to say the longer it takes—the more I seems to get mixed up in other folks' business. But you've done me a good turn, Sam Bossom; an' you've been open with me; an' I reckon I got to keep you straight in this 'ere. There! put up yer verses while I sit an' think it out."

"You don't like 'em?"

Sam was evidently dashed.

"If on'y I 'ad Bill 'ere—"

"Ha, yes: *'im!' E*'d put a boiler inside 'em, no doubt; an' a donkey-engin', an'—"

"What'yer talkin' about? . . . Oh, yer verses! Bless the man, I wasn' thinkin' of yer verses. I was wantin' Bill 'ere, to advise somethin' practical. Lor' sake! Look at Arthur Miles there, the way 'e's leanin' overboard! The child'll drown' isself, nex' news!" She rose up and ran to prevent the disaster. "'Pears to me there's a deal o' motherin' to be done aboard this boat. Trouble aft, an' trouble forrard—"

She was hurrying aft when Mr. Mortimer intercepted her amidships. He held a book in one hand, and two slips of paper in the other.

"Child," he asked, "could you learn a part?—a very small part?"

"'Course I could," answered Tilda promptly; "but I ain't goin' to play it, an' don't yer make any mistake. 'Ere, let me get to Arthur Miles before 'e tumbles overboard."

She darted aft and dragged the boy back by his collar.

"What d'yer mean by it, givin' folks a shock like that?" she demanded.

"I was looking at the pictures," he explained, and showed her.

The *Success to Commerce* bore on her stern panels two gaily painted landscapes, the one of Warwick Castle, the other of ruined Kenilworth. Tilda leaned over the side and saw them mirrored in the still water.

"And then," the boy pursued, "down below the pictures I saw a great ship lying in the seaweed with guns and drowned men on the deck and the fishes swimming over them. Deep in the ship a bell was tolling—"

"Nonsense!" Tilda interrupted, and catching up a pole, thrust it down overside. "Four feet at the most," she reported, as the pole found bottom. "You must be sickenin' for somethin'. Put out your tongue."

"A child of imagination," observed Mr. Mortimer, who had followed her. "Full fathom five thy father lies—"

"'Ush!" cried Tilda.

"—Of his bones are coral made. Those are pearls that were his eyes—"

The boy sat and looked up at the speaker, staring, shivering a little.

"You know? You know too?" he stammered.

"He knows nothin' about it," insisted Tilda. "Please go away, Mr. Mortimer?"

"A young Shakespearian? This is indeed delightful! You shall have a part, sir. Your delivery will be immature, doubtless; but with some tuition from me—"

"If you try it on, I'll tell 'Ucks," the girl threatened, by this time desperate. "You're like all the actors—leastways you're like all that ever I met; an', take it 'ow you will, I got to say it. Once get started on yer own lay, an' everything elst goes out o' yer 'eads. You don't mean to 'urt, but selfish you are and 'eedless, an' somebody 'as al'ays the world's trouble clearin' up the mess. 'Ere, 'and me the part you was tellin' about; an' I'll learn it an' say it, though not within a 'undred miles of Glasson—which," she added, "I'll be an old woman before that, at the rate we're goin'. But you don't drag Arthur Miles into it, an' I give you fair warnin'. For, to start with, 'e's 'idin', an' 'tis only to keep 'im 'id that I got 'Ucks to let yer loose. An' nex' 'e's a gentleman, and why you should want to mix 'im up with yer Shakespeares I can't think."

It is doubtful if Mr. Mortimer heard the conclusion of her outburst. At the mention of Mr. Hucks he pressed a palm dramatically to his forehead; and now, withdrawing it, he handed her the two slips of paper with great politeness.

"True, I had forgotten," he murmured. "Take your time, child—you will take your time, I beg."

He waved his hand, and withdrew to rejoin his wife on the cabin-top. Tilda studied the slips of paper, while Arthur Miles edged away again towards the gunwale for another look into the magic water.

"Stop that!" she commanded, glancing up and catching him in the act. "Stop that, and read these for me: I can't manage handwriting."

The boy took the first slip obediently and read aloud—

"*Madam, a horseman comes riding across the hill. The sun flashes full on his arms. By my halidame 'tis the Knight Hospitaller!*"

"That seems pretty fair rot," criticised Tilda. "Let's 'ave the other."

"*Madam, he has reined up his steed. He stands without.*"

Here Arthur Miles paused and drew breath.

"Without what?"

"It doesn't say. *He stands without: he waves a hand. Shall I go ask his errand?*"

"Is that all? . . . And Mortimer reckons I'll take from 'ere to Stratford learnin' that little lot! Why, I can do it in arf-a-minute, an' on my 'ead. You just listen. *Madam, a 'orseman*—No, wait a moment. *Madam, a Norseman*—" Tilda hesitated and came to a halt. "Would you mind sayin' it over again, Arthur Miles?" she asked politely.

"*Madam, a horseman comes riding*—"

"That'll do. *Madam, a*—H—h—*horseman*—Is that better?"

"You needn't strain at it so," said the boy. "Why, you're quite red in the face!"

"Oh, yes, I need," said Tilda; "first-along, any'ow." She fell silent for a space. "That Mortimer," she conceded, "isn' quite the ass that 'e looks. This 'as got to take time, after all." She paused a moment in thought, and then broke out, "Oh, Arthur Miles, the trouble you're layin' on me—First, to be a mother—an' that's not 'ard. But, on top o' that, lady!"

"Why should you be a lady?" he asked.

"Why?" Tilda echoed almost bitterly. "Oh, you needn' think I'll want to marry yer when all's done. Why? Oh, merely to 'elp you, bein' the sort you are. All you've got to do, bein' the sort you are, is to sit quiet an' teach me. But I got to be a lady, if it costs me my shift."

CHAPTER XII.

PURSUED.

At ten o'clock Sam harnessed up again, and shortly before noon our travellers left the waterway by which they had travelled hitherto, and passed out to the right through a cut, less than a quarter of a mile long, where a rising lock took them into the Stratford-on-Avon Canal.

Said Sam as he worked the lock, the two children standing beside and watching—

"Now see here, when you meet your clever friend Bill, you put him two questions from me. First, why, when the boat's through, am I goin' to draw the water off an' leave the lock empty?"

Before Tilda could answer, Arthur Miles exclaimed—

"I know! It's because we 're going uphill, and at the other locks, when we were going downhill, the water emptied itself."

"Right, so far as you go," nodded Sam. "But why should a lock be left empty?"

The boy thought for a moment.

"Because you don't want the water to waste, and top gates hold it better than lower ones."

"Why do the top gates hold it better?"

"Because they shut *with* the water, and the water holds them fast; and because they are smaller than the bottom gates, and don't leak so much."

"That's very cleverly noticed," said Sam. "Now you keep your eyes alive while we work this one, an' tell me what you see."

They watched the operation carefully.

"Well?" he asked as, having passed the *Success to Commerce* through, he went back to open the lower paddles—or slats, as he called them.

"I saw nothing," the boy confessed disappointedly, "except that you seemed to use more water than at the others."

"Well, and that's just it. But why?"

"It has something to do, of course, with going up-hill instead of down . . . And—and I've got the reason somewhere inside my head, but I can't catch hold of it."

"I'll put it another way. This boat's mod'rate well laden, an' she takes more water lockin' up than if she was empty; but if she was empty, she'd take more water lockin' down. That's a fac'; an' if you can give me a reason for it you'll be doin' me a kindness. For I never could find one, an' I've lain awake at nights puzzlin' it over."

"I bet Bill would know," said Tilda.

Sam eyed her.

"I'd give somethin'" he said, "to be sure this Bill, as you make such a gawd of, is a real person—or whether, bein' born different to the rest of yer sex, you've 'ad to invent 'im."

Many locks encumber the descending levels of the Stratford-on-Avon Canal, and they kept Sam busy. In the intervals the boat glided deeper and deeper into a green pastoral country, parcelled out with hedgerows and lines of elms, behind which here and there lay a village half hidden—a grey tower and a few red-tiled roofs visible between the trees. Cattle dotted the near pastures, till away behind the trees—for summer had passed into late September—the children heard now and again the guns of partridge shooters cracking from fields of stubble. But no human folk frequented the banks of the canal, which wound its way past scented meadows edged with willow-herb, late meadow-sweet, yellow tansy and purple loosestrife, this last showing a blood-red stalk as its bloom died away. Out beyond, green arrowheads floated on the water; the Success to Commerce ploughed through beds of them, and they rose from under her keel and spread themselves again in her wake. Very little traffic passed over these waters. In all the way to Preston Bagot our travellers met but three boats. One, at Lowsonford Lock, had a pair of donkeys ("animals" Sam called them) to haul it; the other two, they met, coming up light by Fiwood Green. "Hold in!" "Hold out!" called the steersmen as the boats met. Sam held wide, and by shouts instructed Mr. Mortimer how to cross the towropes; and Mr. Mortimer put on an extremely knowledgeable air, but obeyed him with so signal a clumsiness that the bargees desired to know where the *Success to Commerce* had shipped her new mate.

The question, though put with good humour, appeared to disturb Sam, who for the rest of the way steered in silence. There are three locks at Preston Bagot, and at the first Mr. Mortimer took occasion to apologise for his performance, adding that practice made perfect.

"I wonder, now," said Sam delicately, "if you could practise leavin' off that fur collar? A little unhandiness'll pass off, an' no account taken; but with a furred overcoat 'tis different, an' I ought to a-mentioned it before. We don't want the children tracked, do we? An' unfort'nitly you're not one to pass in a crowd."

"You pay me a compliment," Mr. Mortimer answered. "Speaking, however, as man to man, let me say that I would gladly waive whatever show my overcoat may contribute to the—er—total effect to which you refer. But"— here he unbuttoned the front of his garment—"I leave it to you to judge if, without it, I shall attract less attention. *Laudatur*, my dear Smiles, *et alget. Paupertas, dura paupertas*—I might, perhaps, satisfy the curious gazer by producing the—er—pawntickets for the missing articles. But it would hardly—eh, I put it to you?"

"No, it wouldn'," decided Sam. "But it's unfort'nit all the same, an' in more ways'n one. You see, there's a nasty 'abit folks 'ave in these parts. Anywheres between Warwick an' Birming'am a native can't 'ardly pass a canal-boat without wantin' to arsk, "Oo stole the rabbit-skin?' I don't know why they arsk it; but when it 'appens, you've got to fight the man—or elst *I* must."

"I would suggest that, you being the younger man—"

"Well, I don't mind," said Sam. "On'y the p'int is I don't scarcely never fight without attractin' notice. The last time 'twas five shillin' an' costs or ten days. An' there's the children to be considered."

During this debate Tilda and Arthur Miles had wandered ashore with 'Dolph, and the dog, by habit inquisitive, had headed at once for a wooden storehouse that stood a little way back from the waterside— a large building of two storeys, with a beam and pulley projecting from the upper one, and heavy folding-doors below. One of these doors stood open, and 'Dolph, dashing within, at once set up a frantic barking.

"Hullo!" Tilda stepped quickly in front of the boy to cover him. "There's somebody inside."

The barking continued for almost half a minute, and then Godolphus emerged, capering absurdly on his hind legs and revolving like a dervish, flung up his head, yapped thrice in a kind of ecstasy, and again plunged into the store.

"That's funny, too," mused Tilda. "I never knew 'im be'ave like that 'cept when he met with a friend. Arthur Miles, you stay where you are—" She tiptoed forward and peered within. "Lord sake, come an' look 'ere!" she called after a moment.

The boy followed, and stared past her shoulder into the gloom. There, in the centre of the earthen floor, wrapped around with straw bands, stood a wooden horse.

It was painted grey, with beautiful dapples, and nostrils of fierce scarlet. It had a tail of real horse-hair and a golden mane, and on its near shoulder a blue scroll with its name *Kitchener* thereon in letters of gold. Its legs were extended at a gallop.

"Gavel's!" said Tilda. "Gavel's, at ten to one an' no takers! . . . But why? 'Ow?"

She turned on 'Dolph, scolding, commanding him to be quiet; and 'Dolph subsided on his haunches and watched her, his stump tail jerking to and fro beneath him like an unweighted pendulum. There was a label attached to the straw bands. She turned it over and read: *James Gavel, Proprietor, Imperial Steam Roundabouts, Henley-in-Arden. Deliver Immediately* . . . "An' me thinkin' Bill 'ad gone north to Wolver'ampton!" she breathed.

Before the boy could ask her meaning they heard the rumble of wheels outside; and Tilda, catching him by the arm, hurried him back to the doors just as a two-horse wagon rolled down to the wharf, in charge of an elderly driver—a sour-visaged man in a smock-frock, with a weather-stained top hat on the back of his head, and in his hand a whip adorned with rings of polished brass.

He pulled up, eyed the two children, and demanded to know what they meant by trespassing in the store.

"We were admirin' the 'orse," answered Tilda.

"An' likewise truantin' from school," the wagoner suggested. "But that's the way of it in England nowadays; the likes o' me payin' rates to eddicate the likes o' you. An' that's your Conservative Government . . . Eddication!" he went on after a pause. "What's Eddication? Did either o' you ever 'ear tell of Joseph Arch?"

"Can't say we 'ave."

"He was born no farther away than Barford—Barford-on-Avon. But I s'pose your schoolmaster's too busy teachin' you the pianner."

Tilda digested the somewhat close reasoning for a moment, and answered—

"It's fair sickenin', the amount o' time spent on the pianner. Between you an' me, that's partly why we cut an' run. You mustn' think we 'ate school—if on'y they'd teach us what's useful. 'Oo's Joseph Arch?"

"He was born at Barford," said the wagoner; "an' at Barford he lives."

"'E must be a remarkable man," said Tilda, "an' I'm sorry I don't know more of 'im. But I know Gavel."

"Gavel?"

"'Im as the 'orse belongs to; an' Bill. Gavel's a remarkable man too in 'is way; though not a patch on Bill. Bill tells me Gavel can get drunk twice any day; separate drunk, that is."

"Liberal or Conservative?"

"Well," hesitated Tilda, playing for safety, "I dunno as he 'd tell, under a pint; but mos' likely it depends on the time o' day."

"I arsked," said the wagoner, "because he's hired by the Primrose Feet; an' if he's the kind o' man to sell 'is princerples, I don't so much mind 'ow bad the news I breaks to him."

"What news?"

The man searched in his pocket, and drew forth a greasy post card.

"He sent word to me there was six painted 'osses comin' by canal from Burning'am, to be delivered at the Wharf this mornin'; an' would I fetch 'em along to the Feet Ground, Henley-in-Arden, without delay?"

"Henley-in-Arden!" exclaimed a voice behind the children; whereat Tilda turned about with a start. It was the voice of Mr. Mortimer, who had strolled across from the lock bank, and stood conning the wagon and team. "Henley-in-Arden? O Helicon! If you'll excuse the remark, sir. OParnassus!"

"Maybe I might," said the wagoner guardedly, "if I understood its bearin's."

"Name redolent of Shakespeare! Of Rosalind and Touchstone, Jaques and Amiens, sheepcrooks and venison feasts, and ballads pinned to oaks! What shall he have who killed the deer, Mr.—?"

"'Olly," said the wagoner.

"I beg your pardon?"

"'Olly—James 'Olly and Son, Carters an' 'Auliers."

"Is it possible? . . . better and better! Sing heigho! the Holly, this life is most jolly. I trust you find it so, Mr. Holly?"

"If you want to know," Mr. Holly answered sourly, "I don't."

"You pain and astonish me, Mr. Holly. The penalty of Adam, the season's difference"—Mr. Mortimer turned up his furred collar—"surely, sir, you will allow no worse to afflict you? You, a dweller on the confines of Henley-in-Arden, within measurable distance, as I gathered?"

"Mile an' a 'arf."

"No more? O Phoebus and the Nine!"

"There *was*," said Mr. Holly, "to 'a been six. An' by consequence here I be with a pair of 'osses an' the big wagon. Best go home-along, I reckon, an' fetch out the cart," he grumbled, with a jerk of his thumb indicating a red-tiled building on the hillside, half a mile away.

"Not so." Mr. Mortimer tapped his brow. "An idea occurs to me—if you will spare me a moment to consult with my—er—partner. A Primrose Fete, you said? I am no politician, Mr. Holly, but I understand the Primrose League exists—primarily—or ultimately—to save our world-wide empire. And how shall an empire stand without its Shakespeare? Our tent and appliances will just load your wagon. As the younger Dumas observed, 'Give me two boards, two trestles, three actors'—but the great Aeschylus did with two—'two actors,' let us say—'and a passion'—provided your terms are not prohibitive . . . Hi, Smiles! Approach, Smiles, and be introduced to Thespis. His charge is three shillings. At the price of three shillings behold, Smiles, the golden age returned! Comedy carted home through leafy ways shall trill her woodnotes—her native woodnotes wild—in Henley-in-Arden!"

The wagon had been packed and had departed, Mrs. Mortimer perched high on a pile of tent cloths, and Mr. Mortimer waving farewells from the tail-board.

The two children, left with instructions to keep near the boat and in hiding, had made a nest for themselves among the stalks of loosestrife, and sat watching the canal for sign of a moorhen or a water-rat. The afternoon was bright and very still, with a dazzle on the water and a faint touch of autumn in the air—the afterglow of summer soon to pass into grey chills and gusts of rain. For many minutes neither had spoken.

"Look!" said Tilda, pointing to a distant ripple drawn straight across the surface. "There goes a rat, and I've won!"

The boy said—

"A boat takes up room in the water, doesn't it?"

"O' course it does. But what's that got to do with rats?"

"Nothing. I was thinking of Sam's puzzle, and I've guessed it. A boat going downwards through a lock would want a lock full, all but the water it pushes out from the room it takes up. Wouldn't it?"

"I s'pose so," said Tilda doubtfully.

"But a boat going up will want a lock full, and that water too. And that's why an empty boat going downhill takes more water than a loaded one, and less going up."

To Tilda the puzzle remained a puzzle. "It *sounds* all right," she allowed. "But what makes you so clever about boats?"

"I've *got* to know about them. Else how shall we ever find the Island?"

She thought for half a minute.

"You're sure about that Island?" she asked, a trifle anxiously.

Arthur Miles turned to her with a confident smile.

"Of course I'm sure."

"Well, we'll arsk about it when we get to Stratford-on-Avon."

She was about to say more, but checked herself at sight of a barge coming down the canal—slowly, and as yet so far away that the tramp of the tow-horse's hoofs on the path was scarcely audible. She laid a hand on 'Dolph's collar and pressed him down in the long grass, commanding him to be quiet, whilst she and the boy wriggled away towards an alder bush that stood a furlong back from the bank.

Stretched at length behind the bush, she had, between the fork of its stem, a clear view of the approaching boat. Its well coverings were loose, and by the upper lock gate the steersman laid it close along shore and put out a gang-plank. His mate, after fitting a nosebag on the horse, came at a call to assist him, and together they lifted out a painted wooden steed wrapped in straw, and carried it to the store.

Having deposited it there, they returned and unloaded another. Five horses they disembarked and housed thus; and then, like men relieved of a job, spat on their hands and turned to work their boat down through the locks. For twenty minutes the children lay prone and watched them, Tilda still keeping a hand on the scruff of 'Dolph's neck. Then, as the boat, having gained a clear reach of water, faded down in the gathering dusk, she arose and stretched herself.

"For anyone but Bill I wouldn' risk it," she said. "But maybe his credit depends on gettin' them 'osses delivered to-night."

She took Arthur Miles by the hand, found the road, and dragged him uphill at a trot towards the group of red brick buildings that showed between the trees.

The buildings consisted of a cottage and a long stable or coach-house contiguous. This presented a blank white-washed wall to the road, but a Gloire de Dijon rose spread itself over the cottage front, almost smothering a board with the inscription: *S. Holly and Son, Carters and Hauliers.*

Tilda knocked, and her knock was answered by a sour-visaged woman.

"Well, an' what can I do for you?" asked the woman, staring down from her doorstep on the children.

"If you please, ma'am, is Mr. 'Olly at 'ome?"

"No, he ain't."

"I knew it," said Tilda tranquilly. "But by all accounts 'e's got a son."

"Eh?"

The woman still stared, divided between surprise and mistrust.

"You're mistakin'," Tilda pursued. "I ain't come with any scandal about the fam'ly. A grown-up son, I mean—with a 'orse an' cart. Because, if so, there's five gallopin' 'orses down at the wharf waitin' to be taken over to Henley-in-Arden."

"Oh?" said the woman. "My 'usband left word Gustavus was to fetch 'em along if they arrived. But who sent you with the message?"

"I've a friend in Gavel's business," Tilda answered with dignity. "'E's what you might call Gavel's right 'and man—an' 'e's 'andy with 'is right, too, when 'e's put out. If 'e should 'ear—I'm advisin' for yer *good*, mind—if 'e should 'ear as five 'orses was 'ung up on the wharf 'ere through S. 'Olly an' Son's neglect, you may look out for ructions. An' that's all I promise."

She turned back towards the wharf, and even as Arthur Miles turned to follow they could hear the woman calling loudly, summoning her son from his tea in the kitchen.

"I reckon," commented Tilda, "I put the fear o' Bill into that woman. You may 'a noticed I didn' like her looks."

She led the way back to the wharf in some elation. Twilight was gathering there and over the canal. She had rounded the corner of the store, when, happening to glance towards the *Success to Commerce*, moored under the bank a bare twenty yards away, she halted, and with a gasp shrank close into the shadow.

"Collar 'Dolph! Grip old on 'im for the Lord's sake!" she whispered, and clutched Arthur Miles by the arm.

On the bank beside the boat stood a man.

"But what's the matter?" the boy demanded.

"'Ush! Oh, 'ush an' lie close! It's Glasson!"

CHAPTER XIII.

ADVENTURE OF THE FURRED COLLAR.

"'*Do you know me, my lord?*' '*Excellent well; you are a fishmonger.*'"—HAMLET.

He stood on the edge of the wharf—a black figure in an Inverness cape—with his back towards the angle of the store where the children hid. There was no mistaking him. For two nights he had haunted Tilda's dreams; and she could have picked him out, even in the twilight, from among a thousand.

She gave another gasp, and with that her presence of mind returned. He had not seen them; he was watching the barge. The angle of the store would still hide them if they tip-toed to the wharf gate. But they must be noiseless as mice; they must reach the road, and then—

She caught up 'Dolph by the scruff of his neck, tucked him under her arm, and whispered to Arthur Miles to steal after her. But before she had taken three paces another fright brought her heart into her mouth.

Footsteps were coming down the road. They could not belong to the wagoner's son. He would be bringing his horse and cart. The footsteps were light, too—light and hurried, and not to be associated with hobnailed boots.

Almost desperate at this cutting off of retreat, Tilda pulled Arthur Miles towards a wooden stairway, unrailed, painted over with Stockholm tar, built against the outside of the store, and leading to its upper chamber.

"Up! and quick!" she commanded, pushing him before her. She followed panting, leaning against the wall for support, for 'Dolph was no light burden, and his weight taxed her hurt leg painfully.

The door of the loft stood ajar. She staggered in after the boy, dropped the dog, and closed all but a chink, at which she posted herself, drawing quick breaths.

In the darkness behind her Arthur Miles listened. The footsteps drew nearer, paused, and after a moment were audible again in the yard below.

"Good Lord—it's Gavel!"

"Eh?" The boy drew closer to her shoulder.

"It's Gavel, come in a sweat for 'is 'orses. I didn' reckernise 'im for the moment—dressed out in a fur coat an' Trilby 'at. But it's Gavel, an' 'e's walkin' straight into Glasson's arms. Stand by to do a bolt soon as 'e turns the corner."

"But I don't see what he has to do with—with—" Arthur Miles hesitated before the terrible name.

"Glasson? Oh, nothin'; on'y ten to one Gavel's met with the Mortimers, an', Glasson bein' on the track already—W'y, what elst is the man 'ere for?"

"He shan't take me," said the boy after a pause, and in a strained low voice which, nevertheless, had no tremor in it. "Not if I throw myself off the ladder."

"You stop that talk, please," threatened Tilda. "It's wicked; an' besides, they 'aven't caught us yet. Do what I tell yer, an' stand by to bolt."

She crept to the other door, which commanded the canal front, unbarred it softly, and opened the upper hatch a few inches. Through this aperture, by standing on tip-toe, she could watch the meeting of the two men.

"When I call, run for yer life."

But a minute—two minutes—passed, and the command did not come. Arthur Miles, posted by the bolt-hole, held his breath at the sound of voices without, by the waterside. The tones of one he recognised with a shiver. They were raised, and although he could not catch the words, apparently in altercation. Forgetting orders, he tip-toed across to Tilda's elbow.

Mr. James Gavel, proprietor of Imperial Steam Roundabouts—as well as of half a dozen side-shows, including a Fat Lady and a Try-your-Strength machine—was a small man with a purplish nose and a temper kept irritable by alcohol; and to-day the Fates had conspired to rub that temper on the raw. He swore aloud, and partly believed, that ever since coming to Henley-in-Arden he was bewitched.

He had come at the instance, and upon the guarantee, of Sir Elphinstone Breward, Baronet, C.B., K.C.V.O., a local landowner, who, happening to visit Warwick on County Council business, which in its turn happened to coincide with a fair day, had been greatly struck by the title "Imperial" painted over Mr. Gavel's show, and with soldierly promptness had engaged the whole outfit—Roundabouts, Fat Lady and all—for his forthcoming Primrose Fete.

If beside his addiction to alcohol Mr. Gavel had a weakness, it was the equally British one of worshipping a title. Flattered by the honest baronet's invitation, he had met it almost more than half-way; and had dispatched six of his shabbiest horses to Birmingham to be repainted for the fete, and labelled "Kitchener," "Bobs," "Cecil Rhodes," "Doctor Jim," "Our Joe," and "Strathcona"—names (as he observed) altogether more up to date than the "Black Prince," "Brown Bess," "Saladin," and others they superseded.

Respect for his patron had further prompted Mr. Gavel, on the morning of the fete, to don a furred overcoat, and to swear off drink for the day. This abstinence, laudable in itself, disastrously affected his temper, and brought him before noon into wordy conflict with his engineer. The quarrel, suppressed for the time, flamed out afresh in the afternoon, and, unfortunately, at a moment when Sir Elphinstone, as chairman, was introducing the star orator from London. Opprobrious words had reached the ears of the company gathered on the platform, and Sir Elphinstone had interrupted his remarks about Bucking Up and Thinking Imperially to send a policeman through the crowd with instructions to stop that damned brawling.

If the great Napoleon may be forgiven for losing his temper when at five in the afternoon from the slope of La Belle Alliance he watched the Prussians breaking through the opposite woods, while Grouchy yet tarried, let it be pleaded in excuse for Mr. Gavel that ever since eleven a.m. he had been awaiting the arrival of his six newly-painted horses. The Birmingham decorator had pledged himself to deliver them early at Preston Bagot, and Mr. Gavel knew him for a man of his word. He had made arrangements for their prompt conveyance to the field. He did not doubt, but he was undeniably anxious.

Imagine, then, his feelings when at four o'clock or a little later a wagon—the wagon of his hiring—rolled into the enclosure bringing one horse only, and in place of the others a pile of tent-cloths and theatrical boxes, on which sat and smiled Mr. and Mrs. Mortimer, his professional rivals.

He had been drinking ginger-ale all day, and in copious draughts. It must be confessed that he lost his temper woefully, and so vociferously that Sir Elphinstone this time descended from the platform, and strode across the meadow to demand what the devil he meant by it. Nor was even this the last drop in the cup of Mr. Gavel's bitterness; for the baronet, struck by Mr. Mortimer's appearance and genteel address, at once invited him to set up his tent and save the situation so desperately compromised.

Sam Bossom, perceiving that the wagon stood on ground well adapted for pitching a tent, cheerfully proceeded to unload. Mr. Gavel watched in speechless rage. Old Holly, the carrier, suggested that there was no need to give up hope of the horses. They might turn up yet before dark. Boats came down the canal at all hours of the day.

"Then why couldn't you have waited and given 'em a chance?" foamed the proprietor; and commanding Holly to turn the empty wagon and follow, he strode off in the direction of the Wharf. The afternoon was hot. His furred coat oppressed him; his shoes—of patent leather, bought ready-made—pinched his feet. On the road he came to a public-house, entered, and gulped down two "goes" of whisky. Still the wagon lagged behind. Re-emerging, he took the road again, his whole man hot within his furred coat as a teapot within a cosy.

In this temper, then, Mr. Gavel came to the wharf at Preston Bagot locks, and finding the *Success to Commerce* moored there with a tall man apparently in charge, demanded if he came from Birmingham.

"Or thereabouts," answered the tall man, eyeing him. "From there or thereabouts. And, if I mistake not, you are the—er—person of whom I came in search."

The man's voice took Mr. Gavel somewhat aback. It did not resemble an ordinary bargee's. But at the moment he could no more check the explosion of his wrath than you can hold back a cork in the act of popping from a bottle of soda-water.

"Curse your laziness!" exploded Mr. Gavel; "and this is your notion of searching for me, is it?"

"It appears to be a pretty successful one," said Dr. Glasson. "I've discovered you, anyhow; and now I suggest to you that swearing won't help the reckoning between us."

"Oh, stow your fine talk! I've heard of sea-lawyers, and I suppose you're a canal specimen. Carriage was paid at the other end, and you know it. I catch you here loafing, and I'm going to dispute the bill— which means that you'll get the sack, my friend, whether I recover the money or no. Pounds out of pocket I am by this, not to speak of reputation. Where are they? Where have you put 'em?"

"That's what I'll trouble *you* to answer, sir."

"My hosses! . . . You don't mean to tell me—" Mr. Gavel smote his brow. "But you said just now you were looking for me!" he cried.

"You act well, sir," said Dr. Glasson sternly. "It is your profession. But, as it happens, I have made inquiries along the canal, and am proof against your bluster. A boat, the *Success to Commerce*—a bargeman in a furred overcoat— the combination is unusual, and not (I put it to you) likely to be repeated on this short stretch of waterway. Confess, Mr.— confess, sir, your game is up. Kidnapping is an ugly offence in this country, and, in short, I advise you without more ado to hand over the two children."

Mr. Gavel leaned back against a crane for support.

"Children? What children?" he repeated, staring.

Clearly here was some hideous blunder, and he perceived at length that the person addressing him in no way resembled a bargee.

"But—but my hosses?" he gasped.

Just then the sound of wheels fell on his ears, and both men faced about. Mr. Gavel made sure that this must be old Holly with his wagon. But no; there came around the corner a cart with a single horse, driven by a lad; and the lad, pulling up before the store, went in, and in less than a minute reappeared staggering under a heavy burden.

"But, Hallo!" cried Mr. Gavel, pulling himself together, and striding towards the cart. "It *is*—" he began incredulously; but after a second look raised his voice in triumphant recognition and demand. "My hosses! What are you doing with my hosses?"

"Yours, be they?" the lad answered. "Well, I'm takin' 'em to Henley, as you sent word."

"*I* sent word?" echoed Mr. Gavel.

"*Somebody* sent word," the lad persisted. "An' in the devil of a 'urry, 'cordin' to the child what brought it. But, as I said to mother, where's the sense in sendin' messages by children?"

"Children?"

"There was two on 'em—a boy an' a girl—"

"Ah!" interrupted Dr. Glasson. "Describe them, please."

The lad scratched his head.

"Mother took the message. I was indoors, havin' tea, an' didn' see more 'n a glimpse. But here comes father," he added briskly, as again wheels were heard on the road, and old Holly drove into the yard with his belated wagon.

"You must admit, sir," said Dr. Glasson, addressing Mr. Gavel, "that circumstances are beginning to look too strong for you."

"Oh, to—with circumstances!" retorted Mr. Gavel. "Mortimer's in this, for a fiver. I don't see how—I don't make head or tail of it; but the tail you've got hold of belongs to the wrong dog. Kidnapping, is it? A couple of children you want? Suspect me, do you? Well, suspect away. *I* don't mind. I've got my hosses; and when we're loaded up you can climb on board the wagon, if you like, and we'll pay a call on Mortimer. I bet he's your man; and the harder you pinch Mortimer to make him squeal, the better you'll please me."

"Arthur Miles," demanded Tilda in a harsh whisper, "what're yer doin' 'ere?"

"Listening," answered the boy simply.

"I 'opes yer likes it! . . . We're in a tight corner, Arthur Miles, an' nothing for it but bolt while they're talkin'."

"We might hide here in the dark—but, of course, you know best."

"O' course I do," Tilda agreed. "'Ide 'ere? An' who's to warn the Mortimers?"

She stooped and again caught 'Dolph under her arm. Then she straightened herself up and stood listening to the voices, clearly audible from the entrance of the store below.

"Tip-toe, mind! There's on'y a board between us—and quiet, for your life!"

They stole to the steps and paused for a moment, peering into the gloom. Here too their enemies' voices were audible, but around the corner of the store, the coast was clear. They crept down the steps and gained the road. In the highway Tilda drew breath.

"Things look pretty bad," she said; "but things ain't altogether so bad as they look. Where we're goin' we'll find Bill; an' Bill's a tower o' strength."

"But we don't even know the way," objected Arthur Miles.

"No, but 'Dolph does. 'Ere, 'Dolph"—she set down the dog—"you got to lead us where the others went; an' at the end of it there's a little surprise for yer. 'Ear?"

'Dolph heard, shook himself, wagged his tail, and padded forward into the gathering darkness; ran a little way and halted, until they overtook him. He understood.

"If they catch up with us we must nip into a gateway," panted Tilda.

But as yet there was no sound of wheels on the road behind. They passed the Hollys' cottage and stable, and braved the undiscovered country. The road twisted between tall hedgerows, black in the shadow of elms. No rain had fallen for many days, and the powdered dust lay so thick underfoot, that twice or thrice Tilda halted—still holding the boy's hand—in doubt if they had wandered off upon turf. But always, as they hesitated thus, 'Dolph came trotting back to reassure them.

In this manner, trotting and pausing, they had covered a bare three-quarters of a mile when there smote on their ears a throbbing of the air—a thud-thud which Arthur Miles took for the beat of a factory engine, so like it was to the echoes that had floated daily, and all day long, across the Orphanage wall; but Tilda, after hearkening a moment, announced it to be the bass of Gavel's steam organ. The hoot of a whistle presently confirmed her guess.

'Dolph was steering them steadily towards the sound; and a glow in the sky, right ahead and easily discernible, would have guided them even without his help. Tilda recognised that glow also.

"And the best is, it means Bill," she promised.

But they did not catch the tune itself until they were close upon the meadow. At the top of a rise in the road it broke on them, the scene almost simultaneously with its music; and a strange scene it was, and curiously beautiful—a slope, and below the slope a grassy meadow set with elms; a blaze of light, here and there in the open spaces; in one space a steam roundabout revolving with mirrors, in another the soft glow of naphtha-lamps through tent cloth; glints of light on the boughs, dark shadows of foliage, a moving crowd, its murmur so silenced by music and the beat of a drum that it seemed to sway to and fro without sound, now pressing forward into the glare, now dissolving into the penumbra.

Arthur Miles paused, trembling. He had never seen the like. But Tilda had recovered all her courage.

"This," she assured him, "is a little bit of all right," and taking his hand, led him down the slope and posted him in the shadow of a thorn-bush.

"Wait here," she enjoined; and he waited, while she descended cautiously towards the roundabout with its revolving mirrors.

He lost sight of her. He lay still where she had commanded him to lie, watching the many twinkling lights, watching the roundabout turn and flash and come to a stop, watching the horseplay of boys and maidens as one set clambered off laughing and another pressed forward into their places. The tune droned in his ears, came to an end, went on again. He drowsed to its recurrent beat. From his couch in the wet shadow he gazed up at the stars riding overhead, above the elms.

At the end of twenty minutes Tilda stole back to him; and, softly though she came, her footfall woke him out of his dreams with a start. Yet, and though he could barely discern her from the shadow of the thorn-bush, he knew on the instant that she brought disappointment.

"What's the matter?" he asked.

"Everything's the matter. Bill's gone!"

CHAPTER XIV.

ADVENTURE OF THE PRIMROSE FETE.

"*Confusion and Exeunt.*"—OLD STAGE DIRECTION.

"Gone?" echoed the boy blankly.

"'Ad a row with Gavel this very aft'rnoon. Got the sack, with a week's pay, an' packed up his kit after tea an' 'ooked it. Bess Burton told me all about it, knowin' me an' Bill to be friends—she's the woman sits at the pay-table an' gives the change. 'E wouldn' tell nobody where 'e was goin'. Ain't cryin' about it, are yer?"

"No," he answered, as she peered close to him in the darkness. "Only we'd built everything on Bill, hadn't we?"

Tilda did not answer this question.

"That's the way with Bill," she said loyally. "Folks never know 'is worth till they miss 'im. Bess allowed to me that before the evenin's out Gavel will be offerin' 'is shirt to 'ave 'im back—an' Bess don't know the worst neither. They've put on a boy to work the engine, an' Bill 'as told me things about that boiler o' Gavel's . . . I couldn' get near enough to read the pressure, but by the way 'e was pilin' in coal—"

She broke off and gazed down the slope. Even as once the poet Gray looked down from the Windsor's heights up the distant prospect of Eton College, so did she regard the cluster of naphtha lights around the galloping horses on which, unconscious of their doom, the little victims played.

"But there's no call to give up an' cry about it," she resumed bravely. "We're in a tight place, but it's our turn to play. (That's another sayin' o' Bill's. Oh, dear, I wish you'd known 'im!) You see, we know where Glasson is an' what 'e's up to, an' can look out accordin'. That's one card to us. An' the next is, I've seen Sam Bossom an' warned 'im. 'E was standin' outside 'is show, an' not darin' to go in; the reason bein' Mortimer 'ad picked up a girl from the shootin' gallery, that used to belong to 'is company, and 'e an' she an' Mrs. Mortimer are doing the last act of *Othello* life size an' tuppence coloured, an' Sam says 'e can't look on an' command 'is feelin's. 'E was considerable surprised to see me, an' started scoldin'; but I left 'im promisin' that 'e'd put a stop to Glasson some'ow, if it had to be on the point o' the jaw; an' we're to nip across and 'ide under the Grand Stand until he comes for us or sends word. See it?"

She pointed across to a crowded platform on the farther slope—a structure of timber draped with scarlet cloth, and adorned with palms and fairy lamps. It stood on the rise a little above and to the left of the roundabout, the flares of which lit up the faces and gay dresses of Sir Elphinstone's guests gathered there to watch the show.

The two children made down the slope towards it, very cautiously, fetching a circuit of the crowd. But as they reached the bottom of the dip, on a sudden the crowd spread itself in lines right across their path. Along these lines three or four men ran shouting, with ropes and lanterns in their hands; and for one horrible moment it flashed on Tilda that all this agitation must be the hue-and-cry.

"Clear the course! Course, course! Just startin'—the great Ladies' Race! Clear the course!"

So it was only a race, after all! Tilda gripped the boy's hand tightly, and held him at stand-still some paces in rear of the crowd. But of this caution there was little need. All the faces were turned the other way; all the crowd pressed forwards against the ropes which the lantern-bearers drew taut to fence off the course. A pistol-shot cracked out. Someone cried, "They're off!" and a murmur grew and rolled nearer—rising, as it approached, from a murmur into great waves—waves of Homeric laughter.

The race went by, and a stranger race Tilda had never beheld. The competitors were all women, of all ages—village girls, buxom matrons, withered crones—and each woman held a ladle before her in which an egg lay balanced. Some were in sun-bonnets, others in their best Sunday headdress. Some had kilted their skirts high. Others were all dishevelled with the ardour of the race. The leader—a gaunt figure with spoon held rigidly before her, with white stockinged legs, and a truly magnificent stride—had come and passed before Tilda could believe her eyes. After a long interval three others tottered by in a cluster. The fifth dropped her egg and collapsed beside it, to be hauled to her feet and revived by the stewards amid inextinguishable laughter from the crowd. In all, fourteen competitors rolled in, some with empty ladles, some laughing and protesting that not a step farther could they stir. But, long before the crowd closed in, Tilda saw the winner breast a glimmering line of tape stretched at the end of the course, and heard the shouts saluting her victory.

"But who is it?"

"Miss Sally!"

"Miss Sally, if ever you heard the like! . . . But there! blood will tell."

"It's years since I seen her," said a woman.

"You don't say! Never feared man nor devil, my mother used to tell. An' to run in a race along with the likes of Jane Pratt! But you never can reckon wi' the gentry—what they'll do, or what they won't."

"With half the county, too, lookin' on from the Grand Stand! I bet Sir Elphinstone's cussin'."

"And I'll bet Miss Sally don't care how hard he cusses. She could do a bit o' that too in her time, by all accounts."

"Ay, a monstrous free-spoken lady always. Swearin' don't sit well upon womankind, I allow—not as a rule. But when there's blood, a damn up or down—what is it? For my part I never knew a real gentleman—or lady for that matter—let out a downright thumper but I want to cry 'Old England for ever!'"

Finding it hopeless to skirt the crowd, the children made a plunge through it, with 'Dolph at their heels. But as the crush abated and they breasted the farther slope, Tilda made two discoveries; the first, that whereas a few minutes since the platform had held a company of people among its palms and fairy-lamps, it was now deserted; the second, that the mob at the winning-post had actually shouldered Miss Sally, and was carrying her in triumph towards the platform, with a brass band bobbing ahead and blaring *See, the Conquering Hero comes!*

This second discovery was serious, for the procession's line of march threatened to intercept them. But luckily the bandsmen, who set the pace, moved slowly, and by taking hands and running the children reached the platform in time, skirted its darker side, and dived under its scarlet draperies into the cavernous darkness beneath the boards.

Here they drew breath, and Tilda again clutched the dog. They were in time, but with a very little to spare. In less than a minute the mob surged all around the platform, shouting, hooraying.

"Three cheers for Miss Sally! The Ham—where's the Ham? Give Miss Sally the Ham! Silence, there—silence for Sir Elphinstone! Speech from Sir Elphinstone! Speech!"

By and by the hubbub died down a little, but still there were cries of "Sir Elphinstone for ever!" "Miss Sally for ever!" and "Your sister's won the Ham, sir!" A high-pitched voice on the outskirts of the throng began to chant—

"For really it was a remarkable 'am!"

But got no further, being drowned first by sporadic, uneasy laughter, and then by a storm of hisses. A tremendous roar of laughter followed, and this (although Tilda could not guess it) was evoked by Miss Sally's finding the ham where it stood derelict on a table among the greenhouse plants, lifting it off its plate and brandishing it before the eyes of her admirers.

Tilda could see nothing of this. But she was listening with all her might, and as the uproar died down again she caught the accents of a man's voice attempting a speech.

"My friends," it was saying, still lifting itself higher against the good-humoured interruptions, "my very good friends—impossible not to be gratified—expression of good will—venture to say, on the whole—thoroughly enjoyable afternoon. My sister"—(interruptions and cheers for Miss Sally)—"my sister begs me to say—highly gratified—spirit of the thing—but, if I may plead, some degree of fatigue only natural— won't misunderstand if I ask—disperse—quietly as possible—eh? Oh, yes, 'God save the King,' by all means—much obliged, reminder— thank you—yes, certainly."

Thereupon the band played the National Anthem, and the throng, after yet another outbreak of cheering, dispersed. Followed a silence in the darkness under the platform, broken only by the distant thudding bass of the roundabout's steam organ; and then between the boards there sounded a liquid chuckle, much like a blackbird's, and a woman's voice said—

"Come, my dear brother, say it out! The Countess has gone; everybody has gone—she must have stampeded 'em, by the way—and as the Jew said, when a thunderstorm broke on the picnic, 'Here's a fuss over a little bit of ham!' Well, my dear, there has always been this about Sally— a man can swear before her *sans gene*. So, to give you a start, how did they take it?"

"If after these years I didn't know you to be incorrigible—" growled the voice of Sir Elphinstone.

"'For ladies of all ages,' the bills said."

"'Ladies!'"

"I am quoting your own bill—I'll bet a fiver, too, that you drafted it. Anyway, I'm rising forty—though I'd defy 'em to tell it by my teeth. And since they passed me for a lady—oh, Elphinstone, it *was* a lark! And I never thought I had the wind for it. You remember Kipling—you are always quoting that young man—"

'The dun he fled like a stag of ten, but the mare like a
   barren doe.'

"Well, that's how it was: 'Like a barren doe,' I give you my word."

"My dear Sally!"

"Shameless, was it? My dear Elphinstone, you've only to bill it, and I'll do Lady Godiva for 'em next year—at *my* time of life. But if you don't like Kipling, what do you say to this?"

> 'For really this was a remarkable Ham,
> A twenty-pound solid Imperial Ham,
> And old Mrs. Liddicott
> Tucked up her petticoat—'

"Which reminds me that the crowd specially cheered my white Balbriggans. They are out of date, but I could never fancy my legs in anything but white."

"What on earth are you reading?"

"The local paper—Opposition. Haven't you seen it? There's a whole column in verse about you, Elphinstone; hits you off to a hair, and none so badly written. I'd a mind to show it to the Countess and Lady Mary, but slipped it under the table cloth and at the last moment forgot it in your eloquence. You really must listen—"

> 'Sir Elphinstone Breward
> He rang for his steward,
> And "Damme," said he, looking up from his letters,
> This side of the county
> That feeds on my bounty
> 's forgotten all proper respect of its betters.'

"The devil!" interrupted Sir Elphinstone. "It's that dirty little Radical, Wrightson."

"You recognise the style? It gets neater, to my thinking, as it goes on—"

> 'Agitators and pillagers
> Stir up my villagers—
> Worst of those fellows, so easily led!
> Some haven't food enough,
> Else it ain't good enough,
> Others object to sleep three in a bed.'
>
> 'Deuce take their gratitude!
> "Life"—that's the attitude—
> "Dullish and hard, on the parish half-crown!"
> Dull? Give 'em circuses!
> Hard? Ain't there work'uses?
> What *can* they see to attract 'em to town?'

"—Neat, in its way," commented Miss Sally, pausing.

"Neat? *I* call it subversive and damnable!"

"Listen! The next is a stinger—"

'Something quite recent, now:
 "Drainage ain't decent," now:
 Damme, when *was* it? I've known, if you please,
 Old tenants, better ones,
 Crimean veterans—
 Never heard *they* required w.c.'s—'

"My *dear* Sally!"

"I read you the thing as it's printed," said Miss Sally, with another liquid chuckle.

["Ain't it just 'eavingly?" whispered Tilda below, clutching the boy's arm while she listened.

"What?"

"The voice of 'er. If I could on'y speak words that way!"]

"He goes on," pursued Miss Sally, "to tell how you and Saunders—that's your new bailiff's name, is it not?—cooked up this woman's race between you as a step towards saving the Empire. The language is ribald in places, I allow; but I shouldn't greatly wonder if that, more or less, is how it happened. And any way I've come to the rescue, and kept the Imperial Ham in the family."

"I have sometimes thought, Sally—if you will forgive my putting it brutally—that you are half a Radical yourself."

Thereat, after a moment's pause, the lady laughed musically. Almost in the darkness you could see her throwing back her head and laughing. She had a noble contralto voice, with a rich mannish purr in it.

"You are mistaken, Elphinstone. But even so, my excellent brother, you might understand it—if your estate lay in the west and ran with Miles Chandon's."

Tilda's small body stiffened with a gasp, 'Miles Chandon'—the name had sounded on her hearing distinct as the note of a bell. There was no mistake: it hummed in her ears yet. Or was it the blood rushing to her ears as she sat bolt upright in the darkness, listening, breathing hard?

Sir Elphinstone, for some reason, had not answered his sister. When at length he spoke, it was in a changed tone, at once careless and more affectionate.

"See anything of Chandon in these days?"

"Nothing at all; or—to put the same thing differently—just so much of him as his tenants see. We were talking of tenantry. Miles Chandon leaves everything to his steward. Now, between ourselves, all stewards, land agents, bailiffs—whatever you choose to call 'em—are the curse of our system, and Miles Chandon's happens to be the worst specimen."

"H'm," said Sir Elphinstone reflectively. "Poor devil!" he added, a few moments later, and then—Miss Sally giving him no encouragement to pursue the subject—"Ten minutes past seven—the car will be waiting. What do you say to getting home for dinner?"

"If I may bring the Ham." Miss Sally laughed and pushed back her chair. "Wait a minute—we will wrap it up in the poem. 'Exit Atalanta, carrying her Ham in a newspaper'—how deliciously vulgar! Elphinstone, you have always been the best of brothers; you are behaving beautifully—and—and I never could resist shocking you; but we're pretty fond of one another, eh?"

"I've consistently spoilt you, if that's what you mean," he grumbled.

They were leaving the platform. Tilda whispered to the boy to take hold of 'Dolph.

"And I'm goin' to leave yer for a bit." She edged past him on hands and knees towards the vallance draperies. "You 'eard what she said?
Well, keep quiet 'ere an' don't be frightened. If Sam comes, tell 'im
I'll be back in five minutes."

She dived out beneath the vallance, caught a glimpse of Miss Sally and Sir Elphinstone making their way at a brisk pace through the crowd, and hurried up the slope in pursuit. It was difficult to keep them in sight, for everyone made way upon recognising them, but showed less consideration for a small panting child; and the head of the field, by the exit gate, was packed by a most exasperating throng pressing to admire a giant motor-car that waited in the roadway with lamps blazing and a couple of men in chauffeurs' dress keeping guard in attitudes of sublime *hauteur*. Sir Elphinstone, with Miss Sally on his arm, reached the car while yet Tilda struggled in the gateway. A policeman roughly ordered her back. She feigned to obey, and dropping out of sight, crawled forth past the policeman's boots, with her head almost butting the calves of a slow-moving yeoman farmer. Before she could straighten herself up Sir Elphinstone had climbed into the car after his sister, and the pair were settling down in their rugs. One of the chauffeurs was already seated, the other, having set the machine throbbing, was already clambering to his seat. The crowd set up three parting cheers, and Miss Sally, remembering her Ham, held it aloft in farewell.

But while Miss Sally waved and laughed, of a sudden, amid the laughter and cheers and throbbing of the motor, a small child sprang out of the darkness and clung upon the step.

"Lady! Lady!"

Miss Sally stared down upon the upturned face.

"Miles Chandon, lady?—where does 'e live?—For the Lord's sake—"

But already Sir Elphinstone had called the order. The car shot away smoothly.

"Elphinstone—a moment, please! Stop! The child—"

"Eh? . . . Stop the car! . . . Anything wrong?"

Miss Sally peered back into the darkness.

"There was a child . . . We have hurt her, I fear. Tell George to jump down and inquire."

But Tilda was not hurt. On the contrary, she was running and dodging the crowd at that moment as fast as her hurt leg permitted. For in the press of it, not three yards away, by the light of the side lamp, she had caught sight of Dr. Glasson and Gavel.

They were on foot, and Gavel had seen her, she could make no doubt. He was bearing down straight upon her.

Not until she had run fifty yards did she pluck up courage to look back. Gavel was nowhere in sight. The car had come to a standstill, and the people were yelling. Was it after her? Was *this* the hue-and-cry?

They were certainly yelling—and behaving too, in the strangest fashion. They seemed by one impulse to be running from the car and crowding back towards the gate. They were fighting—positively fighting—their way into the field. The police could not stop them, but were driven in with a rush; and in the centre of this rush Tilda caught sight of Gavel again. His back was turned to her. He was struggling for admission, and like a maniac. Glasson she could not see.

Sir Elphinstone had climbed out of the car, and came striding back demanding to know what was the matter. It stuck in his head that a child had been hurt, perhaps killed.

A dozen voices answered—

"The roundabouts!" "Explosion at the roundabouts!" "Engine blown up—twenty killed an' injured, they say!"

"Explosion? . . . Nonsense!"

Tilda saw him thrust his way into the gateway, his tall figure towering above the pack there as he halted and gazed down the hill. In the darkness and confusion it was easy enough for her to scramble upon the hedge unobserved, and at the cost of a few scratches only. From the top of the hedge she too gazed.

The roundabout had come to a standstill. Around it, at a decent distance, stood a dark circle of folk. But its lights still blazed, its mirrors still twinkled. She could detect nothing amiss.

What had happened? Tilda had forgotten Miss Sally, and was anxious now but for Arthur Miles. A dozen fears suggested themselves. She ought never to have left him. . . .

She dropped from the hedge into the field, and ran downhill to the platform. It stood deserted, the last few fairy-lamps dying down amid the palms and greenery. In the darkness at its rear there was no need of caution, and she plunged under the vallance boldly.

"Arthur! Arthur Miles! Are you all right? . . . Where are you?"

A thin squeal answered her, and she drew back, her skin contracting in a shudder, even to the roots of her hair. For, putting out her hand, she had touched flesh—naked, human flesh.

"Wh—who are you?" she stammered, drawing back her fingers.

"I'm the Fat Lady," quavered a voice. "Oh, help me! I'm wedged here and can't move!"

CHAPTER XV.

ADVENTURE OF THE FAT LADY.

"*Gin a body meet a body.*"—BURNS.

"But what's 'appened?" demanded Tilda, recovering herself a little.
"And ow? And oh! what's become of the boy, Arthur Miles?"

"There *is* a boy, somewhere at the back of me," the Fat Lady answered; "and a dog too. You can talk to them across me; but I couldn't move, not if I was crushin' them ever so."

Tilda called softly to the prisoners, and to her relief Arthur Miles answered out of the darkness, assuring her, albeit in a muffled voice, that they were both safe.

"But what's the *meanin'* of it?" Tilda demanded again.

"The igsplosion's the meanin' of it."

"But there ain't *been* no explosh'n. And anyway," said Tilda, "you ain't tellin' me you been *blown* 'ere?"

"Igsplosion or no igsplosion," replied the Fat Lady incontestably, "'ere I h'am."

"*Sure* yer can't move?" Tilda coaxed.

At this the Fat Lady showed some irritation.

"I ought to know what I'm capable of by this time. . . . If you could run along and fetch somebody with a tackle and pulley now—"

"I got a friend comin' presently. 'E's quite a 'andy young feller, *an'* tender-'earted: 'e won't leave yer like this, no fear. . . . But, o' course, it'll be a shock to 'im, 'appenin' in upon us an' findin'— well, so much *more*'n 'e expected. I'm thinkin' 'ow to break it to 'im gently, 'ere in the dark." Tilda considered for a while. "It might 'elp if I knew yer name. 'Twouldn' be fair—would it?—to start off that we'd got a surprise for 'im, an' would 'e guess?"

"He'll find out, fast enough, when he strikes a light," said the Fat Lady between resigned despair and professional pride. "But my name's Mrs. Lobb, when you introjuice him."

"Widow?"

"I don't know why you should suppose it."

"No," said Tilda after musing a moment; "there ain't no real reason, o' course. On'y I thought—An' you not mentionin' a nusband, under the circumstances."

To her astonishment, Mrs. Lobb gave way and shook with mountainous sobs.

"I'm a maiden lady," she confessed, "and I'll conceal it no longer, when, God knows, I may be lyin' here punished for my vanity. . . . But 'twasn't all vanity, neither: it sounded more comfortable. If it had been vanity, I'd ha' chosen Montmorency or St. Clair—not Lobb. Wouldn't I now? . . . Of course, you won't understand, at your age; but there's a sort of *sheltered* feelin'. An' I'm a bundle of nerves. You should see me," wound up Mrs. Lobb enigmatically, "with a mouse."

But at this moment Tilda whispered "'Ush!" Someone was stealthily lifting the vallance. "Is that you, Sam?" she challenged.

"Aye, aye, missie. All safe?"

"*And* snug. . . . Can yer risk striking a match? Fact is, we got a lady friend 'ere, an' she wants yer 'elp badly."

Sam struck a sulphur match.

"Good Lord!" he breathed, staring across the blue flame, and still as he stared his eyes grew larger and rounder.

"'Er name's Lobb," explained Tilda. "I oughter a-told yer."

"'Ow did it 'appen?" asked Sam in an awed voice.

"Igsplosion," said the Fat Lady.

"Is—is there *goin'* to be one?"

The match burned low in Sam's trembling fingers, and he dropped it with an exclamation of pain.

"There *was* one," said the Fat Lady. "At Gavel's roundabouts. Leastways, the folks came chargin' into my tent, which is next door, cryin' out that the boiler was blowin' up. I travel with Gavel, sir—as his Fat Lady—"

"Oh!" Sam drew a long breath.

"Which, when I heard it, sir, and the outcries, I burst out through the back of the tent—bein' a timorous woman—and ran for shelter. My fright, sir, I'll leave you to imagine. And then, as I crawled under the boards here, a dog flew at me—and bein' taken unawares—on all fours, too—I rolled over with my legs twisted—and here I am stuck. There's one joist pinnin' my left shoulder, and my leg's jammed under another; and stir I cannot."

Sam lit another match.

"I was fearin'—" he began, but broke off. "If you could manage, ma'am, to draw up your knee an inch or so—or if you wouldn' mind my takin' a pull—"

"Not at all," said Mrs. Lobb. "I'm used to bein' pinched."

Sam gripped the knee-pan firmly, and hauled.

"O-ow!" cried Mrs. Lobb. But the wrench had set her free to uncross her legs, and she did so, murmuring her gratitude.

There had been (Sam now explained) a false alarm. In the midst of the merry-making, and while the roundabouts were crowded and going at full speed, the boy in charge of the engine had taken occasion to announce to the lady at the pay-table that his pressure was a hundred-and-forty-seven, and what had taken the safety valve he couldn't think. Whereupon the lady at the pay-table had started up, scattering her coins, and shrieked; and this had started the stampede. "Which," added Sam in a whisper to Tilda, "was lucky for us in a way; becos Glasson, after tacklin' Mortimer be'ind the scenes an' threatenin' to have his blood in a bottle, had started off with Gavel to fetch the perlice. An' the question is if they won't be watchin' the gates by this time."

"In *my* young days," announced the Fat Lady, with disconcerting suddenness, "it was thought rude to whisper."

Tilda took a swift resolution.

"The truth is, ma'am, we're in trouble, an' 'idin' 'ere. I wouldn' dare to tell yer, on'y they say that people o' your—I mean, in your—"

"Profession," suggested the Fat Lady.

"—Are kind-'earted by nature. I belongs, ma'am—leastways, I *did*,— to Maggs's Circus—if you know it—"

"I've heard Maggs's troupe very well spoken of. But, as you'll understand, I do very little visitin'."

"I was 'appy enough with Maggs's, ma'am. But first of all a pony laid me up with a kick, an' then I stole Arthur Miles 'ere out of the 'Oly Innercents—"

Tilda broke down for a moment, recovered herself, and with sobs told her story.

For a while, after she had ended it, the Fat Lady kept silence. Sam, breathing hard, still doubtful of the child's bold policy, feared what this silence might portend.

"Give me your hand, young man," said the Fat Lady at length.

Sam reached out in the darkness, and grasped hers fervently.

"I didn't ask you to shake it. I want to be helped out to the fresh air, and then these children'll march straight home with me to my caravan."

"But," stammered Sam, not yet clear that he had found an ally, "—but that's leadin' 'em straight into Gavel's arms!"

"Young man," replied the lady austerely, "it leads into no man's arms." But a moment later she dropped her voice, and added with a touch of pathos, "I'm the loneliest woman in the world, outside of show hours; and if you thought a little you might know it."

"I see," said Sam contritely.

"And, what's more, inside my own caravan I've my wits about me. Outside and among folks—well, maybe you've seen an owl in the daylight with the small birds mobbin' him. . . . Now about yourself and the Mortimers—from this child's story there's no evidence yet to connect her or the boy with either of you. The man Hucks knows, and that carrier fellow at the wharf saw them for a minute, with Mortimer standin' by. But that's no evidence for the police; and, anyway, this Glasson can't touch you until he gets hold of the children. If you'll leave it to me, he shan't do that for twenty-four hours. And now—isn't it time you were packing up your show? You'll be gettin' back to the boat to-night, I suppose? What about the Mortimers?" Sam explained that he would be driving back with the tent, and intended to sleep on board. The Mortimers would repose themselves at a small public-house, "The Vine Leaf." In the morning they would join forces again and proceed to Stratford. Address there: "The Red Cow."

He delivered this explanation jerkily, in the intervals of lugging the lady forth from her durance. Tilda, scrambling forth ahead of her, noted with inexpressible relief that the aspect of the field was entirely changed. The crowd had melted away, the flares of the roundabout were extinguished, and a faint glow of lamplight through canvas told where the Mortimer's tent, far to the left, awaited dismemberment. Five or six lanterns dotted the lower slopes, where the smaller shows—the Aunt Sally, the coconut shies and the swing-boats— were being hastily packed. Overhead, in a clean heaven, rode the stars, and by their glimmer the children saw their new protectress draw herself up in all her Amazonian amplitude. She wore a low bodice of pink, with spangles, and a spangled skirt descended to her knees. Beneath them her columnar calves were bare as an infant's. She extended an arm, and pointed towards her caravan.

"Bear around to the right," she commanded. "Keep a look-out on me when I get to the van, and creep up as quietly as you can when I reach the step and bend to pull up my socks. Good night, young man—one good turn deserves another: and now be off, you two . . . Yes, you may bring the dog. Only I hope he doesn't suffer from fleas, for a flea with me is a serious matter."

They ran around, gained the steps in safety, and were admitted to the Fat Lady's virgin bower. It lay in darkness, and enjoining them to stand still and keep silence, she drew the blinds discreetly before lighting her lamp. She did this (Tilda noted) with extreme deftness, reaching out a hand to a dark shelf and picking up the match-box as accurately as though she saw it. At once, too, Tilda noted that in the lamp's rays the whole interior of the caravan shone like a new pin. A stove stood at the end facing the doorway, and beside the stove a closed washstand of polished teak. A dressing-table, a wardrobe, and a dresser-sideboard fitted with lockers occupied one side; along the other ran a couch with a padded back, which, let down, became a mattress and converted the couch into a bed. All the lockers gleamed with brasswork; all the draperies were of muslin or dimity, immaculately white; and looking-glass panelled the doors of every cupboard. These many mirrors caused the interior to appear even fuller of the Fat Lady than it actually was. They reflected her from every angle, and multiplied her into a crowd.

"Dear me!" she said, glancing around on these reflections, "I'll have to turn you out again while I undress. But that won't take long, and you'll be safe enough beneath the van."

So after providing them with a hunk of cake apiece from one of the sideboard lockers, and peeping forth to make sure the coast was clear, she dismissed them with instructions to creep into the darkness under the steps, and there lie quiet until she summoned them.

Ten minutes later she leaned forth again and called "Coo-ee!" very softly, and they returned to find her in the white bed, recumbent in a coquettish nightgown. She had folded and stowed her day garments away— Tilda could not imagine where—and a mattress and rugs lay on the floor, ready spread for the children. Nor was this all. On the sideboard stood a plateful of biscuits, and on the stove a spirit-lamp, with a kettle already beginning to sing, and a teapot and three cups and saucers.

With a turn of the hand, scarcely stirring from her recumbent posture, the Fat Lady closed the door and shot its small brass bolt. Then with a quick series of movements, reaching forward as soon as the kettle boiled, she filled the teapot, emptied the rest of the boiling water into the flashing nickel basin of the washstand, set down the kettle, turned and shut a cold-water tap, and invited the children to wash before supping.

The aroma of the tea—real China tea it was—and the fragrance of scented soap—genuine Old Brown Windsor—went straight through their senses to the children's hearts. In all their lives they had known no experience so delicious.

Mrs. Lobb noted with approval that the boy drew aside and yielded Tilda the first turn at the basin. When his came she watched him, and by and by observed, "He washes like a gentleman, too."

"Not," she explained as the children drank their tea—"not that I have ever seen a gentleman wash. But women know what's dainty." Here she fell into a muse. "I've often pictered Mr. Lobb washing. These little things make so much difference." She sighed. "Well now, if you've finished your supper, we'll say our prayers and get to sleep."

"Prayers?" queried Tilda.

As a rule, when anything happened outside her experience she sat quiet and let it happen, reserving criticism. But, chancing to look up, she had seen the boy wince at the word.

Mrs. Lobb, less observant, had taken down a Bible from the shelf above her. She opened it and read—

> 'And they departed from Kibroth-hattaavah, and encamped at Hazeroth. And they departed from Hazeroth, and pitched in Rithmah. And they departed from Rithmah, and pitched at Rimmoth-parez—'

"It don't always apply," she explained, breaking off, "but takin' it straight through, you'd be surprised how often it sends you to sleep with a bit of comfort."

She read half a dozen verses, closed the book, and recited the Lord's Prayer—

"' . . . For Thine is the kingdom, the power, and the glory, for ever and ever. Amen.' Now we'll go to sleep, and don't be frightened when they harness up in an hour or two. We'll be in Stratford before daybreak. Good night, my dears—you may reach up and give me a kiss apiece if you're so minded; and I hope to goodness you don't snore!"

When they awoke, sure enough Mrs. Lobb announced that they had reached Stratford. In their dreams they had felt the van moving; but now it had come to a standstill, and, peeping forth, they saw that it stood in a broad green meadow and but a little way from a river. There were swans on the river, paddling about or slowly drifting in the pale light; and across the river they saw many clustered roofs, with a church spire to the left set among noble elms.

"That's where Shakespeare's buried," said the Fat Lady; "and the great brick building yonder—to the right, between us and the bridge—that's the Memorial Theatre where they act his plays. There's his statue, too, beside the water, and back in the town they keep the house he was born in. You can't get away from Shakespeare here. If you buy a bottle of beer, he's on the label; and if you want a tobacco-jar, they'll sell you his head and shoulders in china, with the bald top fitted for a cover. It's a queer place, is Stratford."

The boy gazed. To him it was a marvellous place; and somewhere it held his secret—the secret of the Island.

"Talkin' of beer," said Tilda, "we mustn' forget Sam Bossom. At the 'Red Cow,' he said."

"But that won't be till evening," the Fat Lady warned her. "And meantime what am I to do with you. You can't hide here all day: for one reason, I got to get up and dress. And it may be dangerous in the town for you before nightfall. Luckily, Gavel don't know either one of you by sight; but there's the chance of this Glasson havin' come along with him. For all I know, Gavel may have given him a shake-down, and Gavel's is the next van but one."

The children implored her to let them forth before the rest of the show-people awoke. They would fend for themselves, Tilda engaged, and remain in hiding all day along the river-bank below the town. Really, when the Fat Lady thought it over, this appeared the only feasible plan. But first she insisted on cooking them a breakfast of fried sausages and boiled eggs, which she managed to do without stirring from her couch, directing Tilda how to light the stove, and where to find the utensils and the provender; and next she packed a basket for them with a loaf of bread and some slices of cold ham.

Thus furnished, they bade her good-bye for the day, left the dubious 'Dolph in her charge, and tip-toeing past the rear of the caravan where slept the dreaded Gavel, gained the meadow's end, passed a weed-grown ruinated lock below the churchyard, and struck into a footpath that led down-stream between the river and a pretty hanging copse. Below this a high road crossed the river. Following it, they passed over a small tributary stream that wound between lines of pollard willows, and so headed off to their right and regained the Avon's bank.

The boy led. It seemed that the westward-running stream called to him, and that his feet trod to the tune of it. Tilda remembered this later. He was always a silent boy, and he gave no explanation; but she saw that the running water woke a new excitement in him. So long as they had followed the stagnant canal he had been curious, alert, inquisitive of every bend and bush. It was as if he had understood water by instinct, and yet the water had hitherto baffled and disappointed him. Now it ran, and he ran too. She had much ado to keep pace with him. By and by she halted by a clump of willows and seated herself, announcing hypocritically that she was tired.

He heard, and came back contritely.

"I forgot," he said. "What has become of your crutch?"

"I left it be'ind yesterday, in the boat. There wasn' no time to go back for it."

"I am very sorry."

Tilda's conscience smote her.

"There ain't no reason to fret about *me*," she said reassuringly. "But what's taken you? There's no catchin' up with the water, however fast you run."

"It leads down to the Island. It *must*," he announced, conning the stream.

"Think so?"

She too conned it, but could read nothing of his faith in the wimpled surface.

"Sure."

The light in his eyes impressed if it did not convince her.

"Well, maybe we'll 'ave a try to-morrow," she conceded after a while. "But business is business. We must get back to Stratford an' consult Sam Bossom. And then there's a letter to be written to 'Ucks. I promised 'im, you know."

They shared their meal by the river bank; and when it was eaten, sat for a time on the scooped-out brink while Avon ran at their feet—Arthur Miles searching again in the thumbed pages of *The Tempest* for a hint that might perchance have escaped him; Tilda as sedulously intent on a page of a ladies' newspaper in which the bread had been wrapped.

It informed her, under the heading of *Answers to Correspondents by "Smart Set,"* of an excellent home for Anglo-Indian children (gravel soil), of a new way to clean Brussels lace, of the number of gowns required in these days for a week-end visit, of a scale of tips for gamekeepers. It directed her to a manicure, and instructed her how to build a pergola for an Italian garden, supposing that she lived in Suffolk and could spare half an acre facing east. She drank in all this information with an impartial appetite.

"What a favourite it is still, the mushroom 'at!" she spelled out slowly. "W'y the other day, at Messrs. Freebody and Williams's in Regent Street, there it confronted me again in a whole bevy of new model shapes. The medium, in brown Ottoman silk, fronted with wings of fine brown or blue lustre, is quite ridiculously cheap at 27s. 6d. And a large hat in black satin, swathed with black chiffon in which lurks just a touch of real ermine, asks you no more than 35s. 9d. Truly age cannot wither nor custom stale the infinite variety of the mushroom.'"

"What nonsense are you reading?" the boy demanded.

"Nonsense?" echoed Tilda. "What's nonsense? It's—it's 'eavingly—and anyway it ain't no farther off than your Island."

They resumed their way, slightly huffed one with another; passed a group of willows; and came to a halt, surprised and irresolute.

In the centre of a small sunny clearing they beheld a tent, with the litter of a camp equipage scattered on the turf about it; and between the tent and the river, where shone the flank of a bass-wood canoe moored between the alders, an artist had set up his easel. He was a young man, tall and gaunt, and stood back a little way from his canvas with paint-brush held at a slope, while across it he studied the subject of his picture—a grey bridge and the butt-end of a grey building, with a sign-board overtopping the autumnal willows.

For a few seconds the children observed him in silence. But some sound must have warned him; for by and by he turned a quick, eager face, and caught sight of them.

"Ah!" he exclaimed, scanning them rapidly up and down. "The very thing!—that is to say"—after a second and more prolonged scrutiny— "the boy. He just fills the bill. 'Youthful Shakespeare Mews his Mighty Youth. The scene: Binton Bridges, beside Avon.'"

"Binton Bridges?" echoed Tilda, and walked forward to scan the sign-board.

"I must put that down," said the artist, drawing out a notebook and pencil. "Ignorance of Juvenile Population in respect of Immediate Surroundings. Implied Reproach against Britain's Primary Schools."

But by this time the girl was standing under the sign-board and staring up at it. Four figures were depicted thereon in gay colours—a king, a priest, a soldier, and a John Bull farmer. Around them ran this legend—

"RULE ALL, PRAY ALL, FIGHT ALL, PAY ALL."

"Do you 'appen to know, sir," she asked, coming back, "if there's a young woman employed 'ere?"

"There is," answered the artist. "I happen to know, because she won't let me paint her, although I offered ten dollars."

"That's a good sign," said Tilda.

"Oh, is it now?" he queried, staring after her as she marched boldly towards the house and was lost to sight between the willow-stems.

CHAPTER XVI.

ADVENTURES OF THE "FOUR ALLS" AND OF THE CELESTIAL CHEMIST

"*'Friend Sancho,' said Don Quixote, 'this Island that I promised you can neither stir nor fly.'*"—CERVANTES.

"Now what precisely did your sister mean by that?" asked the artist, withdrawing his gaze and fixing it on Arthur Miles.

"She is not my sister," said the boy.

The artist—he was an extraordinarily tall young man, with a keen hatchet face, restless brown eyes, and straight auburn hair parted accurately in the middle—considered for a moment, then nodded.

"That's so. It comes out, soon as you talk . . . Well, see here now, we'll start right away. That's how Art hits me—once I take hold of a notion, I must sling in and get going. It's my temperament; and what's Art—right *there*, please—what's Art, after all, but expressed temperament? You catch the idea? You're the Infant Shakespeare, the youth to fortune and to fame unknown—"

'His listless length at noontide would he stretch'—

"Stretch what you have of it—"

'And pore upon the brook that babbles by.'

"But I don't want you to paint me," rebelled the boy.

"Goodness! Why not?"

For a moment or two Arthur Miles faced the question almost sullenly.

"I don't want my likeness taken," he explained at length.

"My young friend," the artist cheerfully assured him, "if that's your trouble, dismiss it. I can't paint a likeness for nuts."

"You are sure?"

"Well, I should say I have a grounded expectation, seeing that I claim a bigger circle of friends than any other fellow that ever studied with Carolus; and apart from their liking for me, their conviction that never under any circumstances could I catch a likeness is about the only thing they have in common. I don't say it's the cement of their friendship; but, anyway, it's an added tie."

"If Tilda doesn't mind—"

The boy hesitated, with a glance over his shoulder.

"We'll consult the lady when the portrait's finished. If she recognises you, I'll destroy the canvas; and I can't say fairer than that . . . No, I shan't regret it. We'll call it an offering to the gods . . . And now," pursued the young man, flinging in a charcoal outline in fiery haste, "we'll consider the brakes open."

It took him perhaps thirty seconds to block in the figure, and at once he fell to mixing his palette, his fingers moving with a nervous, delicate haste. He held a brush between his teeth during the operation; but no sooner was it over, and the gag removed, than his speech began to gush in quick, impetuous jerks, each jerk marking an interval as, after flinging a fresh splash of paint upon the canvas, he stepped back half a pace to eye its effect.

"That's my theory—what's Art but temperament? expressed temperament? Now I'm a fellow that could never stick long to a thing—never in my life. I've not told you that I'm American, by the way. My name's Jessup—George Pulteney Jessup, of Boise City, Idaho. My father—he's about the most prominent citizen in the State of Idaho. You don't get any ways far west of the Rockies before you bump against Nahum P. Jessup—and you'll be apt to hurt yourself by bumping too hard. . . . My father began by setting it down to fickleness. He said it came of having too much money to play with. Mind you, he didn't complain. He sent for me into his office, and 'George,' he said, 'there's some fathers, finding you so vola_tile_, would take the line of cutting down your allowance; but that's no line for me. To begin with,' he said, 'it would set up a constraint between us, and constraint in my family relations is what, God helping me, I'll never allow. And next, whatever I saved on you I'd just have to re-invest, and I'm over-capitalised as it is—you 'd never guess the straits I'm put to daily in keeping fair abreast of fifteen per cent., which is my notion of making two ends meet. And, lastly, it ain't natural. If a man's born vola_tile_, vola_tile_ he is; and the sensible plan, I take it, is to lean your ear to Nature, the Mighty Mother, and find a career that has some use for that kind of temperament. Now,' said my father, 'I know a little about most legitimate careers, from ticket-punching up to lobbying, and there's not one in which a man would hand in testimonials that he was vola_tile_. But,' says my father, 'what about Art? I've never taken stock of that occupation, myself: I never had time. But I remember once in New York going to a theatre and seeing Booth act William Shakespeare's *Macbeth*; and not twenty minutes later, after all the ghosts and murderings, I happened into a restaurant, and saw the same man drinking cocktails and eating Blue Point oysters—with twice my appetite too. And Booth was at the very top of his profession.'"

"Yes," said Arthur Miles, by this time greatly interested. "That's like Mr. Mortimer, too."

"Mortimer?" Mr. Jessup queried; and then, getting no answer, "Is he an actor?"

The boy nodded.

"A prominent one?"

"I—I believe so. I mean, he says he *ought* to be."

"I'd like to make his acquaintance. It's queer, too, a child like you knowing about actors. What's your name?"

"I don't know," said Arthur Miles, with another glance in the direction of the inn, "that Tilda would like me to tell."

The young artist eyed him.

"Well, never mind; we were talking about my father. That's how he came to send me to Paris to study Art. And since then I've done some thinking. It works out like this," he pursued, stepping back and studying his daub between half-closed eyes, "the old man had struck ore as usual. I never knew a mind fuller of common sense—just homely common sense—but he hadn't the time to work it. Yet it works easy enough if you keep hold of the argument. The Old Masters—we're always having it dinned into us—didn't hustle; they mugged away at a Saint, or a Virgin and Child, and never minded if it took 'em half a lifetime. Well, putting aside their being paid by time and not by the job—because comparisons on a monetary basis ain't fair, one way or another—for better or worse, Carpaccio hadn't a dad in the Oil Trust—I say, putting this aside, the credit goes to their temperament, or, if you like, part to that and part to their environment. It wasn't *in* them to hustle: they felt no call for it, but just sat and painted and took their meals regular. Now that spacious holy sauntering don't figure in my bill. When I get hold of a notion—same as this Infant Shakespeare, f'r instance—it's apt to take hold on me as a mighty fine proposition; and then, before I can slap it on canvas, the thing's gone, faded, extinct, like a sunset." He paused and snapped his fingers expressively. "I paint like Hades, but it beats me by a head every time."

—"And what's the reason? I'm fickle, you say. But that's my temperament, and before a man kicks against *that* he ought to be clear whether it's original sin or the outcome of his environment. See what I mean?"

Arthur Miles was too truthful to say that he did. Indeed, he understood next to nothing of this harangue. But the young American's manner, so eager, so boyishly confidential, set him at his ease; while beneath this voluble flow of talk there moved a deeper current for which, all unconsciously, the child's spirit thirsted. He did not realise this at all, but his eyes shone while he listened.

"I'll put it this way: We're in the twentieth century. Between the old masters and us something has happened. What? Why Speed, sir—modern civilisation has discovered Speed. Railways—telegraphs—'phones— elevators— automobiles—Atlantic records. These inventions, sir"—here as will happen to Americans when they philosophise, Mr. Jessup slipped into an oratorical style—"have altered man's whole environment. Velasquez, sir, was a great artist, and Velasquez could paint, in his day, to beat the band. But I argue that, if you resurrected Velasquez to-day, he'd have to alter his outlook, and everything along with it, right away down to his brush-work. And I go on to argue that if I can't paint like Velasquez—which is a cold fact—it's equally a fact that, if I could, I oughtn't. Speed, sir: that's the great proposition—the principles of Speed as applied to the Fine Arts—"

Here he glanced towards the clearing between the willows, where at this moment Tilda reappeared in a hurry, followed—at a sedater pace—by a young woman in a pale blue sunbonnet.

"Oh, Arthur Miles, it's just splendid!" she announced, waving a letter in her hand. And with that, noting the boy's attitude, she checked herself and stared suspiciously from him to the artist. "Wot yer doin' to 'im?" she demanded.

"Painting his portrait."

"Then you didn't ought, an' 'e'd no business to allow it!"

She stepped to the canvas, examined it quickly, anxiously, then with a puzzled frown that seemed to relax in a sigh of relief—

"Well, it don't seem as you've done much 'arm as yet. But all the same, you didn't ought."

"I want to know what's splendid?" the artist inquired, looking from her to the girl in the sun-bonnet, who blushed rosily.

Tilda, for her part, looked at Arthur Miles and to him addressed her answer—

"'Enery's broke it off!"

"Oh!" said the boy. He reflected a moment, and added with a bright smile, "And what about Sam?"

"It's all 'ere"—she held out the letter; "an' we got to take it to 'im. 'Enery says that waitin's a weary business, but 'e leaves it to 'er; on'y 'e's just found out there's insanity on *'is* side o' the family. That's a bit 'ard on Sam, o' course; but 'Enery doesn' know about Sam's feelin's. 'E was just tryin' to be tactful."

"You'll pardon my curiosity," put in young Mr. Jessup; "but I don't seem to get the hang of this. So far as I figure it up, you two children jump out of nowhere and find yourselves here for the first time in your lives; and before

I can paint one of you—and I'm no snail—the other walks into a public-house, freezes on to an absolute stranger, bustles her through one matrimonial affair and has pretty well fixed her with another. As a student of locomotion"—he turned and stared down upon Tilda—"I'd like you to tell me how you did it."

"Well," she answered, "I felt a bit nervous at startin'. So I walked straight in an' ordered two-penn'orth o' beer—an' then it all came out."

"Was that so?" He perpended this, and went on, "I remember reading somewhere in Ruskin that the more a man can do his job the more he can't say how. It's rough on learners."

But Tilda was not to be drawn into a disputation on Art.

"Come along," she called to the boy.

"You mean to take him from me in this hurry? . . . Well, that breaks another record. I never up to now lost a model before I'd weakened on him: it's not their way."

"That young man," said Tilda as, holding Arthur Miles by the hand, she drew him away and left the pair standing where the level sun slanted through the willows—"that young man," she repeated, turning for a last wave of the hand to the girl in the sunbonnet, "is 'e a bit touched in 'is 'ead, now?"

The dusk gathered as they retraced their way along Avon bank, and by the time they reached the fair meadow the shows were hanging out their lights. The children gave the field a wide berth, and fetching a circuit, reached a grey stone bridge over which the road led into the town.

They crossed it. They were now in Stratford, in a street lit with gas-lamps and lined with bright shop-windows; and Tilda had scarcely proceeded a dozen yards before she turned, aware of something wrong with the boy. In truth, he had never before made acquaintance with a town at night. Lamps and shop-fronts alike bewildered him. He had halted, irresolute. He needed her hand to pilot him.

She gave it, puzzled; for this world so strange to him was the world she knew best. She could not understand what ailed him. But it was characteristic of Tilda that she helped first and asked questions afterwards, if she asked them at all. Usually she found that, given time, they answered themselves. It was well, perhaps, that she asked none now. For how could the boy have explained that he seriously believed these shops and lighted windows to be Eastcheap, Illyria, Verona, and these passers-by, brushing briskly along the pavements, to be Shakespeare's people—the authentic persons of the plays? He halted, gazing, striving to identify this figure and that as it hurried between the lights. Which was Mercutio ruffling to meet a Capulet? Was this the watch passing?—Dogberry's watch? That broad-shouldered man—could he be Antonio, Sebastian's friend, lurking by to his seaport lodging? . . .

They were deep in the town, when he halted with a gasp and a start that half withdrew his hand from her clasp. A pale green light shone on his face. It shone out on the roadway from a gigantic illuminated bottle in a chemist's shop; and in the window stood three similar bottles, each with a gas-jet behind it—one yellow, one amethystine violet, one ruby red.

His grip, relaxed for a second, closed on her fingers again. He was drawing her towards the window. They stared through it together, almost pressing their faces to the pane.

Beyond it, within the shop, surrounded by countless spotlessly polished bottles, his features reflected in a flashing mirror, stood an old man, bending over a mahogany counter, while with delicate fingers he rearranged a line of gallipots in a glass-covered case.

"Is—is he—"

The boy paused, and Tilda heard him gulp down something in his throat.

"Suppose," he whispered, "if—if it should be God?"

"Ga'r'n!" said Tilda, pulling herself together.

"You're sure it's only Prospero?" he asked, still in a whisper.

Before she could answer him—but indeed she could have found no answer, never having heard of Prospero—the boy had dragged her forward and thrust open one of the glass swing-doors. It was he who now showed the courage.

"My lord!"

"Hey?" The old chemist looked up over his spectacles, held for an instant a gallipot suspended between finger and thumb, and set it down with nice judgment. He was extremely bald, and he pushed his spectacles high up on his scalp. Then he smiled benevolently. "What can I do for you, my dears?"

The boy stepped forward bravely, while Tilda—the game for once taken out of her hands—could only admire.

"If you would tell us where the Island is—it is called Holmness—"

Tilda caught her breath. But the old chemist still bent forward, and still with his kindly smile.

"Holmness?—an island?" he repeated in a musing echo. "Let me see—"

"We ain't *sure* it's an island, sir," put in Tilda, plucking up her courage a little.

"It will be in the Gazetteer, of course," said the old chemist with a happy thought; "and you'll find that in the Free Library."

"Gazetteer"—"Free Library." To Tilda these were strange words—names of wide oceans, perhaps, or of far foreign countries. But the boy caught at the last word: he remembered Prospero's—

> "Me, poor man, my library
> Was dukedom large enough,"

And this made him more confident than ever.

"But why do you want to know?" the old chemist went on. "Is it home lessons?"

"'E," said Tilda, indicating Arthur Miles, "'e wants to find a relation 'e's got there—a kind of uncle—in 'Olmness, w'ich is in the Gazetteer," she repeated, as though the scent lay hidden in a nest of boxes, "'w'ich is in the Free Library."

"If you don't mind waiting a moment, I'll take you there."

The children gasped.

He turned and trotted around the back of his mirrored screen. They heard him call and announce to someone in the back parlour—but the boy made sure that it was to Miranda in her inner cave—that he was going out for a few minutes; and by and by he reappeared, wearing a dark skull-cap, with an Inverness cape about his shoulders, and carrying in his hand a stout staff. He joined them by lifting—another marvel—a mahogany flap and walking straight through the counter! and so led the way out of the shop and up the street to the right, while the children in delicious terror trotted at his heels.

They came to an open doorway, with a lamp burning above it. Dark wavering shadows played within, across the threshold; but the old man stepped through these boldly, and pushed open the door of a lighted room. The children followed, and stood for a moment blinking.

The room was lined with books—shelves upon shelves of books; and among their books a dozen men sat reading in total silence. Some held thin, unbound pages of enormous size—Arthur Miles was unacquainted with newspapers—open before them; all were of middle age or over; and none of them showed surprise at the new-comers. The old chemist nodded to one or two, who barely returned his nod and forthwith resumed their studies.

He walked straight across the room—this was wonderful too, that he should know, among so many books, exactly where to search—adjusted his spectacles, stooped with palms on knees, peered for ten seconds or so along the backs of a row of tall volumes, drew forth one, and bearing it to the table, laid it open under the lamplight.

"Let me see—let me see," he muttered, turning the pages rapidly. "H—H.O.—here we are! Hockley—Hoe—no." He turned another three or four pages. "Holbeach—Hollington—Hollingwood—Holme—ah, here we have it!—Holmfirth, Holme Fell, Holme Moss, HOLMNESS."

He paused for a moment, scanning the page while they held their breath. Then he read aloud, yet not so as to disturb the other students—

"'*Holmness*. An Island or Islet in the Bristol Channel—'"

"Ah!" The boy let his breath escape almost in a sob.

"'Uninhabited—'"

The old chemist looked up over the rims of his spectacles; but whether questioning or because the sound had interrupted him, Tilda could not determine.

"Yes," said the boy eagerly. "They thought that about—about the other Island, sir. Didn't they?"

The old man, either not hearing or not understanding, looked down at the page again. He read out the latitude and longitude—words and figures which neither of the children understood.

"'Extreme length, three-quarters of a mile; width at narrowest point, 165 yards. It contains 356 acres, all of short grass, and affords pasturage in summer for a few sheep from the mainland. There is no harbour; but the south side affords fair anchorage for vessels sheltering from N.W. winds. The distance from nearest point of coast is three and three-quarter miles. Reputed to have served anciently as *rendezvous* for British pirates, and even in the last century as a smugglers' *entrepot*. Geological formation—'"

"Is that all?" asked Tilda as the old man ceased his reading.

"That is all."

"But the river will take us to it," said the boy confidently.

"Hey? What river?"

"Why *this* river—the Avon. It leads down to it—of course it must!"

"Why, yes," answered the old chemist after considering a while. "In a sense, of course, it does. I hadn't guessed at your age you'd be so good at geography. The Avon runs down to Tewkesbury, and there it joins the Severn; and the Severn leads down past Gloucester and into the Bristol Channel."

"I was sure!"

The boy said it in no very loud tone: but something shook in his voice, and at the sound of it all the readers looked up with curiosity—which changed, however, to protest at sight of the boy's rags.

"S—sh—sh!" said two or three.

The old chemist gazed around apologetically, closed the volume, replaced it, and shepherded the children forth.

CHAPTER XVII.

BY WESTON WEIR.

"Down below the Weir Brake
Journeys end in lovers' meeting:
You and I our way must take,
You and I our way will wend
Farther on, my only friend—
Farther on, my more than friend—
My sweet sweeting."—COUNTRY SONG.

In a private apartment of the Red Cow Public-house Sam Bossom sat doggedly pulling at a short pipe while Mr. Mortimer harangued him.

On the table stood a cheap, ill-smelling oil-lamp between two mugs of beer. Sam had drawn his chair close, and from time to time reached out a hand for his mug, stared into its depths as though for advice, and gloomily replaced it. For the rest, he sat leaning a little forward on his crossed arms, with set, square chin, and eyes fixed on a knot in the deal table top.

Mr. Mortimer stood erect, in a declamatory attitude, with his back to the exiguous fire. In the pauses of his delivery, failing to draw response from Sam, he glanced down at his wife for approval. But she too, seated on a low stool, made pretence to be absorbed in her knitting; and her upward look, when her lord compelled it, expressed deep sympathy rather than assent.

"Consequently," perorated Mr. Mortimer, "I conceive my personal obligations to Mr. Hucks to be satisfied; practically satisfied, even in law; as keen men of business, and allowing for contingencies, satisfied abundantly. To liquidate the seven pounds fifteen and six owing to your master you have, on your own admission, six-seven-nine in hand. We—my Arabella and I—are offered a fortnight here at forty-four shillings *per* week between us. Not princely, I own. But suffer me to remind you that it realises the dream, as perchance it affords the opportunity, of a lifetime. She will be Ophelia. She, the embodiment (I dare to say it) of Shakespeare's visionary heroine, will realise his conception here, on this classic ground. And if, at short notice, I must content myself with doubling the parts of Guildenstern and First Gravedigger, believe me I do so cheerfully, pending fuller—er—recognition."

"My Stanislas demeans himself by accepting them," said Mrs. Mortimer, still with her eyes on her knitting.

"I should hope so, my poppet. Still, there is Fat in the First Gravedigger; and as our Gallic neighbours put it, everything comes to him who knows how to wait."

"All very well," observed Sam, withdrawing the pipe from his mouth. "But 'ow about the children? I put it to *you*, ma'am."

"Ah, poor things!" sighed Mrs. Mortimer, and hesitated. She was about to say more, when her husband interrupted—

"I trust—I sincerely trust—that my failings, such as they are, have ever leaned to the side of altruism. Throughout life I have been apt to injure myself in befriending others; and you see "—Mr. Mortimer flourished a hand—"where it has landed me. We have convoyed these children to Stratford, to use the language of commerce, as *per* contract. To ask me—to ask Mrs. Mortimer— to dance attendance upon them indefinitely, at the sacrifice of these golden prospects—"

But at this point someone tapped at the door.

"Come in!" called Sam, swinging around in his chair, and with that, jumping to his feet, let out a cheerful "hooray!"

"Same to you," said Tilda, nodding, as she admitted Arthur Miles and closed the door behind him. "Anything to eat in this public?"

"I'll order in supper at once," said Sam.

"No you won't; not for five minutes any'ow. Well, 'ere we are—and 'ow 'ave you three been gettin' along since I saw yer last?"

"Oh, *we're* all right; but all the better for seein' you. That's understood."

"W'ich I looks towards yer, and I likewise bows," said Tilda graciously. "But what's the matter?" she asked, glancing from one to the other. "A stranger might say as you wasn' the best o' friends."

"Nothin'," answered Sam after a slight pause. "Bit of a argymint— that's all."

"Wot about?"

"'Tisn worth mentionin'." Sam glanced at the other two. "The theayter 'ere's offered Mr. and Mrs. Mortimer an engagement."

"Well?"

"We was discussin' whether they ought to take it."

"W'y not?"

"Well, you see—Glasson bein' about—"

"After them too, is 'e? Don't mean ter say *they've* been an' lost their fathers an' mothers? No? Then I don't see."

"Them 'avin' contracted to look after you—"

He paused here, as Tilda, fixing him with a compassionate stare, began to shake her head slowly.

"You don't deserve it—you reelly don't," she said, more in sorrow than in anger; then with a sharp change of tone, "And you three 'ave been allowin', I s'pose, that our best chance to escape notice is travellin' around with a fur coat an' a sixty-foot Theayter Royal? . . . W'y, wot was it put Glasson on our tracks? . . . Oh, I'm not blamin' yer! Some folks—most folks, I'm comin' to think—just can't 'elp theirselves. But it's saddenin'."

"0' course," suggested Sam, "I might take on the job single-'anded. My orders don't go beyond this place; but the beer'll wait, and 'Ucks per'aps won't mind my takin' a 'oliday—not if I explain."

Tilda regarded him for a while before answering. When at length she spoke, it was with a fine, if weary, patience—"Got pen-an'-ink, any of yer?"

Mrs. Mortimer arose, stepped to a bundle of shawls lying in a Windsor chair, unwrapped a portable writing-case which appeared to be the kernel of the bundle, and laid it on the table—all this with extreme docility.

"I'll trouble you to do the writin'," said Tilda, laying a sheet of paper before Sam after she had chosen a pen and unsnapped the ink-case.

"Why not Mortimer?" he protested feebly.

"I wouldn' make Arguin' a 'abit, if I was you."

Sam collapsed and took the pen from her, after eyeing the palms of his hands as though he had a mind to spit on them.

"Now write," she commanded, and began to dictate slowly.

She had taken command of the room. The Mortimers could only stand by and listen, as helpless as Arthur Miles. She spoke deliberately, patiently, indulging all Sam's slowness of penmanship—

"'DEAR Mr. 'UCKS,—This comes 'opin' to find you well as it leaves us all at present. I promised to write in my own 'and; but time is pressin', as I am goin' to tell you. So you must please put up with Mr. Bossom, and excuse mistakes. I will sign this to let you know there is no fake. We are at Stratford-on-Avon: w'ich for slow goin' must be a record: but all well an' 'earty. Mr. M. 'as 'ad luck with 'is actin'—' 'Ow much?"

"Six-seven-nine," answered Sam as he caught up with her.

"Clear?"

Sam nodded. "Barrin', o' course, the bill for to-night's board an' lodgin'."

"'—Up to date 'e 'as paid S. Bossom over six pound, and 'as picked up with an engagement 'ere. Dear sir, you will see there's no risk, and S. Bossom will stay 'ere a week an' collect the balance.'"

"The Lord forbid!" Sam protested, laying down his pen.

"I'd like to know oo's writin' this letter—you or me?" She pointed to the paper. "Go on, please. 'Dear sir, a party as we will call W. B. 'as joined the company. W'ich is strange to say—'"

"Who's *he?*"

Sam looked up again, but Tilda's finger still pointed firmly.

"'W'ich 'e too continues 'earty; but You-know-Oo is close after 'im; and so, dear sir, 'avin' 'eard of an Island called 'Olmness, we are off there to-morrow, and will let you know further. W'ich I remain yours respectfully—' Now 'and over the pen an' let me sign."

"'Olmness? Where's 'Olmness?"

She took the pen from him and slowly printed TILDA, in roman capitals; examined the signature, made sure it was satisfactory, and at length answered—

"It's a Island, somewhere in the Bristol Channel, w'ich is in the Free Library. We've just come from there."

"An' you reckon I got nothin' better to do than go gallivantin' with you, lookin' for islands in the Bristol Channel?"

"—W'en I said, on'y a minute back," she answered with composure, "that we were leavin' you in Stratford for a week."

"Ho!" he commented scornfully. "Leavin' me, are you? *You* leavin' *me?* . . . Well, if that ain't good, I declare!"

She looked at him as one disdaining argument.

"I'll tell you all about it termorrow. Let's 'ave in supper now; for we're 'ungry, Arthur Miles an' me, an' the Fat Lady'll be expectin' us. Between two an' three miles down the river there's a lock, near a place they call Weston—you know it, I reckon? Well, meet us there termorrow—say eight o'clock—an' we'll 'ave a talk."

"The child," said Mr. Mortimer, "has evidently something up her sleeve, and my advice is that we humour her."

Tilda eyed him.

"Yes, that's right," she assented with unmoved countenance. "'Ave in supper and 'umour me."

The supper consisted of two dishes—the one of tripe-and-onions, the other of fried ham. There were also potatoes and beer, and gin, Mr. Mortimer being a sufferer from some complaint which made this cordial, as Mrs. Mortimer assured them, "imperative." But to-night, "to celebrate the reunion," Mr. Mortimer chose to defy the advice of the many doctors—"specialists" Mrs. Mortimer called them—who had successively called his a unique case; and after a tough battle—his wife demurring on hygienic, Sam on financial, grounds—ordered in a bottle of port, at the same time startling the waitress with the demand that it must not be such as that—

"She set before chance-comers,
 But such whose father-grape grew fat
 On Lusitanian summers."

That the beverage fulfilled this condition may be doubted. But it was certainly sweet and potent, and for the children at any rate a couple of glasses of it induced a haze upon the feast—a sort of golden fog through which Mr. Mortimer loomed in a halo of diffusive hospitality. He used his handkerchief for a table-napkin, and made great play with it as they do in banquets on the stage.

He pronounced the tripe-and-onions "fit for Lucullus," whatever that might mean. He commended the flouriness of the potatoes, in the cooking of which he claimed to be something of an amateur—"being Irish, my dear Smiles, on my mother's side." He sipped the port and passed it for "sound, sir, a wine of unmistakable body," though for bouquet not comparable with the contents of a famous bin once the pride of his paternal cellars at Scaresby Hall, Northamptonshire. He became reminiscential, and spoke with a break in his voice of a certain—

"Banquet hall deserted,
 Whose lights were fled,
 Whose garlands dead,
 And all but he [Mr. Mortimer] departed."

Here he wiped his eyes with the handkerchief that had hitherto done duty for napkin, and passed, himself, with equal adaptability to a new *role*. He would give them the toast of "Their Youthful Guests."—

"They are, I understand, about to leave us. It is not ours to gaze too closely into the crystal of fate; nor, as I gather, do they find it convenient to specify the precise conditions of their departure. But of this"—with a fine roll of the voice, and a glance at Mrs. Mortimer—" of this we may rest assured: that the qualities which, within the span of our acquaintance, they have developed, will carry them far; yet not so far that they will forget their fellow-travellers whose privilege it was to watch over them while they fledged their wings; and perhaps not so far but they may hear, and rejoice in, some echo of that fame which (if I read the omens aright)"—here again he glanced at his wife— "the public will be unable much longer to withhold."

Altogether, and in spite of his high-flown language, Mr. Mortimer gave the children an impression that he and his wife were honestly sorry to part with them. And when the supper—protracted by his various arts to the semblance of a banquet of many courses—came at length to an end, Mrs. Mortimer dropped a quite untheatrical tear as she embraced them and bade them good-bye.

Sam Bossom walked with them to the bridge and there took his leave, promising to meet them faithfully on the morrow by Weston Lock.

"Though," said he, "there be scenes hereabouts that I finds painful, and I'm doin' a great deal to oblige you."

"It's a strange thing to me," said Tilda reflectively, gazing after him until his tall figure was lost in the darkness between the gas-lamps, "'ow all these grown-ups get it fixed in their 'eads that *they're* doin' the pertectin'. I reckon their size confuses 'em."

They found the Fat Lady sitting up and awaiting them in some anxiety.

"It's on account of the dog," she explained while 'Dolph devoured them with caresses. "I managed to keep him pretty quiet all day, but when the time came for me to perform, and I had to leave him locked in the van here, he started turnin' it into a menagerie. Gavel has sent around twice to say that if it's a case of 'Love me, love my dog,' him and me'll have to break contracts."

"Leadin' this sort o' life don't suit 'im," said Tilda.

"No," Mrs. Lobb agreed; "he's drunk as a lord again, and his temper something awful."

Tilda stared.

"I meant the dog," she explained.

So the children, looking forth and judging the coast clear, took Godolphus for a scamper across the dark meadow. They returned to find their hostess disrobed and in bed, and again she had the tea-equipage arrayed and the kettle singing over the spirit-lamp.

"It's healthful, no doubt—all this exercise," she remarked with a somewhat wistful look at their glowing faces; "but it's not for me," she added. "There's another thing you've taught me. I've often wondered, sittin' alone here—

supposin' as there had really been a Mr. Lobb—how I could have done with the children. Now, my dears, it's pleasant havin' your company; but there's an anxiety about it that I find wearin'. A week of it, and I'd be losin' flesh. And the moral is, if you're an artist you must make sacrifices."

The Fat Lady sighed. She sighed again and more heavily as, having extinguished the lamp, she composed herself to sleep.

Early next morning they bade her farewell, and departed with her blessing. Now Tilda the match-maker had arranged in her mind a very pretty scene of surprise and reconciliation. But, as she afterwards observed, "there's times when you worrit along for days together, an' no seemin' good of it; an' then one mornin' you wakes up to find everything goin' like clockwork, an' yerself standin' by, an' watchin', an' feelin' small."

So it happened this morning as they drew near to Weston. There in the morning light they saw the broken lock with a weir beside it, and over the weir a tumble of flashing water; an islet or two, red with stalks of loosestrife; a swan bathing in the channel between. And there, early as they came, Sam Bossom stood already on the lock-bank; but not awaiting them, and not alone. For at a distance of six paces, perhaps, stood the girl of the blue sun-bonnet, confronting him.

Tilda gasped.

"And I got 'er promise to wait till I called 'er. It's—it's unwomanly!"

Sam turned and caught sight of them. He made as though to leave the girl standing, and came a pace towards them, but halted. There was a great awe in his face.

"'Enery's broke it off!" he announced slowly, and his voice trembled.

"I could a-told yer that." Tilda's manner was short, as she produced the letter and handed it to him. "There—go to 'im," she said in a gentler voice as she slipped past the girl. "'E's good, as men go; and 'e's suffered."

She walked resolutely away down the path.

"But where are you going?" asked Arthur Miles, running and catching up with her.

"Farther on, as usual," she snapped. "Can't yer see they don't want us?"

"But why?"

"Because they're love-makin'."

He made no answer, and she glanced at his face. Its innocent wonderment nettled her the more, yet she had no notion why. She walked on faster than ever. In the clearing by the "Four Alls" they came on the young American. He had packed up his camp furniture, and was busy stowing it in the canoe.

"Hullo!" he greeted them. "Can't stay for another sitting, if that's what you're after."

With Tilda in her present mood the boy felt a sudden helplessness. The world in this half-hour—for the first time since his escape—had grown unfriendly. His friends were leaving him, averting their faces, turning away to their own affairs. He stretched out his hands.

"Won't you take us with you?"

Mr. Jessup stared.

"Why, certainly," he answered after a moment. "Hand me the valise, there, and nip on board. There's plenty of room."

He had turned to Tilda and was addressing her. She obeyed, and handed the valise automatically. Certainly, and without her help, the world was going like clockwork this morning.

CHAPTER XVIII.

DOWN AVON.

" *O, my heart! as white sails shiver,*
 And crowds are passing, and banks stretch wide,
 How hard to follow, with lips that quiver,
 That moving speck on the far-off side."—JEAN INGELOW.

They were afloat: Arthur Miles in the bows, Tilda amidships, and both facing Mr. Jessup, who had taken the stern seat, and there steered the canoe easily with a single paddle, as the Indians do.

They shot under the scour of a steep bank covered with thorns and crab-apple trees and hummocks of sombre grass. Beyond this they drifted down to Welford Weir and Mill, past a slope where the yellowing chestnuts all but hid Welford village. They had to run the canoe ashore here, unlade her of the valises and camp furniture, and carry her across the weir. The children enjoyed this amazingly.

"Boy, would you like to take a paddle?" asked Mr. Jessup.

Now this was what Arthur Miles had been desiring for twenty minutes past, and with all his soul. So now, the canoe having been launched again and Tilda transferred to the bows, he found himself perched amidships, with his gaze fixed on the reaches ahead, and in his hand a paddle, which he worked cautiously at first, following Mr. Jessup's instructions. But confidence soon grew in him, and he began to put more vigour into his strokes. "Right, sonny," and "Better and better" commented his instructor, for the child took to it as a duck to water. In twenty minutes or so he had learnt to turn his paddle slantwise after the stroke, and to drag it so as to assist the steering; which was not always easy, for here and there a snag blocked the main channel, or a pebbly shallow where the eye had to search for the smooth V that signals the best water. Tilda watched him, marvelling at his strange aptitude, and once, catching her eye, he nodded; but still, as he mastered the knack, and the stroke of the paddle became more and more mechanical, his attention disengaged itself from the moment—from the voice of Mr. Jessup astern, the girl's intent gaze, the swirl about the blade, the scent and pageant of the green banks on either hand—and pressed forward to follow each far curve of the stream, each bend as it slowly unfolded. Bend upon bend—they might fold it a hundred deep; but somewhere ahead and beyond their folding lay the Island.

In this wise they passed under a grassy hillside set with trimmed elms, and came to Grange Mill and another portage; and below Grange to Bidford, where there is a bridge of many arches carrying the old Roman road called

Icknield Street; and from the bridge and grey little town they struck into a long reach that ran straight into the dazzle of the sun—through flat meadows at first, and then, with a turn, under the steep of Marcleeve Hill, that here borders Avon to the south for miles. Here begin the spurs of the Cotswolds—scars of green and red marle dotted with old thorn trees or draped with ash and maple, or smothered with trails of the Traveller's Joy.

Mr. Jessup, whose instructions had become less and less frequent, and indeed were by this time patently superfluous, so quick the boy showed himself to anticipate the slightest warning, hereabouts engaged Tilda in converse.

"He's a wonder, this child! I don't know where he comes from, or you, or how far you're willing I should take you. In fact, there's an unholy flavour of kidnapping about this whole adventure. But I guess, if I wanted to return you, there are no railways hereabouts. We must strike the first depot we come to, and I'll frank you back, with apologies to your parents."

"We got none," Tilda assured him.

"For a steady-going country like England that's unusual, eh?"

"There is a bit o' that about us," she conceded after a pause.

"But you must belong to somebody?" he urged.

"*He* do . . . And that's what I got to find out. But it'll be all right when we get to 'Olmness."

"Holmness?" queried Mr. Jessup. "Where's Holmness?"

"It's an Island, in the Bristol Channel, w'ich is in the Free Library. We're goin' that way, ain't we?"

"That's our direction, certainly; though we're a goodish way off."

"No 'urry," said Tilda graciously. "We'll get there in time."

Mr. Jessup smiled.

"Thank you. I am delighted to help, of course. You'll find friends there—at Holmness?"

She nodded.

"Though, as far as that goes," she allowed yet more graciously, "I'm not conplainin'. We've made friends all the way yet—an' you're the latest."

"I am honoured, though in a sense I hardly deserve it. You did—if I may say—rather take charge of me, you know. Not that I mind. This is my picnic, and I don't undertake to carry you farther than Tewkesbury. But is does occur to me that you owe me something on the trip."

Tilda stiffened.

"You can put us ashore where you like," said she; "but one d. is all I 'ave in my pocket, as may be 'twould a-been fairer t' a-told yer."

The young man laughed outright and cheerfully as he headed the canoe for shore. They were close upon another weir and an ancient mill, whence, as they landed for another portage, clouds of fragrant flour-dust issued from the doorway, greeting their nostrils.

"It's this way," he explained. "I'm here to sketch Shakespeare's Country, and the trouble with me is, I've a theory."

"It's—it's not a bad one, I 'ope?"

She hazarded this sympathetically, never having heard of a theory. It sounded to her like the name of an internal growth, possibly malignant.

"Not half bad," he assured her. He was cheerful about it, at any rate. "I'm what they call an Impressionist. A man—I put it to you—has got to hustle after culture in these days and take it, so to speak, in tabloids. Now this morning, before you came along, I'd struck a magnificent notion. As I dare say you've been told, the way to get at the essence of a landscape is to half-close your eyes—you get the dominant notes that way, and shed the details. Well, I allowed I'd go one better, and see the whole show in motion. Have you ever seen a biograph—or a cinematograph, as some call it?"

"'Course I 'ave," said Tilda. "There was one in Maggs's Circus."

"Then you'll have no trouble in getting the hang of my idea. My complaint with Art is that it don't keep itself abreast of modern inventions. The cinematograph, miss, has come to stay, and the Art of the future, unless Art means to get left, will have to adopt its principles . . . Well, I couldn't put Shakespeare's country into motion; but on the river I could put myself in motion, which amounts to the same thing. With the cinematograph, I grant you, it's mostly the scene that's that in motion while *you* sit still; but there's also a dodge by which *you're* in the railway car and flying past the scenery."

Tilda nodded.

"Maggs 'ad 'old of that trick too. 'E called it *A Trip on the Over'ead Railway, New York.*"

"Right; and now you see. I allowed that by steering down Avon and keeping my eyes half closed, by the time I reached Tewkesbury I'd have Shakespeare's environment all boiled down and concentrated; and at Tewkesbury I 'd stop and slap in the general impression while it was fresh. But just here I ran my head full-butt against another principle of mine, which is *plein air.*"

"Wot's that?"

"Why, that a landscape should be painted where it stands, and not in the studio."

"You couldn' very well paint with one 'and an' paddle with the other," she began; but added in a moment, "Why there's Arthur Miles, o' course! doin', as ush'al, while the others are talkin'. That child brings luck w'erever 'e goes."

"You think that I could change places and trust him to steer."

"Think? Why for the las' ten minutes 'e *'as* been steerin'?"

So below Cleeve they changed places, Mr. Jessup settling himself amidships with his apparatus for sketching, while Arthur Miles was promoted—if the word may be allowed—to the seat astern. For a while he took his new responsibility gravely, with pursed lips and eyes intent on every stroke of the paddle, watching, experimenting, as a turn of the wrist more or less righted or deflected the steering. But in a few minutes he had gained confidence, and again his gaze removed itself from the swirl around the blade and began to dwell on the reaches ahead.

They were entering the rich vale of Evesham. On their left the slopes of Marcleeve Hill declined gradually to the open plain; on their right, behind a long fringe of willows, stretched meadow after meadow, all green and flat as billiard-tables. They were passing down through the scene of a famous battle. But the children had never heard of Evesham fight; and Mr. Jessup had mislaid his guide-book. He sat with half-closed eyes, now and again dipping his brush over the gunwale, and anon, for a half-minute or so, flinging broad splashes of water-colour upon his sketching-pad.

They were nearing the ferry at Harvington, and already began to lift the bold outline of Bredon Hill that shuts out the Severn Valley, when without warning the boy broke into song . . .

It was the strangest performance. It had no tune in it, no intelligible words; it was just a chant rising and falling, as the surf might rise and fall around the base of that Island for which his eyes sought the green vale right away to the horizon.

Mr. Jessup looked up from his work. His eyes encountered Tilda's, and Tilda's were smiling. But at the same time they enjoined silence.

The boy sang on. His voice had been low and tentative at first; but now, gathering courage, he lifted it upon a note of high challenge. He could not have told why, but he sang because he was steering towards his fate. It might lie far, very far, ahead; but somewhere ahead it lay, beyond the gradually unfolding hills; somewhere in the west these would open upon the sea, and in the sea would be lying his Island. His song already saluted it.

"I am coming!" it challenged. "O my fate, be prepared for me!"

So they floated down to Harvington Mill and Weir; and as Mr. Jessup half-turned his head, warning him to steer for shore, the boy's voice faltered and dropped suddenly to silence, as a lark drops down from the sky. Tilda saw him start and come to himself with a hot blush, that deepened when she laughed and ordered 'Dolph to bark for an encore.

They ported the canoe and luggage down a steep and slippery overfall, launched her again, and shot down past Harvington Weir, where a crowd of small sandpipers kept them company for a mile, flitting ahead and alighting but to take wing again. Tilda had fallen silent. By and by, as they passed the Fish and Anchor Inn, she looked up at Mr. Jessup and asked—

"But if you want to paint fast, why not travel by train?"

"I thought of it," Mr. Jessup answered gravely. "But the railroad hereabouts wasn't engineered to catch the sentiment, and it's the sentiment I'm after—the old-world charm of field and high-road and leafy hedgerow, if you understand me." Here he paused of a sudden, and laid his sketch-block slowly down on his knee. "Je-hosaphat!" he exclaimed, his eyes brightening. "Why ever didn't I think of it?"

"Think of wot?"

He nodded his head.

"You'll see, missie, when we get to Evesham! You've put a notion into me—and we're going to rattle up Turner and make him hum. The guide-books say he spent considerable of his time at Tewkesbury. I disremember if he's buried there; but we'll wake his ghost, anyway."

So by Offenham and Dead Man Eyot they came to the high embankment of a railway, and thence to a bridge, and a beautiful bell-tower leapt into view, soaring above the mills and roofs of Evesham.

At Evesham, a little above the Workman Gardens, they left the canoe in charge of a waterman, and fared up to the town, where Mr. Jessup led them into a palatial hotel—or so it seemed to the children—and ordered a regal luncheon. It was served by a waiter in a dress suit; an ancient and benign-looking person, whose appearance and demeanour so weighed upon Tilda that, true to her protective instinct, she called up all her courage to nod across the table at Arthur Miles and reassure him. To her stark astonishment, the boy was eating without embarrassment, as though to be waited on with this pomp had been a mere matter of course.

When the cheese was brought, Mr. Jessup left them on a trivial pretext, and absented himself so long that at length she began to wonder what would happen if he had "done a bilk," and left them to discharge the score. The waiter hovered around, nicking at the side-tables with his napkin and brushing them clean of imaginary crumbs.

Tilda, eking out her last morsel of biscuit, opined that their friend would surely be back presently. She addressed the remark to Arthur Miles; but the waiter at once stepped forward.

"It is to be 'oped!" said he, absent-mindedly dusting the back of a chair.

Just at this moment a strange throbbing noise drew him to the window, to gaze out into the street. It alarmed the children too, and they were about to follow and seek the cause of it, when Mr. Jessup appeared in the doorway.

"I've managed it!" he announced, and calling to the waiter, demanded the bill.

The waiter turned, whisked a silver-plated salver apparently out of nowhere, and presented a paper upon it.

"Nine-and-six—*and* one is ten-and-six. I thank you, sir," said the waiter, bowing low.

He was good enough to follow them to the doorway, where Mr. Jessup waved a hand to indicate a motor standing ready beside the pavement, and told the children to tumble in.

"I've taken your tip, you see."

"My tip?" gasped Tilda.

"Well, you gave me the hint for it, like Sir Isaac Newton's apple. I've hired the car for the afternoon; and now, if you'll tuck yourselves in with these rugs, you two'll have the time of your lives."

He shut the door upon them, and mounted to a seat in front. The car was already humming and throbbing, and the hired chauffeur, climbing to a seat beside him, started her at once. They were off.

They took the road that leads northward out of Evesham, and then, turning westward, rounds the many loops and twists of Avon in a long curve. In a minute or so they were clear of the town, and the car suddenly gathered speed. Tilda caught her breath and held tight; but the pace did not seem to perturb the boy, who sat with his lips parted and his gaze fixed ahead. As for Mr. Jessup, behind the shelter of the wind-glass he was calmly preparing to sketch.

They had left the pastures behind, and were racing now through a land of orchards and market gardens, ruled out and planted with plum trees and cabbages in stiff lines that, as the car whirled past them, appeared to be revolving slowly, like the spokes of a wheel. Below, on their left, the river wandered—now close beneath them, now heading south and away, but always to be traced by its ribbon of green willows. Thus they spun past Wyre, and through Pershore—Pershore, set by the waterside, with its plum orchards, and noble tower and street of comfortable red houses—and crossed Avon at length by Eckington Bridge, under Bredon Hill. Straight ahead of them now ran a level plain dotted with poplars, and stretched—or seemed to stretch—right away to a line of heights, far and blue, which Mr. Jessup (after questioning the chauffeur) announced to be the Malverns.

At Bredon village just below, happening to pass an old woman in a red shawl, who scurried into a doorway at the toot-toot of their horn, he leant back and confided that the main drawback of this method of sketching (he had discovered) was the almost total absence of middle distance. He scarcely saw, as yet, how it could be overcome.

"But," said he thoughtfully, "the best way, after all, may be to ignore it. When you come to consider, middle distance in landscape is more or less of a convention."

Nevertheless Mr. Jessup frankly owned that his experiments so far dissatisfied him.

"I'll get the first principles in time," he promised, "and the general hang of it. Just now I'm being fed up with its limitations."

He sat silent for a while gazing ahead, where the great Norman tower and the mill chimneys of Tewkesbury now began to lift themselves from the plain. And coming to the Mythe Bridge, he called a halt, bade the children alight, and sent the car on to await him at an hotel in the High Street, recommended by the chauffeur.

"This," said he, examining the bridge, "appears to be of considerable antiquity. If you'll allow me, I'll repose myself for twenty minutes in the hoary past." Unfolding a camp stool, he sat down to sketch.

The children and 'Dolph, left to themselves, wandered across the bridge. The road beyond it stretched out through the last skirts of the town, and across the head of a wide green level dotted with groups of pasturing kine; and again beyond this enormous pasture were glimpses of small white sails gliding in and out, in the oddest fashion, behind clumps of trees and—for aught they could see—on dry land.

The sight of these sails drew them on until, lo! on a sudden they looked upon a bridge, far newer and wider than the one behind them, spanning a river far more majestic than Avon. Of the white sails some were tacking against its current, others speeding down stream with a brisk breeze; and while the children stood there at gaze, a small puffing tug emerged from under the great arch of the bridge with a dozen barges astern of her in a long line—boats with masts, and bulkier than any known to Tilda. They seemed to her strong enough to hoist sail and put out to sea on their own account, instead of crawling thus in the wake of a tug.

There was an old road-mender busy by the bridge end, shovelling together the road scrapings in small heaps. He looked up and nodded. His face was kindly, albeit a trifle foolish, and he seemed disposed to talk.

"Good day!" said Tilda. "Can you tell us where the boats are goin'?"

The old road mender glanced over the parapet.

"Eh? The trows, d'ee mean?"

"Trows? Is that what they are?"

"Aye; and they be goin' down to Glo'ster first, an' thence away to Sharpness Dock. They go through the Glo'ster an' Berkeley, and at Sharpness they finish."

"Is that anywhere in the Bristol Channel?" The old man ruminated for a moment.

"You may call it so. Gettin' on for that, anyway. Fine boats they be; mons'rously improved in my time. But where d'ee come from, you two?—here in Tewkesbury, an' not to know about Severn trows?"

"We've—er—jus' run over here for the afternoon, in a motor," said Tilda—and truthfully; but it left the old man gasping.

The children strolled on, idling by the bridge's parapet, watching the strong current, the small boats as they tacked to and fro. Up stream another tug hove in sight, also with a line of trows behind her. This became exciting, and Tilda suggested waiting and dropping a stone—a very small one—upon the tug's deck as she passed under the archway.

"If only she could take us on!" said Arthur Miles.

"We'd 'ave to drop a big stone for *that*," Tilda opined.

And with that suddenly 'Dolph, who had been chasing a robin, and immersed in that futile sport, started to bark—uneasily and in small yaps at first, then in paroxysms interrupted by eager whines.

"W'y wot the matter with 'im?" asked Tilda.

"Look now!"

For the dog had sprung upon the parapet and stood there, with neck extended and body quivering as he saluted the on-coming tug.

"'E can't see . . . No, surely, it can't be—" said Tilda, staring.

The tug was so near by this time that they could read her name, *Severn Belle*, on the bows. Two men stood on her deck—one aft at the tiller (for she had no wheel-house), the other a little forward of midships, leaning over the port bulwarks; this latter a stoker apparently, or an engineer, or a combination of both; for he was capless, and wore a smoke-grimed flannel shirt, open at the breast.

Tilda could see this distinctly as the tug drew near; for the man was looking up, staring steadily at the dog on the parapet. His chest was naked. A cake of coal-dust obscured his features.

"It can't be," said Tilda; and then, as the tug drew close, she flung herself against the parapet. "Bill! Oh, Bill!"

"Cheer-oh!" answered a voice, now already among the echoes of the arch.

"Oh, Bill! . . . *Where?*" She had run across the roadway. "Oh, Bill— take us!"

The boy running too—yet not so quickly as 'Dolph—caught a vision of a face upturned in blankest amazement as tug and barges swept down stream out of reach. But still Tilda hailed, beating back the dog, to silence his barking.

"Oh, Bill! Where're yer goin'?"

As she had cried it, so in agony she listened for the response. It came; but Arthur Miles could not distinguish the word, nor tell if Tilda had heard better. She had caught his hand, and they were running together as fast as their small legs could carry them.

The chase was hopeless from the first. The tug, in midstream, gave no sign of drawing to shore. Somehow—but exactly how the boy could never tell—they were racing after her down the immense length of the green meadow.

It seemed endless, did this meadow. But it ended at last, by a grassy shore where the two rivers met, cutting off and ending all hope. And here, for the first and only time on their voyage, all Tilda's courage forsook her.

"Bill! Oh, Bill!" she wailed, standing at the water's edge and stretching forth her hands across the relentless flood.

But the dog, barking desperately beside her, drowned her voice, and no answer came.

CHAPTER XIX.

THE S.S. EVAN EVANS

"Then three times round went our gallant ship."—OLD SONG.

The time is next morning, and the first grey hour of daylight. The scene, an unlovely tidal basin crowded with small shipping— schooners and brigantines dingy with coal-dust, tramp steamers, tugs, Severn trows; a ship lock and beyond it the river, now grown into a broad flood all grey and milky in the dawn.

Tilda and Arthur Miles sat on the edge of the basin, with Godolphus between them, and stared down on the deck of the *Severn Belle* tug, waiting for some sign of life to declare itself on board. By leave of a kindly cranesman, they had spent the night in a galvanised iron shed where he stored his cinders, and the warmth in the cinders had kept them comfortable. But the dawn was chilly, and now they had only their excitement to keep them warm. For some reason best known to himself the dog did not share in this excitement, and only the firm embrace of Tilda's arm around his chest and shoulders held him from wandering. Now and again he protested against this restraint.

Tilda's eyes never left the tug; but the boy kept intermittent watch only, being busy writing with the stump of a pencil on a scrap of paper he had spread on the gritty concrete. Somewhere in the distance a hooter sounded, proclaiming the hour. Still but the thinnest thread of smoke issued from the tug's funnel.

"It's not like Bill," Tilda muttered. "'E was always partic'lar about early risin' . . . An' I don't know what *you* feel like, Arthur Miles, but *I* could do with breakfast."

"And a wash," suggested the boy.

"It don't look appetisin'—not even if we knew 'ow to swim," said Tilda, relaxing her watch for an instant only, and studying the water in the basin. "We must 'old on—'old on an' wait till the clouds roll by—that was one of Bill's sayin's. An' to think of 'im bein' so near!" Tilda never laughed, but some mirth in her voice anticipated Bill's astonishment. "Now read me what yer've written."

"It's no more than what you told me."

"Never mind; let's 'ear if it's c'rect."

Arthur Miles read—

'DEAR MR. HUCKS,—This comes to say that we are not at Holmness yet, but getting on. This place is called Sharpness, and does a big trade, and the size of the shipping would make you wonder, after Bursfield. We left S.B. and the M.'s at Stratford, as *per* my favour—'

"What does that mean?" asked the scribe, looking up.

"It's what they always put into business letters."

"But what does it mean?"

"It means—well, it means you're just as sharp as th' other man, so 'e needn't try it on."

'—as *per* my favour of yesterday. And just below Stratford we picked up with a painter from America, but quite the gentleman, as you will see by his taking us on to a place called Tukesberry in a real moter car.'

[Let it be pleaded for Arthur Miles that his spelling had been outstripped of late by his experience. His sentences were as Tilda had constructed them in dictation.]

'Which at Tukesberry, happening to come across a gentleman friend of mine, as used to work for Gavel, and by name William, this American gentleman—'

"Sounds odd, don't it?" interposed Tilda.

"There's too much about gentlemen in it," the boy suggested.

"Well, but *you're* a gentleman. We shall find that out, right enough, when we get to 'Olmness. 'Ucks don't know that, and I'm tonin' 'im up to it. . . . You 'aven't put in what I told yer—about me tellin' Mr. Jessup as Bill was my brother-in-law an' 'is callin' back to us that 'e'd look after us 'ere."

"No."

"W'y not?"

There was reason for Tilda's averted gaze. She had to watch the tug's deck. But why did her face flush?

"Because it isn't true."

"It got us 'ere," she retorted. "True or not, 'twouldn't do yer no 'arm to allow *that*, seemin' to me."

Although she said it defiantly, her tone carried no conviction.

Arthur Miles made no response, but read on—

'—this American gentleman paid our fares on by railway to join him, and gave us half a suffering for X.'s.'

"Is that right?"

"Sure," said Tilda. "Gold money is all sufferin's or 'arf-sufferin's. I got it tied in a corner o' what Miss Montagu taught me to call my shimmy—shifts bein' vulgar, she said."

> '—So here we are, and W.B. capital. Which we hope to post our next from Holmness, and remain,'
> 'Yours respectfully,'
> 'TILDA.

'William will post this.'

"But you're not sure of that, you know," he urged. Hereat Tilda found the excuse she wanted for losing her temper (for her falsehood—or, rather, the boy's pained disapproval of it—yet shamed her).

"'Oo brought yer 'ere, I'd like to know? And where'd yer be at this moment if 'twasn't for me an' 'Dolph? In Glasson's black 'ole, that's where yer'd be! An' now sittin' 'ere so 'igh-an'-mighty, an' lecturin'!"

The boy's eyes had filled with tears.

"But I'm not—I'm not!" he protested. "Tilda!—"

"As if," she jerked out between two hard, dry sobs (Tilda, by the way, never wept)—"as if I wasn' *sure*, after chasin' Bill all this way on purpose, and 'im the best of men!"

Just at this moment there emerged from the after-companion of the *Severn Belle*, immediately below them, a large head shaped like an enormous pear—shaped, that is, as if designed to persuade an upward passage through difficult hatchways, so narrow was the cranium and so extremely full the jowl. It was followed by a short bull neck and a heavy pair of shoulders in a shirt of dirty grey flannel; and having emerged so far, the apparition paused for a look around. It was the steersman of yesterday afternoon.

"'Ullo, below there!" Tilda hailed him.

"'Ullo yerself!" The man looked up and blinked. "W'y, if you ain't the gel and boy?"

"Where's Bill?" she asked, cutting him short.

"Bill?"

"Yes, Bill—w'ich 'is full name is William; an' if 'e's sleepin' below I'd arsk yer to roust 'im out."

"Oh," said the stout man slowly, "Bill, is it?—Bill? Well, he's gone."

"Gone?"

"Aye; 'e's a rollin' stone, if you wants my pinion—'ere ter-day an' gone ter-morrow, as you might put it. There's plenty o' that sort knockin' around."

"D'yer mean—ter say as Bill's—*gone?*"

"Maybe I didn' make myself clear," answered the stout man politely. "Yes, gone 'e 'as, 'avin' only shipped on for the trip. At Stourport. Me bein' short-'anded and 'im fresh off the drink."

"But Bill doesn't drink," protested Tilda, indignant in dismay.

"Oh, doesn't 'e? Then we're talkin' of two different parties, an' 'ad best begin over again. . . . But maybe," conceded the stout man on second thoughts, "you only seen 'im sober. It makes a difference. The man I mean's dossin' ashore somewhere. An', I should say, drinkin' 'ard," he added reflectively.

But here Godolphus interrupted the conversation, wriggling himself backwards and with a sudden yap out of Tilda's clutch. Boy and girl turned, and beheld him rush towards a tall, loose-kneed man, clad in dirty dungaree, dark-haired and dark-avised with coal-dust, who came slouching towards the quay's edge.

"Bill! Oh, Bill!" Tilda sprang up with a cry. Perhaps the cry was drowned in the dog's ecstatic barking. The man—he had obviously been drinking—paid no attention to either; or, rather, he seemed (since he could not disregard it) to take the dog's salutation for granted, and came lurching on, fencing back 'Dolph's affectionate leaps.

"G'way!"

He advanced unsteadily towards the edge of the basin, not perceiving, or at any rate not recognising the children, though close to them.

"Let my cap be'ind," he grumbled; "elst they stole it."

He drew himself up at the water's edge, a dozen yards or so wide of the *Severn Belle's* stern.

"Oh, Bill!" Tilda flung herself before him as he stood swaying.

"'Ullo!" He recognised her slowly. "And wot might *you* be doin' 'ere? Come to remember, saw you yesterday—you *and* your frien'. Yes, o' course—ver' glad t' meet yer—*an'* yer friend—any friend o' yours welcome, 'm sure."

He stretched out a hand of cordiality towards Arthur Miles.

"Oh, Bill—we've been countin' on yer so—me an' 'Dolph. This is Arthur Miles, an' I've told 'im all along as you're the best and 'elpfullest o' men—an' so you are, if you pull yourself together. 'E only wants to get to a place called 'Olmness, w'ich is right below 'ere—"

"'Olmness?"

"It's an Island, somewhere in the Bristol Channel. It—it *can't* be far, Bill—an' I got 'arf-a-sufferin'—"

"Where?" asked Bill with unexpected promptness.

"Never you mind, just now."

Bill assumed an air of injured but anxious virtue.

"'Course, if you don't *choose* to trust me, it's another matter . . . but I'd like to know you came by it honest."

"Of course she did!" Arthur Miles spoke up to the rescue hotly.

Bill turned a stare on him, but dropped it, somewhat abashed.

"Oh, well, I'm not sayin' . . ." he muttered sulkily, and then with a change of tone, "But find yer an Island—somewheres in the Bristol Channel—me! It's ridicklus."

Tilda averted her face, and appeared to study the masts of the shipping. Her cheek was red and something worked in her throat, but in a few seconds she answered quite cheerfully—

"Well, the first thing is to pick up a breakfast. If Bill can't find us an Island, maybe 'e can show us a respectable 'ouse, where they make their cawfee strong—an' not the 'ouse where 'e slept last night, if it's all the same to 'im."

They found a small but decent tavern—"The Wharfingers' Arms, *Shipping Gazette* daily"—and breakfasted on coffee and boiled eggs. The coffee was strong and sticky. It did Bill good. But he persisted in treating the adventure as a wild-goose chase. He had never heard of Holmness. It was certainly not a port; and, that being so, how—unless they chartered a steamer—could they be landed there?

"That's for you to find out," maintained Tilda.

"Well," said he, rising from the meal, "I don't mind lookin' around an' makin' a few inquiries for yer. But I warn yer both it's 'opeless."

"You can post this letter on yer way," she commanded. "I'll pay fer the breakfast."

But confidence forsook her as through the small window they watched him making his way—still a trifle unsteadily—towards the docks. For a little distance 'Dolph followed him, but halted, stood for a minute wagging his tail, and so came trotting back.

"'E'll manage it," said Tilda at length.

Arthur Miles did not answer.

"Oh, I know what you're thinkin'!" she broke out. "But 'tisn' everyone can look down on folks bein' born with *your* advantages!" She pulled herself up sharply, glancing at the back of the boy's head: for he had turned his face aside. "No—I didn' mean that. An'—an' the way you stood up fer me bein' honest was jus' splendid—after what you'd said about tellin' lies, too."

They wandered about the docks all day, dodging official observation, and ate their midday crust behind the cinder-shed that had been their shelter overnight. Tilda had regained and kept her old courage, and in the end her faith was justified.

Towards nightfall Bill sought them out where he had first found them, by the quay-edge close above the *Severn Belle*.

"It's all right," he said. "I done it for yer. See that boat yonder?" He jerked his thumb towards a small cargo steamer lying on the far side of the basin, and now discernible only as a black blur in the foggy twilight. "She's the *Evan Evans* of Cardiff, an' bound for Cardiff. Far as I can larn, Cardiff's your port, though I don't say a 'andy one. Fact is, there's no 'andy one. They seem to say the place lies out of everyone's track close down against the Somerset coast—or, it may be, Devon: they're not clear. Anyway," he wound up vaguely, "at Cardiff there may be pleasure steamers runnin', or something o' the sort."

"Bill, you're an angel!"

"I shipped for a stoker," said Bill.

"But what'll it cost?"

"I don't want ter speak boas'ful, after the tone you took with me this mornin'"—Bill spoke with scarcely dissembled pride—"but that's where the cleverness comes in. You see, there ain't no skipper to 'er— leastways not till ter-morrow. The old man's taken train an' off to Bristol, to attend a revival meetin', or something o' the sort—bein' turned pious since 'is wife died, w'ich is about eighteen months ago. I got that from the mate, when 'e shipped me. The mate's in charge; with the engineer an' two 'ands. The engineer—'e's a Scotchman—'as as much whisky inside 'im already as a man can 'old an' keep 'is legs; an' the 'ole gang'll be goin' ashore again to-night—all but the mate. The mate 'as to keep moderate sober an' lock 'er out on first 'igh water ter-morrow for Kingroad, where she'll pick up the old man; and as natcher'lly 'e'll want *somebody* sober down in the engine-room, 'e's got to rely on me. So now you see."

"I think I see," said Tilda slowly. "We're to ship as stowaways."

"You may call it so, though the word don't 'ardly seem to fit. I've 'eard tell of stowaways, but never as I remember of a pair as 'ad the use of the captain's cabin, and 'im a widower with an extry bunk still fitted for the deceased. O' course we'll 'ave to smuggle yer away somewheres before the old man comes aboard. But the mate'll do that easy. 'E promised me."

"Bill, you *are* an angel!"

It was, after all, absurdly easy, as Bill had promised; and the easier by help of the river-fog, which by nine o'clock—the hour agreed upon— had gathered to a thick grey consistency. If the dock were policed at this hour, no police, save by the veriest accident, could have detected the children crouching with 'Dolph behind a breastwork of paraffin-casks, and waiting for Bill's signal— the first two or three bars of *The Blue Bells of Scotland* whistled thrice over.

The signal came. The gang-plank was out, ready for the crew's return; and at the head of it Bill met the fugitives, with a caution to tread softly when they reached the deck. The mate was nowhere to be seen. Bill whispered that he was in his own cabin "holding off the drink," whatever that might mean.

He conducted them to the after-companion, where, repeating his caution, he stepped in front of the children and led the way down a narrow twisting staircase. At the foot of it he pushed open a door, and they gazed into a neat apartment, panelled with mirrors and bird's-eye maple. A swing-lamp shone down upon a white-covered table; and upon the table were bread and cheese and biscuits, with a jug of water and glasses. Alongside the table ran two bunks, half-curtained, clean, cosy and inviting.

"Say what yer like," said Tilda half an hour later as, having selected their bunks, the children composed themselves to sleep, "but Bill 'as the 'ead of the two."

"Which two?" asked the boy, not quite ingenuously.

"As if I didn' know yer was comparin' 'im with Sam Bossom all day! W'y, I seen it in yer face!" Getting no answer, she went on after a pause, "Sam 'd never a' thought o' this, not if 'e'd lived to be a 'undred."

"All the same, I like Sam better," said the boy sleepily.

They slept soundly after their wanderings. The crew returned shortly before half-past eleven, and tumbled aboard "happy and glorious"—so Bill afterwards described their condition, in the language of the National Anthem. But the racket was mainly for'ard, and did not awake the children. After this, silence descended on the *Evan Evans*, and lasted for five long hours. Still they slept; and the voice of the mate, when a little before dawn he started cursing and calling to the men to tumble up, was a voice heard in dreams and without alarm.

It was, as a matter of fact, scarcely more operative in the forecastle than in the cabin. But Bill in the intervals of slumber had visited the furnaces, and kept up a good head of steam; and in the chill of dawn he and the mate cast off warps and (with the pilot) worked the steamer out through the ship lock, practically unaided. The mate, when not in liquor, was a first-class seaman; and Bill, left alone between the furnaces and the engines, perspired in all the glory of his true vocation.

The noise of hooting, loud and protracted, awoke Tilda at last, and she raised herself in her bunk to stare at the apparition of Bill in the cabin doorway—a terrifying apparition, too, black with coal-dust and shining with sweat.

"Wot's 'appened?"

For one moment her sleepy brain confused him with the diabolical noise overhead.

"Nothin'," he answered, "'cept that you must tumble out quick, you two. We're off Avonmouth, an' the whistle's goin' for the old man."

They tumbled out and redded up the place in a hurry, folding away the rugs and linen—which Bill, with his grimed fingers, did not dare to touch—and stowing them as he directed. A damp fog permeated the cabin. Even the engine-room (Bill reported) was full of it, and how the mate had brought her along through it and picked up Avonmouth was a marvel.

"Single-'anded too, as you may say. 'E's a world's wonder, that man."

The children too thought it marvellous when they reached the deck and gazed about them. They could spy no shore, not so much as a blur to indicate it, but were wrapped wholly in a grey fog; and down over the steamer's tall sides (for she was returning light after delivering a cargo of Welsh coal) they stared upon nothing but muddy water crawling beneath the fog.

They heard the mate's voice calling from the bridge, and the fog seemed to remove both bridge and voice to an immeasurable height above them.

It was just possible to descry the length of the ship, and they saw two figures bestir themselves forward. A voice answered, "Aye, aye, sir!" but thickly and as if muffled by cotton wool. One of the two men came running, halted amidships, lifted out a panel of the bulwarks, set in a slide between two white-painted stanchions, and let down an accommodation ladder.

"*Evan Evans*, ahoy!" came a voice from the fog.

"Ahoy, sir!" sang out the mate's voice high overhead, and between two blasts of the whistle, and just at this moment a speck—a small blur— hove out of the grey on the port side. It was the skipper arriving in a shore boat.

The children dodged behind a deck-house as he came up the ladder—a thin little man habited much like a Nonconformist minister, and wearing—of all amazing head-gear—a top-hat, the brim of which shed moisture in a steady trickle. A grey plaid shawl swathed his shoulders, and the fringe of this dripped too, as he gained the deck and stepped briskly aft, without so much as a word to the men standing at the head of the ladder, to whom after a minute the mate called down.

"Sam Lloyd!"

"Aye, aye, sir!"

"What did 'e say?"

"Nothin', sir."

Apparently the children were not alone in finding this singular, for after another minute the mate descended from the bridge, walked aft, and followed his chief down the companion. He stayed below for close on a quarter of an hour, the steamer all this while moving dead slow, with just a lazy turn now and then of her propeller. When he returned it was with a bottle in his hand and a second bottle under his arm.

"Cracked as a drum," he announced to the seaman Lloyd on his way back to the bridge. "Says 'e's 'ad a revelation."

"A wot?"

"A revelation. Says 'e 'eard a voice from 'eaven las' night, tellin' 'im as Faith was dead in these times; that if a man only 'ad faith 'e could let everything else rip . . . and," concluded the mate heavily, resting his unoccupied hand on the ladder, "'e's down below tryin' it."

The seaman did not answer. The mate ascended again, and vanished in the fog. After a pause a bell tinkled deep down in the bowels of the ship. Her propeller began to churn the water, very slowly at first, then with gathering speed, and the *Evan Evans* forged ahead, shouldering her way deeper and deeper into the fog.

It had certainly grown denser. There was not the slightest reason for the children to hide. No one came near them; they could see nothing but the wet and dirty deck, the cook's galley close by (in which, as it happened, the cook lay in drunken slumber) and a boat swinging on davits close above their heads, between them and the limitless grey. Bill had disappeared some time before the skipper came aboard and was busy, no doubt, in the engine-room. In the shrouded bows one of the crew was working a fog-horn at irregular intervals, and for a while every blast was answered by a hoot from the steam-whistle above the bridge.

This lasted three hours or more. Then, though the fog-horn continued spasmodically, the whistle fell unaccountably silent. The children scarcely noted this; they were occupied with staring into the fog.

Of a sudden the bridge awoke to life again, and now with the bell. *Ting* . . . *ting, ting, ting—ting—ting, ting, ting* then *ting, ting* again.

The fog-horn stopped as though to listen. By and by, as from minute to minute the bridge continued this eccentric performance, even the children became aware that something was amiss.

Abruptly the ringing ceased, ceased just as a tall man—it was the Scotch engineer—emerged from somewhere below and stood steadying himself by the rail of the ladder.

"What the deevil?" he demanded angrily, staring aloft. "What the deev—"

Here he collapsed on the lowest step. (A Glasgow man must be drunk indeed before he loses his legs.)

The seaman Sam Lloyd came running, jumped over the engineer's prostrate body and climbed to the bridge. There was a brief silence, and then he shouted down—

"Dave! Dave Morgan!"

"Ahoy! What's wrong there?"

Another seaman came staggering aft.

"Run, one o' you an' fetch up th' old man. Mate 'e's dead drunk 'ere, an' the ship pointin' any way this 'arf hour."

"I—I canna," said the engineer, raising himself erect from the waist and collapsing again; but the other staggered on and disappeared down the companion hatchway. Two or three minutes passed before he re-emerged.

"It's no go," he shouted up. "Skipper says as we must 'ave Faith. Called me an onbelievin' generation o' vipers, an' would I kindly leave 'im alone to wrastle."

"Faith?" fairly yelled the voice from the bridge. "Tell 'im the man's lyin' 'ere outside o' three pints o' neat Irish—tell 'im she's been chasin' 'er own tail for this two—three hours—tell 'im the sound o' breakers is distinkly audibble on the lee bow—tell 'im—oh, for Gawd's sake tell 'im anythink so's it'll fetch 'im up!"

Dave Morgan dived down the companion again, and after a long interval returned with the skipper at his heels. The old man was bare-headed now, and the faint breeze, blowing back his grey locks, exposed a high intellectual forehead underset with a pair of eyes curiously vague and at the same time introspective.

The old man clutched at the coaming that ran around the hatchway, steadied himself, and gazed around upon the fog.

"'Eavenly Father!" he said aloud and reproachfully, "*this* won't do!"

And with that he came tripping forward to the bridge with a walk like a bird's. At the sight of Tilda and Arthur Miles, who in their plight had made no effort to hide, he drew himself up suddenly.

"Stowaways?" he said. "I'll talk to you presently." He stepped over the engineer. "Heh? What's the matter?" he called up as he put his foot on the ladder.

"Mate's drunk an' 'ncapable, sir," answered the seaman from above.

"What o' that?" was the unexpected reply. "Let the poor body lie, an' you hold her to her course."

"But she's chasin' 'er tail, sir. She's pointin' near as possible due south at this moment, an' no tellin' 'ow long it's lasted—"

"Then bring her round to west—west an' a point south, an' hold her to it. You've got no *Faith*, Samuel Lloyd,—an' me wrestlin' with the Lord for you this three hours. See yonder!"—the skipper waved a hand towards the bows, and his voice rose to a note of triumph.

Sure enough, during the last two or three minutes the appearance of the fog had changed. It was dense still, but yellower in colour and even faintly luminous.

From the bridge came no answer.

"Liftin', that's what it is, an' I ask the Lord's pardon for lettin' myself be disturbed by ye."

The skipper turned to leave the ladder, of which he had climbed but half a dozen steps.

"Liftin' it may be "—Lloyd's voice arrested him—"but we're ashore somewheres, or close upon it. I can 'ear breakers—"

"Eh?"

"Listen!"

The skipper listened, all listened, the fog the while growing steadily more golden and luminous.

"Man, that's no sound of breakers—it's voices!"

"Voices!"

"Voices—voices of singin'. Ah!"—the skipper caught suddenly at the rail again—"a revelation! Hark!"

He was right. Far and faint ahead of the steamer's bows, where the fog, meeting the sun's rays, slowly arched itself into a splendid halo— a solid wall no longer, but a doorway for the light, and hung with curtains that momentarily wore thinner—there, where the water began to take a tinge of flame, sounded the voices of men and women, or of angels, singing together. And while the crew of the *Evan Evans* strained their ears the hymn grew audible—

> 'Nearer—and nearer still,
>   We to our country come;
> To that celestial Hill,
>   The weary pilgrim's home! . . .'

Arthur Miles had clutched Tilda's hand. She herself gazed and listened, awestruck. The sound of oars mingled now with the voices, and out of the glory ahead three forms emerged and took shape—three boats moving in solemn procession.

They were of unusual length, and black—at any rate, seen against that golden haze, they appeared black as Erebus. In the bows of each sat a company of people singing as they pulled at the long oars; and in the stern of each, divided from the rowers by the cargo—but what that cargo was could not yet be distinguished—stood a solitary steersman.

Patently these people were unaware of the steamer's approach. They were heading straight across her path—were, in fact, dangerously close—when at length the seaman on the bridge recovered presence of mind to sound her whistle, at the same time ringing down to stop the engines.

As the whistle sounded the singing ceased abruptly, the steersmen thrust over their tillers in a flurry, and of the rowers some were still backing water as the boats drifted close, escaping collision by a few yards.

"Ahoy there!"

"Ahoy!" came the answer. "Who are you?"

"The *Evan Evans*, of Cardiff," responded the skipper between his hollowed palms.

"Whither bound?"

"Cardiff."

The foremost boat was close now and drifting alongside. Arthur Miles and Tilda stared down upon the faces of the rowers. They were eight or ten, and young for the most part—young men of healthy brown complexions and maidens in sun-bonnets; and they laughed, with upturned eyes, as they fell to their oars again to keep pace with the steamer's slackening way. The children now discerned what cargo the boats carried—each a score or two of sheep, alive and bleating, their fleeces all golden in the strange light.

An old man stood in the stern of the leading boat. He wore a long white beard, and his face was extraordinarily gentle. It was he who answered the skipper.

"For Cardiff?" he echoed.

"Aye, the *Evan Evans*, of Cardiff, an' thither bound. Maybe you've heard of him," added the skipper irrelevantly. "A well-known Temperance Reformer he was."

The old steersman shook his head.

"You're miles away out o' your course, then—five an' twenty miles good."

"Where are we?"

"Right south-west—atween Holmness and the land. You've overshot *everything*. Why, man, are ye all mazed aboard? Never a vessel comes hereabouts, and 'tis the Lord's mercy you han't run her ashore."

"The Lord will provide," answered the skipper piously, "Which-a-way lies Cardiff, say you?"

The old man pointed. But while he pointed Tilda ran forward.

"'Olmness? Is it 'Olmness?"

He stared up.

"Holmness it is, missie? But why?"

"An' you'll take us off? We're 'ere with a message. It's for Miles Chandon, if you know 'im."

"Surely," the old man answered slowly. "Yes, surely—Sir Miles. But who can have a message for Sir Miles?"

"For Miss Sally, then. You know Miss Sally?"

The old man's look changed in a moment.

"Miss Sally? Why o' course—Do we know Miss Sally?" he was appealing to the crew of men and maidens forward, and they broke into a chime of laughter.

"What's this?" demanded the skipper, stepping forward. "Here's a couple of stowaways. I know nothing about 'em. It's your risk if you choose to take 'em off."

"If she've a message for Miss Sally—" answered the old steersman after a pause.

"It's life an' death!" pleaded Tilda.

The steamer, the upturned faces below, the fog all around—she saw it as in a dream, and as in a dream she heard herself pleading . . .

"Get out the ladder, there!" called the skipper.

They were in the boat, still as in a dream, sitting among these strange, kindly people. In a dream, too, she was waving to Bill, who had come up from below and leant over the bulwarks, staring as steamer and boats fell apart in the fog. Then, at a word from the bridge, he waved his hand for the last time and ran below. In a minute or so the *Evan Evans* began to feel around and edge away for the northward.

She faded and was lost in the vaporous curtain. Still the children gazed astern after her over the backs of the huddled sheep. The rowers had fallen to singing again—men and maidens in harmony as they pulled—

> 'The ransom'd sons of God,
>   All earthly things we scorn,
> And to our high abode
>   With songs of praise return! . . .'

Of a sudden, while they sang and while the children gazed, the fog to northward heaved and parted, pierced by a shaft of the sinking sun, and there in a clear hollow lay land—lay an Island vignetted in the fog, with the light on its cliffs and green slopes—an Island, resting like a shield on the milky sea.

"Look!"

Arthur Miles clutched Tilda by the arm and pointed.

The old steersman turned his head.

"Aye," said he, "she looks pretty of an evening sometimes, does Holmness."

CHAPTER XX.

INISTOW FARM.

"Clean, simple livers."—CRASHAW.

The rowers in the leading boat were seven—four young men and three young women; and they pulled two to an oar—all but the bowman, a young giant of eighteen or thereabouts, who did without help. A fourth young woman sat beside, suckling a baby. And so, counting the baby and the two children and the old steersman, whom they all addressed as "Father," and omitting 'Dolph and the sheep, they were twelve on board. The second and third boats had half a dozen rowers apiece. The second was steered by a wizened middle-aged man, Jan by name. Tilda learned that he was the shepherd. More by token, he had his three shaggy dogs with him, crowded in the stern.

At first these dogs showed the liveliest interest in 'Dolph, raising themselves with their forepaws on the gunwale, and gazing across the intervening twenty yards of water. But they were dignified creatures, and their self-respect forbade them to bark. 'Dolph, who had no breeding, challenged back loudly, all his bristles erect—and still the more angrily as they forbore to answer; whereat the young men and women laughed. Their laughter would have annoyed Tilda had it been less unaffected; and, as it was, she cuffed the dog so sharply that he ceased with a whine.

She had never met with folk like these. They gave her a sense of having reached the ends of the earth—they were so simple and strong and well-featured, and had eyes so kindly. She could understand but a bare third of what they said, their language being English of a sort, but neither that of the gentry—such as Arthur Miles spoke—nor that of the gypsies; nor, in short, had she heard the human like of it anywhere in her travels. She had never heard tell of vowels or of gutturals, and so could not note how the voices, as they rose and fell, fluted upon the one or dwelt, as if caressingly, on the other. To her their talk resembled the talk of birds, mingled with liquid laughter.

Later, when she came to make acquaintance with the Scriptures and read about the patriarchs and their families, she understood better. Laban with his flocks, Rebekah and her maidens, the shepherds of Bethlehem—for all of them her mind cast back to these innocent people, met so strangely off an unknown coast.

For she had come by water; and never having travelled by ship before, and being wholly ignorant of geography and distances, she did not dream that the coast towards which they were rowing her could be any part of England.

It loomed close ahead now—a bold line of cliff, reddish brown in colour, but with patches of green vivid in the luminous haze; the summit of the cliff-line hidden everywhere in folds of fog; the dove-coloured sea running tranquilly at its base, with here and there the thinnest edge of white, that shone out for a moment and faded.

But now the cliffs, which had hitherto appeared to run with one continuous face, like a wall, began to break up and reveal gullies and fissures; and as these unfolded, by and by a line of white cottages crept into view. They overhung a cove more deeply indented than the rest, and close under them was a diminutive grey pier sheltering a diminutive harbour and beach.

And now the voyage was soon ended. The boat shot around the pier-end and took ground upon firm shingle. The others, close in her wake, ran in and were beached alongside, planks were laid out from the gunwales, and in half a minute all hands had fallen to work, urging, persuading, pushing, lifting the sheep ashore, or rounding them up on the beach, where they headed hither and thither, or stood obstinately still in mazed fashion, all bleating. The middle-aged shepherd took command of these operations, no man gainsaying, and shouted here, there and everywhere, sparing neither age nor sex, but scolding all indiscriminately, hallooing to his dogs and waving his arms—as his master described it later—"like a paper man in a cyclone." And the dogs were silent no longer, but coursed the beach with short, fierce yelps, yet always intent on their business, as 'Dolph discovered when, spurred on by his theatrical instincts, he made a feint of joining in the sport. A snap of teeth close to his fore-legs sent him back yelping, and he retired in dudgeon to a heap of seaweed; but by and by, when the sheep were gathered into a compact crowd, he made a really heroic effort to divert attention back to his own talents.

"Look to the dog, there—look to 'en!" cried a maiden of eighteen, pointing and then resting a hand on either hip while she laughed.

This was Chrissy (short for Christiana), the prettiest, though not the youngest of the girls. Beside her there were Dinah (it was she who suckled the baby) and Polly, and Rose and Sabina, and Charity; and of the young men John Edward, and William, 'Rastus, Donatus and Obed. These were of the sons and daughters of the old steersman, with others of whom Tilda had not yet learnt the names. There was Old William also—Dinah's husband—a young man of thirty or so, but serious for his years; and Old William's two sisters, Sheba and Bathsheba—the younger a maiden, but the elder married to a youth they called Daniel; and Festus, who appeared to be courting Chrissy; and Roger, the young giant who had pulled the bow oar, and was courting nobody as yet. Quick though Tilda was to find her feet in a crowd and distinguish names and faces, she found the numbers bewildering. To Arthur Miles they were but a phantom throng. He stood on the beach amid the small tumult and, while the sheep blundered by, gazed back upon the Island, still in view, still resting like a shield out yonder upon the milky, golden sea.

As yet Tilda could not know that the old man had been married twice, that these stalwart youths and maidens were his offspring by two mothers. Indeed, they might all have been his, and of one womb, so frankly and so gently spoken they were one to another. Only the shepherd kept scolding all the while, and with vigour, using his brief authority which no one—not even his master—attempted to dispute. While this was going on two farm-boys from the rearmost boat had run up the hill, and by and by returned, each cracking a whip and leading a pair of horses harnessed to a lumbering hay-wagon. All scrambled on board, romping and calling to Tilda and Arthur Miles to follow their example; and so, leaving the shepherd to follow with his collected flock, the procession started, the horses plunging at the first steep rise from the beach.

Half-a-dozen children had collected on the beach and ran with them, cheering, up the hill, and before the cottage doorways three or four women, wives and widows, stood to watch the procession go by. These (someone told Tilda) were all the inhabitants left, their men-folk having sailed away west and north a month ago for the fishery.

"Wish 'ee well, Farmer Tossell!" cried one or two. "Sheep all right, I hope?"

"Right as the bank, my dears!" called back the old patriarch, waving a whip he had caught from one of the farm-boys. "The same to you, an' many of 'em!"

They mounted the hill at a run, and when the horses dropped to a walk Farmer Tossell explained to Arthur Miles, who had been thrust forward into a seat—or rather perch—beside him, that this bringing home of the sheep from Holmness was a great annual event, and that he was lucky, in a way, to have dropped in for it.

"The whole family turns out—all but the Old Woman an' Dorcas. Dorcas is my eldest. They're t'home gettin' the supper. A brave supper you'll see, an' the preacher along with it. I dunno if you 're saved. . . . No? P'r'aps not, at your age. I was never one for hurryin' the children; bruisin' the tender flax, as you might say. . . But you mustn't be upset if he *alloods* to you. . . . A very powerful man, when you're used to 'en. So you've a message for Miss Sally? Know her?"

The boy had to confess that he did not.

"Curious!" the farmer commented. "She's one of the old sort, is Miss Sally. But you can't get over to Culvercoombe to-night: to-morrow we'll see. . . . What's your name, by the way?"

"Arthur Miles."

"And your sister's?"

"She's called Tilda; but she—she isn't really—"

Farmer Tossell was not listening.

"You'll have to sleep with us to-night. Oh," he went on, misinterpreting the boy's glance behind him (he was really seeking for Tilda, to explain), "there's always room for one or two more at Inistow: that's what you might call our motto; and the Old Woman dotes on children. She ought to—havin' six of her own, besides nine of my first family."

The wagon had reached a short break in the ascent—you might liken it to a staircase landing—where the road ran level for about fifty yards before taking breath, so to speak, for another stiff climb. Here a by-road led off to the right, and here they turned aside.

The road ran parallel, or roughly parallel, with the line of the cliffs, between low and wind-trimmed hedges, over which, from his perch beside Farmer Tossell, the boy looked down across a narrow slope of pasture to the sea. The fog had lifted. Away and a little above the horizon the sun was dropping like a ball of orange flame in a haze of gold; and nearer, to the right of the sunset, lay the Island as if asleep on the waves, with glints of fire on the pointed cliffs at its western end, and all the rest a lilac shadow resting on the luminous water.

He gazed, and still gazed. He heard no longer, though the farmer was speaking. There was indeed some excuse, for the young men and girls had started another hymn, and were singing with all their voices. But he did not even listen.

The road rose and dipped.... They came to a white-painted gate, which one of the young men sprang down to open. The last glow of the sunset fell on its bars, and their outline repeated itself in dazzling streaks on the sky as the horses wheeled to the left through the gateway, and the boy turned for a last look. But Holmness had disappeared. A brown ridge of stubble hid it, edged and powdered with golden light.

Turning from the sea, the wagons followed a rutted cart-track that wound downhill in a slow arc between an orchard hedge and an open meadow dotted with cattle. High beyond the orchard rose a cluster of elms, around which many rooks were cawing, and between the elms a blue smoke drifted. There too the grey roof of the farmhouse crept little by little into sight; and so they came to a second gate and the rick-yard; and beyond the ricks was a whitewashed doorway, where a smiling elderly woman stood to welcome them. This was Mrs. Tossell, forewarned many minutes since by their singing.

She had come straight from preparing the feast, and her face was yet flushed with the heat of the kitchen fire. The arrival of the extra mouths to be fed did not put her out in the least. But she looked the children over with eyes at once benevolent and critical—their clothes and their faces—and said frankly that they wanted a wash, which was only too evident, the *Evan Evans* being a peculiarly grimy boat, even for a collier.

"The sooner the better," agreed Tilda with the utmost alacrity.

"Well, and I'm glad you take it like that," said their hostess, nodding approval. She called "Hepsy! Hepsy!" and an elderly serving-woman answered the summons. "Run, Hepsy, and fill the wash-house boiler," she commanded.

Within twenty minutes two long wash-trays stood ready and steaming—one for Tilda in the wash-kitchen itself, the other for Arthur Miles in a small outhouse adjoining; and while the children revelled in this strange new luxury, Mrs. Tossell bethought her of certain garments in a press upstairs—a frock and some underclothing long since outgrown by Sabina, a threadworn shirt and a suit that had formerly habited Obed, her youngest, all preserved and laid away on the principle (as she put it) that "Store is no Sore."

It was Chrissy, the pretty girl, who carried his clean garments to Arthur Miles; and he, being caught naked in the wash-tub, blushed furiously. But Chrissy was used to brothers, and took stock of him composedly.

"My!" she exclaimed, "what pretty white skin you've got!" And with that her quick eyes noted the mark on his shoulder. "Well, I never—but that's funny!"

"What's funny?" asked the boy.

"I'll tell you later, in the kitchen," she promised, and went off to Tilda.

The kitchen was of noble size—far larger even than the refectory at Holy Innocents' Orphanage—and worthy of the feast Mrs. Tossell had arrayed there to celebrate the sheep-bringing. The table, laden with hot pies, with dishes of fried rasher and hog's-puddings, black-puddings, sausages, with cold ham and cold ribs of beef, with apple tarts, junkets, jellies, syllabubs, frumenties, with mighty tea-pots and flagons of cider, ran close alongside the window-seat where the children were given their places, and whence, turning their heads, they looked out upon a garden set with clipped box-trees, and bordered with Michaelmas daisies, and upon a tall dove-cote of many holes and ledges crowded with pigeons settling down to their night's rest. On the outside of the table ran an unbacked bench, and at top and bottom stood two ample elbowed chairs for the farmer and his wife; but Mrs. Tossell had surrendered hers to a black-coated man whom all addressed as "Minister," though in talk among themselves they spoke of him rather as The Rounder.

Before the company sat he delivered a long grace with much unction. Tilda—a child of the world, and accustomed to take folks as she found them—eyed him with frank curiosity; but in Arthur Miles his black coat and white tie awoke a painful association of ideas, and for a while the child sat nervous and gloomy, without appetite to eat . . . Tilda for once was unobservant of him. The Minister, with his long thin neck, straggling black beard, weak, eloquent mouth and black, shining eyes—the eyes of a born visionary—failed, as well they might, to suggest a thought of Dr. Glasson. She was hungry, too, and her small body glowing deliciously within her clean garments. Amid all this clatter of knives and forks, these laughing voices, these cheerful, innocent faces, who could help casting away care?

Now and again her eyes wandered around the great kitchen—up to the oaken roof, almost black with age, and the hams, sides of bacon, bundles of potherbs, bags of simples, dangling from its beams; across to the old jack that stretched athwart the wall to the left of the fireplace—a curious apparatus, in old times (as Chrissy explained to her) turned by a dog, but now disused and kept only as a relic; to the tall settle on the right with the bars beneath the seat, and behind the bars (so Chrissy averred) a couple of live geese imprisoned, and quietly sitting on their eggs amid all this uproar; to the great cave of the fireplace itself, hung with pothooks and toothed cramps, where a fire of logs burned on a hearthstone so wide that actually—yes, actually—deep in its recess, and behind the fire, were set two smoke-blackened seats, one in each farther angle under the open chimney.

Before the feast had been twenty minutes in progress the farmer looked up and along the table and called for lights. His eyes, he explained, were not so young as they had been. Roger—tallest of the young men— jumped up and lit two oil-lamps that hung from the beams. The lamps had immense reflectors above them, made of tin; but they shone like silver, and Tilda took them for silver.

"That's cheerfuller!" shouted Farmer Tossell with a laugh of great contentment, and fell-to again.

But as the light wavered and anon grew steady, Chrissy leaned over Tilda, touched Arthur Miles on the shoulder, and pointed to the wall opposite. Tilda stared also, following the direction of her finger.

The lamp-light, playing on the broad chimney-piece with its brass candlesticks and china ornaments, reached for a yard or so up the wall, and then was cut off by the shadow of the reflectors. But in that illuminated space, fronting the children, stood out a panel of plaster, moulded in high relief, overlaid with a wash of drab-coloured paint. The moulding was of a coat-of-arms—a shield surrounded by a foliated pattern, and crossed with the same four diamond device as was tattooed on Miles Arthur's shoulder—

this with two antlered stags, collared, with hanging chains for supporters; above it a cap of maintenance and a stag's head coupe for crest; and beneath a scroll bearing some words which Tilda could not decipher. She glanced at Chrissy, alert at once and on the defensive. She had recognised the four diamonds, but all the rest was a mere mystery to her.

"He's got just that mark on his shoulder," said Chrissy, meeting her gaze and nodding towards the shield.

"Has he?" said Tilda disingenuously.

But she was jealous already, and by habit distrustful of her sex.

"Didn't you know? I noticed it, just now, when he was stripped. And I thought for a moment . . . you two coming and asking for Sir Miles. . . . But I'm always supposing some secret or other. Mother says it comes of muzzing my head with books, and then putting two and two together and making 'em five. . . . It's fanciful, of course"—here Chrissy sighed—"things don't happen like that in real life. . . . But there's always been stories about Sir Miles; and when I saw the mark—it *is* queer, now—"

But Tilda kept a steady face, her eyes fixed on the escutcheon.

"What does it mean?" she asked. "I don't know about these things."

"Why it's Sir Miles's coat-of-arms; of the Chandons, that is. Inistow Farm used to belong to them—belonged to them for hundreds of years, right down to the time Miss Sally bought it. Father farmed it under them for thirty years before that, and his father, and his grandfather, and his great-greats—back ever so long. He was terribly put out when it changed hands; but now he says 'Thank the Lord' when he talks of it."

"Changed hands?" Tilda found herself echoing.

"Yes. Inistow has belonged to Miss Sally these five years now. I thought maybe you'd be knowing all about her and Sir Miles—coming like this and inquiring for them. She's a good one, is Miss Sally; but when a woman sees a man poor—well, of course, that's her revenge."

"Is—is Sir Miles *poor?*"

Tilda's hopes were tottering, falling about her, she hardly knew how or why. Vaguely she had been building up a fabric of hope that she was helping Arthur Miles home to a splendid inheritance. Such things happened, almost as a matter of course, in the penny fiction to which her reading had been exclusively confined. To be sure, they never happened—they were wildly unlikely to happen—in the world of her own limited experience. But in the society to which the boy belonged by his gentle manners and his trick of speech, which could only come as a birthright—in that rarefied world where the ladies wore low gowns, with diamonds around their necks, and the gentlemen dined in fine linen with wide shirt-fronts—all life moved upon the machinery of romance. The books said so; and after that romance she had been pursuing, by degrees more consciously, from fugitive hints almost to certainty that a few hours would give it into her grasp. And now—

"Is—is he poor?" she repeated. She could not understand it. The story-books always conducted the long-lost heir to rank and wealth in the end.

"Well, he don't *spend* money, they say," answered Chrissy. "But nobody knows for certain. His tenants never see him. He's always abroad: he's abroad now—"

"Abroad?"

This was worse and worse.

"Or else shut up at Meriton—that's the great house—with a lot of nasty chemicals, trying to turn copper pennies into gold, they say."

Tilda caught at this hope.

"P'r'aps 'e'll manage it, one of these days."

"That's silly. Folks have been trying it for hundreds of years, and it'll never be done."

"And 'Olmness? 'As Miss Sally bought 'Olmness too?"

"No; he wouldn't part with it, for some reason. But father rents the grazing from him; same as before, when th' island belonged to Inistow Farm. There's a tale—"

But Tilda was not to hear the tale, for just now Mrs. Tossell pushed back her chair, and at her signal the feast ended. All left the table, and exchanged their benches for the settle or for chairs which they drew in a wide semicircle around the fireplace. Across the warm chord of this semicircle the sheep-dogs, stretched before the blaze, looked up lazily, and settled themselves to doze again. 'Dolph, lying a little apart (for they declined to take notice of him), copied their movements in an ingratiating but not very successful attempt to appear bred to the manner.

Tilda remarked that the company took their new positions with some formality. The shepherd alone comported himself carelessly, slouching around to the back of the fire, where he lit a clay pipe from the embers and seated himself on one of the ingle-ends, so that his tobacco smoke had a clear passage up the chimney. Then, almost before the children knew what was happening, the Minister gave out a hymn.

All sang it lustily, and when it was ended all dropped on their knees. The Minister broke into prayer—at first in smooth, running sentences, formal thanksgivings for the feast just concluded, for the plenty of seedtime and harvest, for the kindly fruits of the earth, with invocations of blessing upon the house and the family. But by and by, as these petitions grew more intimate, his breath came in short gasps. "O the Blood!" he began to cry; "the precious Blood of Redemption!" And at intervals one or other of his listeners answered "Amen!" "Hallelujah!" Tilda wondered what on earth it was all about; wondered too—for she knelt with her back to the great fireplace—if the shepherd had laid by his pipe and was kneeling among the ashes. Something in the Minister's voice had set her brain in a whirl, and kept it whirling.

"Glory! Glory! The Blood! Glory be for the Blood!"

And with that, of a sudden the man was shouting a prayer for *her*—for her and Arthur Miles, "that these two lambs also might be led home with the flock, and sealed—sealed with the Blood, with the precious Blood, with the ever-flowing Blood of Redemption—"

Her brain seemed to be spinning in a sea of blood . . . Men and women, all had risen from their knees now, and stood blinking each in the other's faces half-stupidly. The Minister's powerful voice had ceased, but he had set them going as a man might twirl a teetotum; and in five or six seconds one of the men—it was Roger, the young giant—burst forth with a cry, and began to ejaculate what he called his "experience." He had been tempted to commit the Sin without Pardon; had been pursued by it for weeks, months, when alone in the fields; had been driven to wrestle with it in hollows and waste places, Satan always at his ear whispering to him to say the words of blasphemy, to cross the line, to have rest of mind though it were in damnation. To Tilda this was all mere gibberish, but to the youth and to his hearers all real and deadly earnest. His words came painfully, from a dry throat; the effort twisted him in bodily contortions pitiful to see; the sweat stood on his handsome young forehead—the brow of a tortured Apollo. And the circle of listeners bent forward to the tale, eager, absorbed, helping out his agony with groans and horrified murmurs. They held their breath, and when he reached the crisis, and in a gush of words related his deliverance—casting up both arms and drawing one long shuddering breath—they could almost see the bonds burst on the muscles of his magnificent chest, and broke afresh into exultant cries: "Glory!" "Hallelujah!" "The Blood—the Blood!" while the shepherd in the ingle-nook slowly knocked out the ashes of his pipe against the heel of his boot. He was a free-thinker, an ex-Chartist, and held himself aloof from these emotions, though privileged, as an old retainer, to watch them. His face was impassive as a carved idol's.

The young giant dropped back into his chair, and doubtless a second spiritual gust was preparing to shake the company—you could feel it in the air—when Godolphus intervened. That absurd animal, abashed by a series of snubbings, probably saw a chance to rehabilitate himself. For certain during the last few minutes he had been growing excited, sitting up with bright eyes, and opening and shutting his mouth as in a dumb effort at barking. Now, to the amazement of all, including the sheep-dogs, he lifted himself upon his hind legs and began to gyrate slowly.

Everyone stared. In the tension nobody yet laughed, although Tilda, throwing a glance toward the chimney-corner, saw the shepherd's jaw relax in a grin. Her head yet swam. She felt a spell upon her that must be broken now or never.

"'Dolph!" she called, and wondered at the shrill sound of her own voice. "'Dolph!" She was standing erect, crooking her arm. The dog dropped on his fore-paws, crouched, and sprang through the hoop she made for him; crouched, sprang back again, alighted, and broke into a paean of triumphant yelps.

Tilda was desperate now. With a happy inspiration she waved her hand to the ancient jack against the wall, and 'Dolph sprang for it, though he understood the command only. But he was a heavy dog, and as the rusty machine began to revolve under his weight, his wits jumped to the meaning of it, and he began to run like a turnspit demented.

"Faster! 'Dolph!"

The Minister had arisen, half-scandalised, on the point of calling for silence; but his eyes fell on Tilda, and he too dropped back into his chair. The child had raised both arms, and was bending her body back—back—until her fingers touched the hem of her skirt behind her. Her throat even sank out of view behind her childish bust. The shepherd's pipe dropped, and was smashed on the hearthstone. There was a silence, while still Godolphus continued to rotate. Someone broke it, suddenly gasping "Hallelujah!"

"Amen! Tis working—'tis working!"

In despite of the Minister, voice after voice took up the clamour. Farmer Tossell's louder than any. And in the height of the fervour Tilda bent her head yet lower, twisted her neck sideways, and stared up at the ring of faces from between her ankles!

CHAPTER XXI.

THE HUNTED STAG.

*"Three hundred gentlemen, able to ride,
 Three hundred horses as gallant and free,
 Beheld him escape on the evening tide
 Far out till he sank in the Severn Sea . . .
 The stag, the runnable stag."*—JOHN DAVIDSON.

Early next morning the two children awoke in clean beds that smelt deliciously of lavender. The feeling was so new to them and so pleasant, that for a while they lay in luxurious ease, gazing out upon so much of the world as could be seen beyond the window—a green hillside scattered with gorse-bushes, sheeted with yellowing brake-fern and crossed by drifting veils of mist: all golden in the young sunshine, and all framed in a tangle of white-flowered solanum that clambered around the open casement. Arthur Miles lay and drank in the mere beauty of it. How should he not? Back at the Orphanage, life—such as it was—and the day's routine had always taken care of themselves; he had accepted, suffered them, since to change them at all lay out of his power. But Tilda, after a minute, sat upright in her bed, with knees drawn up beneath the bedclothes and hands clasped over them.

"This is a good place," she announced, and paused. "*An'* decent people, though rummy." Then, as the boy did not answer, "The best thing we can do is stay 'ere, if they'll let us."

"Stay here?" he echoed. There was surprise in the echo and dismay. "But why should we stay here?"

"W'y not?"

She had yet to break it to him that Sir Miles Chandon was abroad, and would (so Miss Chrissy had told her) almost certainly remain abroad for months to come. She must soften the blow.

"W'y not?" she repeated. "They're kind 'ere. If they'll keep us we can look about an' make inquiries."

"But we must get to the Island."

"The Island? Oh, yes, I dessay we'll get there sometime or another. What're you doin'?" she asked, for he had leapt out of bed and run to the window.

"Looking for it."

But the Island was not visible. This gable of the house fronted a steep coombe, which doubtless wound its way to the sea, since far to the right a patch of sea shone beyond a notch in the enfolding slopes.

"It'll stay there, don't you fret," Tilda promised. "'Wish I could be as sure that *we'd* stay *'ere*: though, far as I can see, we're safe enough for a few days. The old lady's puzzled about me. I reckon she don't attend circuses—nor the Minister neither—an' that Child-Acrobat turn fairly fetched 'em. They set it down to the 'fects of grace. I 'eard them talkin' it over, an' that was 'ow the Minister put it— whatever 'e meant."

"Well, but wasn't it?"

Arthur Miles had come back from the window, and stood at the foot of the bed in a nightshirt many sizes too large for him.

"Wasn't it *wot?*"

"Hadn't—hadn't it anything to do with the praying?"

"Garn!" Tilda chuckled. "But I'm glad it took *you* in too. The foolishness was my overdoin' it with 'Dolph. Dogs don't 'ave any religion, it seems; and it rattled 'em a bit, 'is be'avin' like a person that 'ad just found salvation. The Minister talked some science about it to Mother Tossell—said as 'ow dogs 'adn't no souls but a 'eap of *sympathy*; and it ended by 'er 'avin' a good cry over me when she tucked me up for the night, an' sayin' as after all I might be a brand plucked from the burnin'. But it didn' take in Miss Chrissy, as I could tell from the look in 'er eyes."

Whatever Miss Chrissy's doubts may have been, she chose a curious and perhaps a subtle method of expressing them. After breakfast she took Tilda to her room, and showed her a small volume with a cloth binding printed over with blue forget-me-nots and a gilt title, *The Lady's Vade-Mecum, or How to Shine in Society*. It put forth a preface in which a lady, who signed herself "One of the Upper Ten Thousand" but gave no further clue to her identity, undertook (as she put it) "to steer the aspirant through the shoals and cross-currents which beset novitiate in the *haut-ton*;" and Miss Chrissy displayed the manual shyly, explaining that she had bought it in Taunton, and in a foolish moment. "It flies too high for me. It says, under 'Cards,' that no lady who respects herself would talk about the 'Jack of Spades'; but when I played *Fives and Sevens* at the last harvest supper but one, and started to call him a Knave, they all made fun of me till I gave it up." She opined, nevertheless, that Tilda would find some good reading in it here and there; and Tilda, sharp as a needle, guessed what Miss Chrissy meant—that a study of it would discourage an aspirant to good society from smiling up at it between her ankles. She forgave the divined intention of the gift, for the gift itself was precisely what her soul had been craving. She borrowed it for the day with affected nonchalance—Tilda never gave herself away—and hugged the volume in her pocket as she and Arthur Miles and 'Dolph explored the coombe's downward windings to the sea.

A moor stream ran down the coombe, dodging and twisting between the overlaps of the hills, and ended in a fairy waterfall, over which it sprang some thirty feet to alight on a beach of clean-washed boulders. Close beside the edge of the fall stood a mud-walled cottage, untenanted and roofless, relic of a time when Farmer Tossell's father had adventured two or three hundred pounds in the fishery, and kept a man here with two grown sons to look after his nets. Nettles crowded the doorway, and even sprouted from crevices of the empty window sockets. Nettles almost breast-high carpeted the kitchen floor to the hearthstone. Nettles, in fact—whole regiments of nettles—had taken possession and defended it. But Tilda, with the book in her pocket, decided that here was the very spot for her—a real house in which to practise the manners and deportment of a real lady, and she resolved to borrow or steal a hook after dinner and clear the nettles away. Farmer Tossell had promised the children that on the morrow he would (as he put it) ride them over to Miss Sally's house at Culvercoombe, to pay a call on that great gentlewoman; to-morrow being Sunday and his day of leisure. But to-day he was busy with the sheep, and the children had a long morning and afternoon to fill up as best they might.

Arthur Miles did not share Tilda's rapture over the ruined cottage, and for a very good reason. He was battling with a cruel disappointment. All the way down the coombe he had been on the look-out for his Island, at every new twist and bend hoping for sight of it; and behold, when they came here to the edge of the beach, a fog almost as dense as yesterday's had drifted up Channel, and the Island was invisible. Somewhere out yonder it surely lay, and faith is the evidence of things not seen; but it cost him all his fortitude to keep back his tears and play the man.

By and by, leaning over the edge of the fall, he made a discovery that almost cheered him. Right below, and a little to the left of the rocky pool in which the tumbling stream threw up bubbles like champagne, lay a boat—a boat without oars or mast or rudder, yet plainly serviceable, and even freshly painted. She was stanch too, for some pints of water overflowed her bottom boards where her stern pointed down the beach— collected rain water, perhaps, or splashings from the pool.

The descent appeared easy to the right of the fall, and the boy clambered down to examine her. She lay twenty feet or more—or almost twice her length—above the line of dried seaweed left by the high spring tides. Arthur Miles knew nothing about tides; but he soon found that, tug as he might at the boat, he could not budge her an inch. By and by he desisted and began to explore the beach. A tangle of bramble bushes draped the low cliff to the right of the waterfall, and peering beneath these, he presently discovered a pair of paddles and a rudder, stored away for safety. He dragged out one of the paddles and carried it to the boat, in the stern-sheets of which he made his next find—five or six thole-pins afloat around a rusty baler. He was now as well equipped as a boy could hope to be for an imaginary voyage, and was fixing the thole-pins for an essay in the art of rowing upon dry land, when Tilda, emerging from the cottage (where the nettles stung her legs) and missing him, came to the edge of the fall in a fright lest he had tumbled over and broken his neck. Then, catching sight of him, she at once began to scold—as folks will, after a scare.

"Come down and play at boats!" the boy invited her.

"Shan't!" snapped Tilda. "Leave that silly boat alone, an' come an' play at houses."

"Boats aren't silly," he retorted; "not half so silly as a house without any roof."

"A boat out of water—bah!"

Here Tilda was forced to stoop and rub her calves, thus in one moment demonstrating by word and action how much she had to learn before qualifying to shine in Society.

So for the first time the two children quarrelled, and on the first day that invited them to cast away care and be as happy as they listed. Arthur Miles turned his back upon Tilda, and would not budge from his boat; while Tilda seated herself huffily upon a half-decayed log by the cottage doorway, with 'Dolph beside her, and perused *The Lady's Vade-Mecum*. "A hostess," she read, "should make her preparations beforehand, and especially avoid appearing *distraite* during the progress of dinner. . . . Small blunders in the service should either be ignored, or, at the worst, glided over with a laughing apology. . . . A trace too much of curacao in the *salade d'oranges* will be less easily detected and, if detected, more readily pardoned, than the slightest suspicion of *gene* on the part of the presiding goddess. . . In England it is customary to offer sherry with the soup, but this should not be dispensed lavishly. Nursed by a careful butler (or parlour-maid, as the case may be), a single bottle will sherry twelve guests, or, should the glasses be economical, thirteen. Remember the Grecian proverb, 'Meden agan,' or 'In all things moderation.'" All this Tilda read in a chapter which started with the sentence, "A dinner is a Waterloo which even a Napoleon may lose; and it is with especial care, therefore, almost with trepidation, that we open this chapter. We will assume that our pupil has sufficiently mastered those that precede it; that she is apparelled for the fray, her frock modest but *chic*, her *coiffure* adequate . . .'" This was going too fast. She harked back and read, under *General Observations*, that "It is the hall-mark of a lady to be sure of herself under all circumstances," and that "A lady must practise self-restraint, and never allow herself to exhibit temper."

"And I'm showin' temper at this moment! Oh, 'Dolph"—she caught the dog close to her in a hug—"the lot we've got to learn!"

'Dolph might have answered that he for his part was practising self-restraint, and practising it hard. He loved his mistress before all the world, but he had no opinion of books, and would have vastly preferred to be on the beach with Arthur Miles, nosing about the boat or among the common objects of the seashore.

By this time Arthur Miles, too, was feeling lonely and contrite. On their way back to dinner—signalled by the blowing of a horn in the farm-place—he ranged up beside Tilda and said gently, "I'm sorry," upon which, to her astonishment, Tilda's eyes filled with tears. She herself could not have said it; but somehow it was just by differing from her and from other folks that this boy endeared himself.

The reconciliation made them both very happy, and after dinner—to which the whole family, the shepherd and half a dozen labourers assembled, so that Tilda marvelled how, even with a fireplace so ample, Mrs. Tossell managed to cook for them all—Arthur Miles boldly approached Chrissy and got her to persuade her sweetheart, Festus, to lend him a hook. Armed with this, the children retraced their steps down the coombe. The fog had lifted a little, and in the offing Holmness loomed out dimly, with a streak of golden light on the water beyond its westernmost cliffs. But the boy nerved himself; he would not loiter to gaze at it, but strode into the cottage and began hacking with great fierceness at the nettles, which Tilda—her hands cased in a pair of old pruning gloves—gathered in skirtfuls and carried out of door. Godolphus, in his joy at this restored amity, played at assisting Arthur Miles in his onslaught, barking and leaping at the nettles, yet never quite closely enough to endanger his sensitive nose.

They had been engaged thus for half an hour, perhaps, when they heard a horn sounded far up the coombe. It had not the note of Mrs. Tossell's dinner-horn; it seemed to travel, too, from a distance beyond the farm, and as Tilda listened, it was followed by a yet fainter sound, as of many dogs baying or barking together. 'Dolph heard it, yapped excitedly, and made a dash out through the doorway. But, when Tilda followed, the sounds had died away. The coombe was silent save for the chatter of the fall and the mewing of an army of sea-gulls up the vale, where, on the farthest slope in sight, young Roger paced to and fro with a team of horses breaking up the stubble.

Tilda whistled 'Dolph back and fell to work again, filling her lap with nettles; but the load was scarcely complete before the dog, who had been whimpering and trembling with excitement, made another dash for the open, his yells all but drowning a thud of hooves with which a dark body hurled itself past the doorway, between the children and the sunshine, and so leapt clear for the beach over the fall.

Tilda, running to the doorway, saw the animal leap, but in so quick a flash that she noted nothing but its size, and mistook it for a riderless, runaway horse. Then as it appeared again and with three bounds cleared the beach and plunged into the sea, she knew that it was no horse but a huge stag— even such a stag as she had seen portrayed on menagerie posters—a huge Exmoor stag leaping dark against the sun, but with a flame along the russet-gold ridge of his back and flame tipping his noble antlers as he laid them back and breasted the quiet swell of the waves.

The hounds were close upon him. Not until they were close had he quitted his hide-hole in the stream, where for the last time he had broken the scent for them. This was the third stream he had used since they had tufted him out of the wood where through the summer he had lorded it, thirty-five miles away; and each stream had helped him, and had failed him in the end. He had weakened the scent over stony ridges, checked it through dense brakes of gorse, fouled and baffled it by charging through herds of cattle and groups of hinds of his own race couching or pasturing with their calves; for the stag-hunting season was drawing close to its end, and in a few weeks it would be the hinds' turn. But the hinds knew that their peril was not yet, and, being as selfish as he, they had helped him but little or not at all. And now his hour was near.

For even while the children gazed after him the hounds came streaming down the coombe in a flood, with a man on a grey horse close behind them; and behind him, but with a gap between, a straggling line of riders broke into sight, some scarlet-coated, others in black or in tweeds. The man on the grey horse shouted up the hill to Roger, who had left his team and was running. Away over the crest above him two labourers hove in sight, these also running at full speed. And all— hounds, horses, men—were pouring down the coombe towards the beach.

The hounds swept down in a mass so solid and compact that Tilda dragged Arthur Miles into the doorway, fearful of being swept by them over the edge of the fall. Past the cottage they streamed, down over the grassy cliff, and across the beach. 'Dolph, barking furiously by the edge of the waves, was caught and borne down by the first line of them—borne down and rolled over into the water with no more ceremony than if he had been a log. They did not deign to hurt him, but passed on swimming, and he found his feet and emerged behind them, sneezing and shaking himself and looking a fool. He was, as we know, sensitive about looking a fool; but just then no one had time to laugh at him.

The riders had arrived, and reined up, crowding the ledge before the cottage, and the most of them stood raising themselves in their stirrups, gazing after the stag that now, with little more than his antlers visible like a bleached bough moving on the flood, swam strongly out into the golden mist still cloaking the Island. Moment by moment he out-distanced the wedge-shaped ripple where the heads of the tired pack bobbed in pursuit; for here, as always in water, the deer held the advantage, being able to float and rest at will while the hound must always ply his forelegs or sink. The huntsman, however, judged it impossible that he could reach Holmness. He and a dozen gentlemen had dismounted, clambered down beside the fall, and were dragging the boat down the beach to launch her, when Roger and the two labourers burst through the throng and took charge; since to recover a deer that takes to the sea means a guinea from the hunt. And the boat was necessary now, for as the Inistow men launched her and sprang aboard the leading hounds realised that their quarry could not be headed, or that their remaining strength would scarcely carry them back to shore, and gave up the chase. By this the hunted stag gained another respite, for as the rowers pulled in his wake they had to pause half a dozen times and haul on board a hound that appeared on the point of sinking.

At the last moment the huntsman had leapt into the stern-sheets of the boat. He had his knife ready, and the rowers too had a rope ready to lasso the stags' antlers when they caught up with him. Ashore the huddled crowd of riders watched the issue. The children watched with them; and while they watched a sharp, authoritative voice said, close above Tilda's ear—

"They won't reach him now. He'll sink before they get to him, and I'm glad of it. He's given us the last and best run of as good a season as either of us can remember—eh, Parson?"

Tilda looked up with a sudden leap of the heart. Above her, on a raw roan, sat a strong-featured lady in a bottle-green riding-habit, with a top hat—the nap of which had apparently being brushed the wrong way— set awry on her iron-grey locks.

The clergyman she addressed—a keen-faced, hunting parson, elderly, clean-shaven, upright as a ramrod on his mud-splashed grey—answered half to himself and in a foreign tongue.

"Latin, hey? You must translate for me."

"A pagan sentiment, ma'am, from a pagan poet . . . If I were Jove, that stag should sleep to-night under the waves on a coral bed. He deserves it."

"Or, better still, swim out to Holmness and reign his last days there, a solitary king."

The Parson shook his head as he gazed.

"They would be few and hungry ones, ma'am, on an island more barren than Ithaca; no shady coverts, no young ash shoots to nibble, no turnip fields to break into and spoil . . . Jove's is the better boon, by your leave."

"And, by Jove, he has it! . . . Use your eyes, please; yours are better than mine. For my part, I've lost him."

They sat erect in their saddles, straining their gaze over the sea.

"It's hard to say—looking straight here against the sun, and with all this fog drifting about—"

But here a cry, breaking almost simultaneously from a score of riders, drew his attention to the boat.

"Yes, the boat—they have ceased pulling. He must have sunk!"

"God rest his bones—if a Christian may say it."

"Why not, ma'am?"

But as he turned to her the lady turned also, bending down at a light eager touch on her stirrup.

"Oh, ma'am! . . . Oh, Miss Sally!"

Miss Sally stared down into the small upturned face.

"Eh? . . . Now where in the world have I seen *you* before? Why, mercy, if it ain't the child Elphinstone ran over!"

CHAPTER XXII.

THE VOYAGE.

"Many a green isle needs must be . . . "—SHELLEY.

The boat had given up its search, and returned to shore. The hunt had wound back up the coombe in a body, and thence homeward in the failing light over the heather, breaking up into small parties as their ways parted, and calling good nights after the best run of the season. But Miss Sally and Parson Chichester sat talking in the best parlour at Inistow, and still sat on while the level sunset shone blood-red through the geraniums on the window-ledge, and faded and gave place to twilight.

They had heard the children's story; had turned it inside out and upside down, cross-questioning them both; and had ended by dismissing them for the time. To-morrow, Miss Sally promised, Farmer Tossell should be as good as his word, and ride them over to Culvercoombe, where perhaps she might have a few more questions to put to them. For the present she and Mr. Chichester had enough to talk over.

The interview had lasted a good hour, and Arthur Miles was glad to regain his liberty. The boy's manner had been polite enough, but constrained. He had stripped and shown the mark on his shoulder; he had answered all questions truthfully, and Miss Sally's readily—with the Parson he had been less at home—but he had managed to convey the impression that he found the whole business something of a bore; and, indeed, he asked himself, Where was the point of it? If only, instead of asking questions, they would take him to the Island now! . . .

But when he would have followed Tilda from the room, she took hold of him, pushed him out, and closing the door upon him, turned back and walked up to the two elders where they sat.

"You mus'n' judge Arthur Miles by to-day," she pleaded, meeting the amused, expectant twinkle in Miss Sally's eye. "'E didn't show at 'is best—along of *'im*."

She nodded towards the Parson.

"Eh, to be sure," said Mr. Chichester, "what you may call my *locus standi* in this affair is just nothing at all. If the child had demanded my right to be putting questions to him, 'faith, I don't know what I could have answered."

"It ain't that at all," said Tilda, after considering awhile. "It's your bein' a clergyman. 'E's shy of clergymen. If ever you'd seen Glasson you wouldn' wonder at it, neither."

"I'd like to persuade him that the clergy are not all Glassons. Perhaps you might ask him to give me a chance, next time?"

"Oh, *you?*" Tilda answered, turning in the doorway and nodding gravely. "*You're* all right, o' course. W'y, you sit a hoss a'most well enough for a circus!"

"That child is a brick," laughed Miss Sally as the door closed.

"At this moment," said Mr. Chichester, "I should be the last man in the world to dispute it. Her testimonial was not, perhaps, unsolicited; still, I never dreamed of one that tickled my secret vanity so happily. I begin to believe her story, and even to understand how she has carried through this amazing anabasis. Shall we have the horses saddled?"

He rang the bell. Mrs. Tossell answered it, bringing with her a tray of cold meats, apple tart, syllabubs, glasses, and a flagon of home-made cider. Yes, to be sure, they might have their horses saddled; but they might not go before observing Inistow's full ritual of hospitality.

Miss Sally plied (as she put it) a good knife and fork, and the Parson was hungry as a hunter should be. They ate, therefore, and talked little for a while: there would be time for talk on the long homeward ride. But when, in Homer's words, they had put from them the desire of meat and drink, and had mounted and bidden Mrs. Tossell farewell, Parson Chichester reopened the conversation.

"You believe the child's story, then?"

"Why, of course; and so must you. Man alive, truth was written all over it!"

"Yes, yes; I was using a fashion of speech. And the boy?"

"Is Miles Chandon's son. On that too you may lay all Lombard Street to a china orange." In the twilight Miss Sally leaned forward for a moment and smoothed her roan's mane. "You know the history, of course?"

"Very little of it. I knew, to be sure, that somehow Chandon had made a mess of things—turned unbeliever, and what not—"

"Is that all?" Miss Sally, for all her surprise, appeared to be slightly relieved. "But I was forgetting. You're an unmarried man: a wife would have taught you the tale and a hundred guesses beside. Of all women in the world, parsons' wives are the most inquisitive."

Mr. Chichester made no reply to this. She glanced at him after a pause, and observed that he rode with set face and looked straight ahead between his horse's ears.

"Forgive me," she said. "When folks come to our time of life without marrying, nine times out of ten there has been a mess; and what I said a moment since is just the flippant talk we use to cover it up. By 'our time of life' I don't mean, of course, that we're of an age, you and I, but that we've fixed our fate, formed our habits, made our beds and must lie in 'em as comfortably as we can manage.... I was a girl when Miles Chandon came to grief; you were a grown man—had been away for years, if I recollect, on some missionary expedition."

"In north-east China."

"To be sure, yes; and, no doubt, making the discovery that converting Chinamen was as hopeless a business as to forget Exmoor and the Quantocks."

"I had put my hand to the plough—"

"—and God by an illness gently released it. I have heard... Well, to get back to Miles Chandon.... He was young—a second son, you'll remember, and poor at that; a second lieutenant in the Navy, with no more than his pay and a trifling allowance. The boy had good instincts," said Miss Sally with a short, abrupt laugh. "I may as well say at once that he wanted to marry me, but had been forced to dismiss the notion."

Again she paused a moment before taking up the story.

"Well, his ship—the *Pegasus*—was bringing him home after two years on the Australian station.... Heaven help me! I'm an old sportswoman now, and understand something of the male animal and his passions. In those days I must have been—or so it strikes me, looking back—a sort of plain-featured Diana; 'chaste huntress'—isn't that what they called her? At any rate, the story shocked, even sickened, me a little at the time.... It appears that the night before making Plymouth Sound he made a bet in the wardroom—a bet of fifty pounds—that he'd marry the first woman he met ashore. Pretty mad, was it not?—even for a youngster coming home penniless, with no prospects, and to a home he hated; for his father and mother were dead, and he and his elder brother Anthony had never been able to hit it off.... On the whole, you may say he got better than he deserved. For some reason or other they halted the *Pegasus* outside the Hamoaze—dropped anchor in Cawsand Bay, in fact; and there, getting leave for shore, the young fool met his fate on Cawsand quay. She was a coast-guard's daughter—a decent girl, I've heard, and rather strikingly handsome. I'll leave it to you what he might have found if he'd happened to land at Plymouth.... He got more than half-drunk that night; but a day or two later, when the ship was paid off, he went back from Plymouth to Cawsand, and within a week he had married her. Then it turned out that fate had been nursing its stroke. At Sidmouth, on the second day of the honeymoon, a redirected telegram reached him, and he learnt that by Anthony's death Meriton was his, and the title with it. He left his bride at once, and posted up to Meriton for the funeral, arriving just in time; and there I saw him, for we all happened to be at Culvercoombe for the shooting, and women used to attend funerals in those days. . . . No one knew of the marriage; but that same evening he rode over to Culvercoombe, asked for a word with me in private, and told me the whole story—pluckily enough, I am bound to say. God knows what I had expected those words in private to be; and perhaps in the revulsion of learning the truth I lashed out on him. . . . Yes, I had a tongue in those days—have still, for that matter; not a doubt but I made him feel it. The world, you see, seemed at an end for both of us. I had no mother to help me, and my brother Elphinstone's best friend wouldn't call him the man to advise in such a business. Moreover, where was the use of advice? The thing was done, past undoing. . . Oh," Miss Sally went on, "you are not to think I broke my heart over it. As I've tried to explain, I was disgusted rather: I loathed the man, and—and—well, this is not the history of Sally Breward, so once more we'll get back to Miles Chandon. . . . He rode off; but he didn't ride back to Sidmouth. In his rage he did a thing that, I now see, was far baser than his original folly. I saw it as soon as my mind cleared; but—since this is a confession of a sort— I didn't see it at the time, for I hated the woman. He wrote her a letter; stuck a cheque inside, I dare say—he was brute enough just then; and told her she might claim her price if she chose, but that he would never see her again. . . . She went back to her coast-guard people."

"It would seem," said Mr. Chichester gravely, as she paused for a while, "that he did not even supply her with alimony—that is, if the child's story be true."

"Probably she refused to accept any. I think we must suppose that, in justice to her—and to him. Let me finish my confession. . . . I thought I could never endure to look on the woman; I have never, as a fact, set eyes on her. I don't know that she ever knew of my existence. If we meet, t'other side of the grave, there'll be a deal to be discussed between us before we straighten things out; but I'll have to start by going up and introducing myself and telling her that, in the end, she beat me. . . . Yes, parson, you'll hardly believe it, but one day, finding myself in Plymouth, I took a boat from Admiral's Hard, and crossed over to Maker Parish to make inquiries. This was two years later, and she had gone—moved with her father (God help her, like me she hadn't a mother) to some station on the east coast—the folk in Cawsand and Kingsand couldn't tell me where. But they told me a child had been born; which was new to me. They weren't sure that it was alive, and were wholly vague about the father—called him Chandon, to be sure, but supposed the name to be spelt with an 'S' as pronounced; told me he was an officer in the Navy, reputed to be an earl's son. Gossip had arrived no nearer. She was respectable, all agreed; no doubt about her marriage lines; and the register confirmed it, with the right spelling—the marriage and, ten months later, the boy's christening. Arthur Miles was the name. That is all, or almost all. It seems that towards the end of his time there her father became maudlin in his wits; and the woman—her maiden name had been Reynolds, Helen Reynolds—relied for help and advice upon an old shipmate of his, also a coast-guard, called Ned Commins. It was Ned Commins they followed when he was moved to the east coast, the father being by this time retired on a pension. And that is really all. I was weary, ashamed of my curiosity, and followed the search no further."

"You must follow it now," said Parson Chichester quietly.

"That's understood."

"What do you propose as the first step?"

"Why, to ride to Meriton to-morrow, and get Miles Chandon's address. He's somewhere in the South of France. It's ten years or so since we parted, that evening of the funeral; but a telegram from me will fetch him, or I am mistaken."

"Let me save you some trouble. To-morrow is Sunday, and my parishioners will be glad enough to escape a sermon at Morning Service. Let me cut the sermon and ride over to Meriton, get the address and bring it to Culvercoombe. I ought to reach there by three in the afternoon, but the precise hour does not matter, since in these parts there's no telegraphing before Monday."

"That's a good neighbourly offer, and I'll accept it," answered Miss Sally. "I could ride over to Meriton myself, of course. But Tossell has promised to bring the children to Culvercoombe in the early afternoon, and this will give you an excuse to be present. Some questions may occur to you between this and then; and, anyway, I'd like to have you handy."

No more was said. They parted, having come to a point where the rising moon showed their paths lying separate across the moor. Their lonely homes lay eight miles apart. Even by daylight one unaccustomed to the moor could hardly have detected the point where the track divided in the smothering heather. But these two could have found it even in the dark; being hunters both, and children of the moor, born and bred.

Had they known it, even while they talked together, something was happening to upset their plans for the morrow, and for days to come.

The children, as they left the parlour, had been intercepted by Mrs. Tossell with the information that tea was ready for them in the kitchen.

"Wot, another meal?" said Tilda.

Twenty-four hours ago a world that actually provided too much to eat would have been inconceivable by her. But already the plenty of Inistow was passing from a marvel into a burden. It seemed to her that the great kitchen fire never rested, as indeed it seldom did. Even when the house slept, great cauldrons of milk hung simmering over the hot wood ashes.

Tea over, the children started once again for their waterfall; and this time in haste, for the hollow of the coombe lay already in shadow, and soon the yellow evening sunlight would be fading on its upper slopes. Arthur Miles hungered for one clear view of his Island before nightfall; Tilda was eager to survey the work accomplished that afternoon in the cottage; while 'Dolph scampered ahead and paused anon, quivering with excitement. Who can say what the dog expected? Perchance down this miraculous valley another noble stag would come coursing to his death; and next time 'Dolph would know how to behave, and would retrieve his reputation—to which, by the way, no one had given a thought. But dogs can be self-conscious as men.

Lo! when they came to the ledge above the fall, Holmness was visible, vignetted in a gap of the lingering fog, and standing so clear against the level sunset that its rocky ledges, tipped here and there with flame, appeared but a mile distant, or only a trifle more. He caught his breath at sight of it, and pointed. But Tilda turned aside to the cottage. This craze of his began to annoy her.

She was yet further annoyed when he joined her there, ten minutes later, and appeared to pay small attention, if he listened at all, to her plans for to-morrow, before the ride to Culvercoombe. There could be no more nettle-clearing to-day. Dusk was gathering fast, and in another hour the moon would rise. So back once more they fared, to find Mrs. Tossell busily laying supper; and close after supper came prayer, and bedtime on the stroke of nine.

An hour later Tilda—who slept, as a rule, like a top—awoke from uneasy dreams with a start, and opened her eyes. A flood of moonlight poured in at the window, and there in the full ray of it stood Arthur Miles, fully dressed.

The boy let drop the window-curtain, and came across to her bed.

"Are you awake?" he whispered. "Get up and dress—we can do it easily."

"Do what?"

"There's a tank just under the window—with a slate cover: we can lower ourselves down to it from the sill, and after that it's not six feet to the ground."

"What's up with you?" She raised herself, and sat rubbing her eyes. "Oh, get yer clothes off an' go back to bed! Walkin' in yer sleep you must be."

"If you won't come with me, I'm going alone."

"Eh?" She stared at him across the moon-ray, for he had gone back to the window and lifted the curtain again. "But *where* in the world?"

"To Holmness."

"'Olmness? . . . It's crazed you are."

"I am not crazed at all. It's all quite easy, I tell you—easy and simple. They've left the boat afloat—I've found out how to get to her—and the night is as still as can be. . . . Are you coming?"

"You'll be drowned, I tell you—drowned or lost, for sure—"

"Are you coming?"

He did not reason with her, or she would have resisted. He spoke very calmly, and for the first time she felt his will mastering hers. One thing was certain—she could not let him go alone. . . . She threw back the bedclothes, slipped out, and began to dress, protesting all the while against the folly of it.

To reach the ground was mere child's-play, as he had promised. From the broad window-ledge to the slate tank was an easy drop, and from the tank they lowered themselves to a gravelled pathway that led around this gable of the house. They made the least possible noise, for fear of awakening the farm-dogs; but these slept in an out-house of the great farmyard, which lay on the far side of the building. Here the moon shone into a diminutive garden with box-bordered flower-beds, and half a dozen bee-skips in row against a hedge of privet, and at the end of the gravelled walk a white gate glimmering.

Arthur Miles tip-toed to the gate, lifted its latch very cautiously, and held it aside for Tilda to pass. They were free.

"Of all the madness!" she muttered as they made for the coombe.

The boy did not answer. He knew the way pretty well, for this was their fourth journey. But the moonlight did not reach, save here and there, the hollows through which the path wound, and each step had to be carefully picked.

"Look 'ere," she essayed again after a while, "I won't say but this is a lark, if on'y you'll put that nonsense about 'Olmness out of yer mind. We can go down to the cottage an' make believe it's yer ancestral 'ome—"

"Wh'st!" he commanded sharply, under his breath.

She listened. Above the murmur of the stream her ears caught a soft pattering sound somewhere in the darkness behind.

"What is it?" She caught at his arm.

"I don't know. . . . Yes I do. 'Dolph?—is it 'Dolph? Here then— *good* dog!"

And sure enough 'Dolph came leaping out of the darkness, heaven knows by what instinct guided. 'Dolph, too wise to utter a single bark, but springing to lick their hands, and fawning against their legs.

The dog's presence put new courage into Tilda, she scarcely knew why, and henceforth she followed more confidently. With a stumble or two, but no serious mishap, they groped their way down the coombe, and coming to the ledge, saw the beach spread at their feet in the moonlight and out on the water the dark boat heaving gently, a little beyond the edge of the waves' ripple. The tide had receded since their last visit, and Arthur Miles knew nothing about tides. But he had discovered the trick of the boat's moorings. The farm-men, returning from their pursuit of the stag, had dropped a small anchor attached to a shore-line, by which at high-water they could draw her in and thus save themselves the present labour of hauling her up the steep beach. But the weather being fair, they had suffered high-water to pass, and let her ride out the night as she lay.

Arthur Miles knew the bush to which the shore-end of the line was attached, and scrambling down beside the fall, found it easily and untied it. As a fact (of which, however, he was quite unaware), he had very little time to lose. In another twenty minutes the boat's keel would have taken ground immovably. He ran down the beach, coiling the slack of the line as he went; tugged at the anchor, which yielded readily; found it; and almost at the same moment heard the boat's nose grate softly on the pebbles. The beach shelved steeply, and her stern lay well afloat; nor was there any run of sea to baffle him by throwing her broadside-on to the stones. He hurried Tilda aboard. She clambered over the thwarts to the stern-sheets, 'Dolph sprang after her, and then with the lightest push the boy had her afloat—so easily indeed that she had almost slid away, leaving him; but he just managed to clutch the gunwale close by the stem and to scramble after.

He seized an oar at once and thrust off. Next came the difficult job of working her round and pointing her nose for the sea. Of rowing he knew nothing at all, nor could Tilda help him. He could but lift the clumsy oar, and ply it with the little skill he had learnt on the voyage down Avon, as one plies a canoe-paddle. Even to do this he was forced to stand erect in the stern-sheets: if he sat, the awkward pole would over-weight his strength completely. But the boy had a native sense of watermanship, and no fear at all; and the boat, being a stable old tub, while taxing all his efforts, allowed a margin for mistakes. Little by little he brought her round, and paddled her clear of the cove into open water.

Even then he might have desisted. For although the moon, by this time high aloft behind his right shoulder, shone fair along the waterway to the Island, the grey mass of which loomed up like the body of a sea-monster anchored and asleep in the offing, he soon discovered that his own strength would never suffice to drive the boat so far. But almost on the moment of this discovery he made two others; the first, that the tide—or, as he supposed it, the current—set down and edged the boat at every stroke a little towards the Island, which lay, in fact, well down to the westward of the cove, and by half a mile perhaps; the second, that out here a breeze, hitherto imperceptible, was blowing steadily off the land. He considered this for a while, and then ordered Tilda, who by this time was shivering with cold, to pull up the V-shaped bottom-board covering the well in the stern and fix it upright in the bows. She did this obediently, and, so placed, it acted as a diminutive sail.

Seeing that she still shivered, he commanded her to take the other oar, seat herself on a thwart forward, and do her best to work it as they had seen the farm-hands pulling after the stag. Again she obeyed, and he fixed the thole-pins for her, and lifted the oar into place between them. But with the first stroke she missed the water altogether, and with the next caught a crab, which checked the boat dead. This would never do; so, and still to busy her and keep her warm with exercise, rather than in hope of help from her, he instructed her to stand with her face to the bows, and push with the oar as she had seen him pushing.

He expected very little from this; but Tilda somehow caught the knack after a few strokes, and for half a mile it helped them greatly. By this time they were both warm enough, but desperately tired. So far as they could judge, half of the distance was accomplished. They could certainly not work back against the breeze blowing more and more freshly off the land.

With a little steering on the boy's part they might even have trusted to this breeze to carry them the rest of the way, had it not been for the ebb tide. This too had steadily increased in strength, and now, unless a miracle happened, would sweep them far to the westward of their goal. Hitherto they had been working their oars one on each side of the boat. Now Tilda shifted hers across, and they pushed together; but all in vain. The tide steadily forced them sideways. They were drifting past the westernmost end of the Island, and the Island still lay more than a mile off.

For the next ten minutes neither spoke; and it may stand to Tilda's credit that she uttered no reproach at all. At slow intervals she lifted the oar and pushed with it; but she had none of the boy's native instinct for managing it, and her strokes grew feebler. At length she lifted the heavy shaft a little way, and let it fall with a thud on the gunwale. She could do no more, and the face she turned to him in the moonlight was white with fatigue.

"I just *can't*," she panted. "It's dead beat I am."

"Lie down," he commanded, pointing to the bottom boards. "Here—take my coat—"

He picked his jacket up from the stern-sheets and tossed it to her. His face was white and wearied almost as hers, yet, strange to say, quite cheerful and confident, although patently every second now was driving the boat down Channel, and wider of its goal. For a moment it appeared that she would resist. But, as she caught the coat, weakness overcame her, her knees gave way, and she dropped in a huddled heap. 'Dolph ran to her with a sharp whine, and fell to licking the hand and wrist that lay inert across the thwart. The touch of his tongue revived her, and by and by she managed to reach out and draw his warm body close to her, where he was content to lie, reassured by the beating of her heart.

"That's right!"

The boy spread his jacket over her, and went aft again. He did not resume his paddling, for this indeed was plainly useless. Already on his right hand the Island was slipping, or seemed to be slipping, away into darkness. But he did not lose it, for after a while the climbing moon stood right above it, linking it to the boat by a chain of light that rippled and wavered as if to mock him.

But he was not mocked. He had faith all the while. He longed for the secret by which that shining chain could be hauled upon, by which to follow up that glittering pathway; but he never doubted. By whatever gods might be, he had been brought thus far, and now sooner or later the last miracle was bound to happen. He had been foolish to struggle so, and to wear Tilda out. He would sit still and wait.

And while he sat there and waited he began, of a sudden and at unawares, to sing to himself. It was the same tuneless chant that had taken possession of him by Harvington-on-Avon; but more instant now and more confident, breaking from him now upon the open sea, with moon and stars above him. Tilda did not hear it, for she slept. He himself was hardly conscious of it. His thoughts were on the Island, on the miracle that was going to happen. He did not know that it had already begun to happen; that the tide was already slackening; nor, had he marked it, would he have understood. For almost an hour he sang on, and so slipped down in the stern-sheets and slept.

By and by, while he slept, the tide reached its ebb and came stealing back, drawing with it a breeze from the south-west.

He awoke to a sound which at first he mistook for the cawing of rooks—there had been many rooks in the trees beyond the wall of Holy Innocents, between it and the Brewery. But, gazing aloft, he saw that these were sea-gulls, wheeling and mewing and making a mighty pother. And then—O wonder!—as he rubbed his eyes he looked up at a tall cliff, a wall of rock rising sheer, and a good hundred feet from its base where the white water was breaking. The boat had drifted almost within the back-draught, and it was to warn him that the gulls were calling.

"The Island! The Island!"

He caught up his oar and called to Tilda. She struggled up sleepily, and gasped at the sight.

"You must take an oar and help!" he called. "There must be a landing near, if we work her round the point—"

And, sure enough, around the point they opened a small cove, running inwards to a narrow beach of shingle. A grassy gully wound up from the head of the cove, broadening as it trended to the left, away from the tall rocks of the headland; and at the sight of this 'Dolph began barking furiously, scaring fresh swarms of sea-birds from their roosting-ledges.

They were in quiet water here, and in less than two minutes—the boy steering—the boat's stem grated softly on the shingle and took ground. 'Dolph sprang ashore at once, but the children followed with some difficulty, for they were cold and stiff, and infinitely weary yet. It seemed to them that they had reached a new world: for a strange light filled the sky and lay over the sea; a light like the sheen upon grey satin, curiously compounded of moonlight and dawn; a light in which the grass shone a vivid green, but all else was dim and ghostly.

Scarcely knowing what they did, they staggered up the beach a little way, and flung themselves down on the shingle.

Two hours passed before Arthur Miles awoke. The sun had climbed over the low cliff to the eastward of the cove, and shone on his lids. It seemed to him that his feet were lying in water.

So indeed they were, for the tide had risen and .was running around his ankles. But while he sat up, wondering at this new marvel, Tilda gave a cry and pointed.

The boat had vanished.

CHAPTER XXIII.

THE ISLAND.

"Be not afraid; the isle is full of noises, Sounds and sweet airs, that give delight and hurt not."—THE TEMPEST.

"Well," said Tilda dolefully, "I guess that about settles us!"

The boy, his hands thrust into his breeches' pockets, stared over the sea for a while.

"I don't see that it matters much," he answered at length, withdrawing his gaze. "You know well enough we could never have worked her back again."

"Oh, indeed? And 'ow are we goin' to pick up our vittles? I don't know what *you* feel like, but I could do with breakfast a'ready."

"Perhaps 'Dolph can catch us a rabbit," he suggested hopefully after a pause. "I heard Roger say last night that Holmness swarmed with rabbits."

"Rabbits?" said Tilda with scorn. "D'yer know 'ow to skin one if we caught 'im?"

"No, I don't," he confessed.

"And when he's skinned, there's the cookin'; and we 'aven't so much as a box of matches. . . . That's the worst of boys, they 're so unpractical."

"Well, then, we can hunt for gulls' eggs."

"That's better; if," she added on an afterthought, "gulls 'appen to lay eggs at this time of year—which I'll bet they don't."

"Look here," said the boy severely, "we haven't searched yet. What's the use of giving in before we've *tried?* Nobody starves on the Island, I tell you; and—and I can't bear your talking in this way. It isn't *like* you—"

"I can't *'elp* it," owned poor Tilda with a dry sob.

"—breaking down," he continued, "just when we've reached, and all the rest is going to happen just as the book says."

"That's likely!"

"It's certain." He pulled out the tattered, coverless volume. "Why, I do believe"—he said it with a kind of grave wonder—"you're hankering after that silly cottage!"

"Of course I am," she confessed defiantly, for he exasperated her. "We'd promised to ride over an' see Miss Sally this afternoon, an' I wanted to spend the 'ole mornin' learnin' 'ow to be a lady. . . . I don't get *too* much time for these little things."

The protest was weak enough, and weakly uttered. Until the moment of embarking on this expedition Tilda had been throughout their wanderings always and consciously the leader—her will the stronger, her's to initiate and to guide. But now he stuck his hands deeper into his pockets.

"That's all very well," he replied; "but you can't get to Miss Sally's to-day. So who's unpractical now? Let's find the cave first, and have breakfast; and then, if you're tired of exploring, you can sit on cushions all day, and read your book and learn how to be a princess— which is ever so much higher than an ordinary lady."

"Cave? *Wot* cave? *Wot* breakfast? *Wot* cushions? Oh, I do believe, Arthur Miles, you've gone stark starin' mad!"

"Why," he reasoned with her, "on a seashore like this there are bound to be caves; the only trouble will be to find the right one. And as for breakfast, it was you that talked about it just now."

His persistence, his gentleness, the careful lucidity of his craze drove her fairly beside herself.

"Oh," she cried again, "if you ain't mad, then I must be, or elst I'm sickenin' for it! It don't much matter, any'ow. We got to starve 'ere an' die, an' the sooner the better."

She walked across the beach to a smooth slab of rock and seated herself sullenly, with her eyes on the distant mainland. They were misty with tears of anger, of despair. But he could not see them, for she had resolutely turned her back on him. Had she broken down—had she uttered one sob even— the boy would have run to her side. As it was, he gazed at her sorrowfully. . . . She had lost her temper again, and it spoiled everything. But the spell of the Island was on him. Above, in the sunlight, the green gully wound upward and inland, inviting him; and here on the shingle at his feet sat 'Dolph and looked up at him, with eyes that appealed for a ramble. The dog's teeth chattered, and small suppressed noises worked in his throat.

"Very well," called the boy, "I am going, and you can sit there or follow, as you like."

He swung on his heel and set forth, 'Dolph scampering ahead and barking so wildly that the noise of it scared the birds again in flock after flock from their ledges.

On the ridge the boy halted for a moment and looked down. But Tilda sat stubbornly on her rock, still with her back turned.

She had pulled out her book, the *Lady's Vade-Mecum*, but only for a pretence. She did not in the least want to read, nor could her eyes just now have distinguished a word of the text. She was wholly miserable; and yet, curiously enough, after the first minute her misery did not rest on despair, or at any rate not consciously. She was wretched because the boy had broken away and gone without her, and 'Dolph with him—'Dolph, her own dog. They were ungrateful. . . . Had not everything gone right so long as they had obeyed her? While now—They would find out, of course. Even Arthur Miles would begin to feel hungry after a while, and then—'Dolph might keep going for a time on rabbits, though as a circus-dog he was not clever at sport.

Yes, she had a right to be indignant. She had lost command for a moment, and Arthur Miles had straightway led her into this trap. . . . This was all very well, but deep down beneath the swellings of indignation there lurked a thought that gradually surmounted them, working upwards until it sat whispering in her ear. . . . They were in a tight place, no doubt, . . . but was she behaving well? Now that the mess was made and could not be unmade, where was the pluck—where was even the sense—of sitting here and sulking? Had she stuck it out, why then at the end she could have forgiven him, and they would have died together. . . . She stared forlornly at the book, and a ridiculous mocking sentence stared back at her: "It is often surprising into what tasty breakfast dishes the cunning housewife will convert the least promising materials." In a gust of temper she caught up the book and hurled it from her.

And yet . . . with all these birds about, there must surely be eggs. She had not a notion how gulls' eggs tasted. Raw eggs! they would certainly be nasty; but raw eggs, after all, will support life. Moreover, deliverance might come, and before long. The Tossells, when they found the boat missing, would start a search, and on the Island there might be some means of signalling. How could she be forgiven, or forgive herself, if the rescuers arrived to find Arthur Miles dead and herself alive?

With that a dreadful apprehension seized her, and she stood erect, listening. . . . She had let him go alone, into Heaven knew what perils. He was searching along the cliffs, searching for a cave, and very likely for gulls' eggs on the way. . . . What easier than to slip and break his neck? She listened—listened. But the sound of 'Dolph's barking had long ago died away. . . . Oh, if he were dead, and she must search the Island alone for him!

Poor child! for the moment her nerve deserted her. With a strangling sob she ran towards the beach-head, and began to clamber up the low cliff leading to the gully.

"Til-da! Hi! Til-da!"

From the ledge of the cliff she stared up, and with another sob. High on the ridge that closed the gully stood Arthur Miles, safe and sound. He was waving both arms.

"I've found it!" he called.

"Found w'ot?"

"The House." He came running down to meet her as she scrambled her way up the gully. "It's not a Cave, but a House." They met, both panting. "You were right, after all," he announced, and in a voice that shook with excitement. He had forgotten their quarrel; he had no room for remembrance of it; sheer joy filled him so full. "It's not a Cave, but a House; and with *such* things to eat!"

"Things to eat?" she echoed dully, and for an instant her heart sank again at the suspicion that after all he was mad, and here was another proof of it. But her eyes were fixed on something he held out in his hand. "What's that you've got?"

"Marmalade—real marmalade! And a spoon too—there are heaps of spoons and cups and glasses, and a fire ready laid. And—see here—biscuits!" He produced a handful from his pocket. "I brought these things along because you said you were hungry."

Still incredulous, distrusting her eyes, Tilda watched him dip out a small spoonful of marmalade and spread it on the biscuit. She took it and ate, closing her eyes. The taste was heavenly.

"Oh, Arthur Miles, where are we?"

"Why, on the Island. Didn't I tell you it was going to be all right?"

He said it in mere elation, without a hint of reproach.

"I'm so sorry."

"Sorry? What is there to be sorry about? Come along."

They climbed the turfy slope in silence, Tilda too deep in amaze for speech. By and by she asked irrelevantly—

"Where is 'Dolph?"

"Eh? 'Dolph? He was with me five minutes ago. Off chasing rabbits, I expect. He has missed catching about two dozen already."

"Isn't that his bark? Listen . . . away to the right."

They stood still for a while.

"Sounds like it," said the boy; "and yet not exactly like."

"It's 'Dolph, and he's in some sort of trouble. That's not 'is usual bark."

"We'd best see what it is, I suppose, and fetch him along." Arthur Miles struck aside from the line they had been following, and moved after the sound, not without reluctance. "It may be only a vision," he said gravely. "Remember the hounds that ran after Caliban and the others?"

But as they trended towards the edge of the cliffs the barking grew louder, and was recognisably 'Dolph's; and so they came to a wide shelving amphitheatre of turf overgrown with furze and blackthorn. It curved almost as smoothly as the slope of a crater, and shelved to a small semi-circular bay. There, on the edge of the tide, danced 'Dolph yelping; and there, knee-deep in water, facing him with lowered head, stood a magnificent stag—yes, the stag of yesterday! When Arthur Miles caught at Tilda's arm and proclaimed this, at first she doubted. But he pointed to the antlers, glinting bright in the sunshine. He did not know the names for them, but whereas the left antler bore brow, bay, tray, and three on top, the top of the right antler, by some malformation, was not divided at all, and even a child could see this and guess it to be unusual. He was a noble stag nevertheless. The sun shone down on his russet-gold flanks as he stood there fronting the dog with his deadly brow-points. And 'Dolph kept to the edge of the water, leaping forward a little and anon leaping back, and at each leap emitting a futile yelp.

The children stared, wondering how he could have driven so noble a quarry; until, as Arthur Miles called down, he lifted his head and gazed up at them for a moment. Then he turned slowly, as it were disdainfully, and they divined the truth—that the long swim of yesterday had broken his gallant strength, and he had come down to the beach to die. He turned and lurched heavily down into deep water, laid himself gently afloat, and struck out as if heading for the main. But the main and his own heathery moors lay far distant, a blue-grey line in the haze to the southward. Perhaps his spirit regained them as his body slowly sank. The children watched it sink until only the antlers showed above water like a forked bough adrift on the tideway. They drifted so for a few seconds; then dipped out of sight, and were gone.

The children stood for a full minute gazing at the water where he had disappeared. Then Arthur Miles whistled to 'Dolph, who came bounding up the slope, and together all three struck inland again, but in silence. They were awed by the Island and its wonders.

The Island, as they climbed to its grassy chine, gradually revealed itself as a hill of two peaks, united by a long saddle-back. The most of this upland consisted of short turf, with here and there a patch of stones. In all the prospect was no single tree, scarcely a furze-bush even—the furze grew only on the southern slopes, low down; and Tilda strained her eyes vainly for sight of the House.

But in the very dip of the saddle was a gully, much like the one by which they had ascended, but steeper and dipping to the north. Before they reached it, before she could detect it even, Arthur Miles pointed to where it lay; and they had scarcely turned aside to follow it before a chimney—a genuine red-brick chimney—rose into sight above the dying bracken.

A minute later, and she was looking down on a broad slated roof, on a building of one story, stuck here in a notch of the gully, and in the lee of almost every wind that could blow. Its front faced her as she descended. It had a deep, red-tiled verandah, and under the verandah a line of windows, close-shuttered all but one. This one stood next to the front door, on the right.

The boy, still leading, ran down the sloping path to the door, and lifted the latch. Tilda halted just within the threshold, and looked about her.

The kitchen, on which the door opened, was well furnished, with an open hearth, and a fire laid ready there, and even a row of saucepans twinkling above the mantel-shelf.

Arthur Miles waved a hand around, and pointed to another door at the end of the kitchen.

"There's a heap of rooms in there. I didn't stay to search. But look at this!"

He unhitched a card which hung above the mantel-shelf. On it was written:—

"The provisions here are left for any mariners who may find themselves shipwrecked on this Island. All such are welcome to make use of what accommodation they find here. Casual visitors will kindly respect the intention with which this house is kept open, and will leave the place strictly as they find it."

"(Signed) MILES CHANDON, Bart."

From the next room came the sound of a window opened and a shutter thrown wide, and Tilda's voice announced—

"Well, I never! Beds!"

"Beds?"

"Beds—*and* sheets—*and* blankets." Tilda reappeared in the doorway. "A 'ole reel 'ouse! But why?—and 'ow in the world?"

Arthur Miles held out the card.

"It's for sailors shipwrecked here."

Tilda studied the notice.

"And we 're shipwrecked! Well, if this ain't the loveliest. A reel 'ouse, with reel beds an' sorsepans!"

Her jaw dropped.

"An' I flung that blessed book away just as it was tellin' about breakfast dishes!"

CHAPTER XXIV.

GLASSON IN CHASE.

"*Prospero: Hey, Mountain, hey! Ariel: Silver, there it goes, Silver!*"—THE TEMPEST.

Like most men of fifty or thereabouts, and like every man who finds himself at that age a bachelor rector of a remote country parish, Parson Chichester had collected a number of small habits or superstitions—call them which you will: they are the moss a sensible stone gathers when it has ceased rolling. He smoked a pipe in the house or when he walked abroad, but a Manila cheroot (he belonged to the age of cheroots) when he rode or drove; and he never rode on a Sunday, but either walked or used a dog-cart. Also by habit—or again, if you please, superstition—he preached one sermon, not necessarily a new one, every week.

To-day he had broken through this last custom, but observed the others. After an abbreviated Morning Service he lit a cheroot, climbed into his dog-cart, and drove off towards Meriton at a brisk pace, being due to perform his errand there and report himself at Meriton by three in the afternoon. For luncheon he carried a box of sandwiches and a flask of whisky and water. His horse—a tall, free-stepping bay, by name Archdeacon—was, properly speaking, a hunter, and the Parson, in driving as in riding him, just rattled him along, letting him feel the rein but seldom, or never using it to interfere with his pace.

The entrance gates at Meriton are ancient and extremely handsome, wrought of the old iron of East Sussex, and fashioned, somewhere in the mid-eighteenth century, after an elaborate Florentine pattern—tradition says, by smiths imported from Italy. The pillars are of weather-stained marble, and four in number, the two major ones surrounded by antlered stags, the two minor by cressets of carved flame, symbolising the human soul, and the whole illustrating the singular motto of the Chandons, "*As the hart desireth.*" On either side of the gates is a lodge in the Ionic style, with a pillared portico, and the lodges are shadowed by two immense cedars, the marvel of the country-side.

But to-day the lodges stood empty, with closed doors and drawn blinds—the doors weather-stained, the blinds dingy with dust. Weeds overgrew the bases of the pillars, and grass had encroached upon all but a narrow ribbon scored by wheel-ruts along the noble drive. Parson Chichester pulled up, and was about to dismount and open the gates for himself, when he caught sight of a stranger coming afoot down the drive; and the stranger, at the same moment catching sight of the dog-cart, waved a hand and mended his pace to do this small service.

"Much obliged to you," nodded Parson Chichester pleasantly, after a sharp and curious scrutiny. For the stranger was a parson too by his dress—a tall, elderly man with grey side-whiskers and a hard, square mouth like the slit of a letter-box. The clergy are always curious about one another by a sort of freemasonry, and Parson Chichester knew every beneficed clergyman in the diocese and most of the unbeneficed. But who could this be? And what might be his business at Meriton, of all places?

The stranger acknowledged his thanks with a slight wave of the hand.

"A fine day. I am happy to have been of service."

It was curious. Each paused for a second or so as if on the point of asking a question; each waited for the other to speak; then, as nothing came of it, each bowed again, and thus awkwardly they parted.

Parson Chichester drove on with a pucker between the eyebrows and a humorous twitch in the corners of his mouth. So when two pedestrians, strangers, meet and politely attempt to draw aside but with misdirected *chasses* that leave them still confronting one another, they disengage at length and go their ways between irritation and amusement.

Meriton, one of "the stately homes of England," is a structure in the Palladian style, injudiciously built on the foundations of an older house dating from the fifteenth century, when sites were chosen for the sake of a handy supply of water, and with little regard to view or even to sunshine. It occupies a cup of the hills, is backed by a dark amphitheatre of evergreen trees, and looks across a narrow valley. The farther slope rises abruptly, and has been converted into a park, so to speak, against its will. The stream that flows down the valley bottom has likewise been arrested by art and forced to form a lake with a swannery; but neither lake nor swannery is entirely convincing. It was not, however, its architect's fault that to Parson Chichester the place looked much more stately than homelike, since every window in its really noble facade was shuttered and sightless.

The great entrance porchway lay at the back of the house, in the gloom of a dripping cliff. Here the Parson climbed down and tugged at an iron bell-handle. The bell sounded far within the house, and was answered pretty promptly by the butler, a grizzled, ruddy-faced man, who (it was understood) had followed Sir Miles out of the Service, and carried confirmation of this in the wrinkles about his eyes—those peculiar, unmistakable wrinkles which are only acquired by keeping look-out in many a gale of wind.

"Ah? Good morning, Matters!" said Parson Chichester. "Sorry to disturb you, but I've driven over to ask for Sir Miles's address."

"Certainly, sir. That's curious too," added Mr. Matters half to himself. "His address . . . yes, to be sure, sir, I'll write it down for you. But you must let me get you something in the way of luncheon after your drive. Sir Miles would be annoyed if you went away without— though, the house being closed, you'll pardon deficiencies. As for the horse, sir—"

"I hope I know how to stable him," struck in the Parson. "But I won't stay— thank you all the same. I've eaten my sandwiches on the road, and couldn't make a second meal if you paid me. What's curious, by the way?"

"I beg your pardon, sir?"

"I am quoting you. 'Curious,' you said."

"Ah, to be sure, sir. Well, less than half an hour ago there was a stranger here—a clergyman too—putting the very same question."

"I met him at the lodge gates. Oldish man, grey whiskers, mouth like a trap."

"That's him, sir."

"It's a coincidence, certainly. The more remarkable, I guess, because Meriton nowadays is not much infested with parsons. 'Wonder who he was, and what he wanted?"

"He would not give his name, sir. He wanted the address."

"You gave it to him?"

"I did not, sir."

"Was he annoyed?"

"He was, sir; very much annoyed. He said words to himself, which unless I'm mistaken—"

Matters paused.

Parson Chichester laughed.

"If you had refused *me*, you 'd have heard 'em quite distinctly."

"Yes, sir. The address is, Grand Hotel, Monte Carlo. I heard from Sir Miles only yesterday. You understand, sir, that as a rule he does not choose for everyone to know his movements."

"I do, and am obliged by your confidence. I want it for Miss Sally Breward; and, if this reassures you, I shall give it to her and to no one else."

"I thank you, sir; it was unnecessary. But I may tell you, sir, that Sir Miles has a very high opinion of Miss Sally, as I happen to know."

"We all have, Matters. . . . Well, I have what I came for, and will be driving back to Culvercoombe with it. So good day, and thank you!"

"I thank *you*, sir."

Mr. Matters bowed.

Parson Chichester turned Archdeacon, and put him at his best trotting speed—by a single hint from the reins, no whip needed. This time he had to descend and open the lodge gates for himself. A mile and a half beyond them the road crossed one of the many high brows of the moor, and here on the rise he discerned a black-habited figure trudging along the road ahead.

He recognised the stranger at once, and reined up as he overtook him.

"Good day again, sir! Can I offer you a lift?"

"I thank you," said the stranger. "I am bound for a place called Culvercoombe."

"Why, and so am I! So you must give me the pleasure."

"You are exceedingly kind."

He clambered up, not very skilfully, and the dog-cart bowled on again.

For a while the two kept silence. Then Parson Chichester made an opening—

"You don't belong to these parts?" he asked.

"No. . . . Pardon my curiosity, but are you a friend of Miss Breward's?"

"I believe she would allow me to say 'yes.' By the way, hereabouts we call her Miss Sally. Everyone does—even the butler at Meriton, with whom I was speaking just now."

"Indeed? . . . I am wondering if you would presently add to your kindness by giving me an introduction to her? Trust me," he went on, staring down the road ahead and answering Parson Chichester's quick glance without seeming to perceive it, "you will incur no responsibility. I am not a mendicant priest, and only ask her to favour me with an address, which I believe she can easily give."

"An address?"

The stranger's somewhat grim mouth relaxed a little at the corners.

"The English language," he said, "is full of distracting homonyms. I am not asking her for a sermon, but to be directed where a certain gentleman resides—at present, I have reason to believe, abroad—where, for instance, a letter will reach him."

"Sir Miles Chandon?"

"Precisely. You have hit it. . . . But, to be sure, you were talking just now with his butler. A worthy fellow, I dare say, though suspicious of strangers."

Parson Chichester felt pretty much of a fool, and the more annoyed because unable to detect anything offensive in the tone of the rebuke— if, indeed, a rebuke had been implied.

"Folk in these parts see few strange faces," he said lamely.

"It was the kinder of you to offer me a lift. I had heard, by the way, that Sir Miles's butler did not come from these parts, but was a much-travelled man."

"That is so."

Mr. Chichester felt that he was getting very markedly the worst of this conversation, and decided to let it drop. But just as he had arrived at this decision the stranger faced around and asked—

"Perhaps *you* know Sir Miles's present address?"

At this point-blank question Mr. Chichester's face grew very red indeed. He had brought it on himself. Denial was useless.

"Perhaps I do," he answered. "But you were going to ask Miss Sally for it, and we will leave it to her."

"Quite right," the stranger assented. "Here is my own card, though it will convey nothing to you."

But it conveyed a great deal. Parson Chichester reached across with his disengaged right hand, took the card and read—

>   The Reverend Purdie J. Glasson, LL.D.,
>   Holy Innocents' Orphanage,
>   Bursfield.

The words danced before his eyes. Imagine some unskilled player pitted against an expert at cards, awake at one moment to his weakness, and the next overwhelmingly aware that his opponent, by an incredible blunder, is delivered into his hands. The elation of it fairly frightened Mr. Chichester, and he so far forgot himself as to take up his whip and administer a sharp flick on Archdeacon's shoulder—an outrage which the good horse, after an instant of amazement, resented by a creditable attempt to bolt. This was probably the best that could have happened. It gave the Parson a job he understood, and for five minutes effectually prevented his speaking.

They had almost reached the entrance gate of Culvercoombe before he reduced the affronted horse to a trot, and Doctor Glasson, who had been clutching the rail of the dog-cart in acutest physical terror, had no nerve as yet to resume the conversation. A lodge-keeper ran out and opened the gate (service under Miss Sally was always alert), and they rolled smoothly down the well-gravelled drive through an avenue of yellowing sycamores.

A couple of aged mastiff bitches—mothers in their time, and now great-grandmothers, of a noble race—lay sunning themselves before the house-porch. They recognised the parson's dog-cart and heaved themselves up, wagging their tails to welcome a respected, if rare, visitor; but growled at sight of his companion. Their names were Tryphena and Tryphosa.

Parson Chichester alighted and rang the bell, after handing the reins to Doctor Glasson with an apology.

"I'll get the groom sent round in a moment," he explained, and to the butler who opened the door, "Miss Sally is expecting me, eh, Butts?"

"In the yellow drawing-room, y'r worship."

The Parson was a magistrate, and, for no known reason, Butts always addressed him as such.

"Very well, I'll find my way to her. Send someone around to take the dog-cart, and as soon as he comes, take this gentleman inside until your mistress rings. Understand?"

"I understand, y'r worship."

"Then be as brisk as you can, for the horse is fresh to-day."

"He 'as aperiently been workin' hisself into a lather, y'r worship," said Butts. "Which I 'ave noticed, sir, your 'abit—or, as I may say, your custom—of bringin' 'im in cool."

But Parson Chichester had left him, and was making his way across the hall to the yellow drawing-room, which he entered with little ceremony. Miss Sally rose to receive him. She had been sitting in its oriel window with a small table before her, and on the table a Bible. This was her rule on a Sunday afternoon, and every Sunday after luncheon she donned a pair of spectacles. Butts, who knew her habits to a hair, brought the spectacles once a week and laid the book open at his favourite passages. For aught it mattered, he might have opened it upside-down.

"You're pretty punctual," said Miss Sally. "Before your time, if anything."

"Yes; the horse bolted, or tried to," Mr. Chichester explained.
"Guess whom I've brought with me."

"Not Miles Chandon?"

"No; he's at Monte Carlo. His address, the Grand Hotel. Guess again."

"Don't be foolish and waste time. The children may be arriving at any minute."

"You must keep 'em out of the way, then."

"Why?"

"Because I've brought him."

"'Him'? You'll excuse me—"

"Glasson."

"Glasson?" Her eyes opened wide. "You've brought Glasson? Well, I must say you're clever."

"On the contrary, I've been infernally stupid. I met him coming down the drive from Meriton. He had been pumping Matters for Sir Miles's present address—which he didn't get. What's his game, do you think?"

"Blackmail."

"That crossed my mind too. He seems a deep one, and I don't like his looks."

"You are sure it is Glasson?"

Parson Chichester produced the card, badly crumpled, from his riding-glove. Miss Sally pushed her Sunday spectacles higher on her brows and examined it with her clear eyes.

"This," she said "is going to be a treat. The man cannot possibly have guessed that the children are in this neighbourhood. You haven't enlightened him, I hope?"

"Certainly not," Mr. Chichester answered indignantly.

"Well, you said a moment since that you'd been infernally stupid, and I don't yet know what form it took."

"I let him know what I'd discovered—that he had been pumping Matters for Sir Miles's address."

"There is no harm in that. He can have the address from me as soon as he likes."

"But surely you see through his game? He has tracked out the boy's parentage, and he's out after blackmail."

"To be sure he is; and, what's more, he's going to have a run for his money. What on earth is the matter outside?"

For a noise of furious barking had broken out suddenly, and, as she spoke, there mingled with it a sound very like a human scream.

Miss Sally hurried out to the hall, the parson close at her heels. They had scarcely crossed the threshold when Doctor Glasson staggered by them like a maniac, with Tryphosa hanging on to his clerical skirts and Tryphena in full cry behind. Butts brought up the rear of the chase, vainly shouting to call them off.

"Down, Tryphosa!" Miss Sally ran in, planted a well-directed kick on the mastiff's ribs, caught her by the scruff of the neck and banged her ears. "Back, you brutes!"

Catching a dog-whip down from the rack, she lashed and drove them yelping; while Glasson flung himself on a couch and lay panting, with a sickly yellow face and a hand pressed to his heart.

"Oh, ma'am, your lady dogs!"

"'Bitches' in the country, Doctor Glasson. I must apologise for them. Butts, bring some brandy and water to the drawing-room. . . . Not bitten, I hope? If the skin's broken we had better cauterise."

Miss Sally confessed afterwards that she would have enjoyed operating on the man with a red-hot poker: "and I'd have used the biggest poker in the house." But Doctor Glasson arose, felt himself, and announced that it was unnecessary.

"Mr. Chichester tells me you wish for Sir Miles Chandon's address. He was, until a couple of days ago, at the Grand Hotel, Monte Carlo, and I have no doubt is there yet."

Doctor Glasson's face fell somewhat.

"I thank you," he murmured. "It is a long distance."

"A letter will reach him in less than two days."

"Yes," said Glasson, and said no more.

"But a letter addressed to him at Meriton would, of course, be forwarded. So I conclude you wish to see him personally. Are you— pardon the question— a friend of his?"

"Not a personal friend, ma'am. I came to see him on a matter of business."

"From Bursfield," said Miss Sally, with a glance at the card.

It was a superstition with Glasson to tell the truth about trifles.

"From Plymouth, to be exact, ma'am. I have been indulging in a—er— brief holiday."

"Ah," thought Miss Sally to herself, "researching, no doubt!"

Aloud she said—

"Well, I am sorry, sir; but Monte Carlo's the address, and that's all I can do for you except to offer you some refreshment, and—yes, let me see—you are returning to-night?"

"As speedily as possible, ma'am."

"Sunday trains are awkward. There is one at Fair Anchor at 4.35, and after that no other until the 7.12, which picks up the evening mail at Taunton. You are on foot, I understand, and will certainly not catch the first unless you let my man drive you over."

Doctor Glasson was evidently anxious to get away at the earliest moment. He protested, with many thanks, that he was trespassing on her kindness.

"Not a bit," said Miss Sally; "and you shall be as comfortable as we can make you in the barouche. Mr. Chichester, would you mind stepping out and ringing them up at the stables, while Butts is bringing the brandy?"

The Parson guessed that she was sending him with a purpose; and he was right, for he had scarcely left the room when, on an excuse, she followed him.

"Tossell and the children are about due. This man must not see them, of course. As you leave the stables you go up on the Inistow road and head 'em off—keep 'em out of sight until the barouche is past the cross-roads and on the way to Fair Anchor."

He nodded, and having left his order with the coachman, climbed by a footpath to a rise of the moor whence he commanded a view of the cross-roads on his right, and on his left of the road running northward like a pale ribbon across the brown heather. Neither vehicle nor horseman was in sight. Nor, though he waited more than half an hour, did any appear coming from the direction of Inistow.

At the end of that time, however, he saw the barouche roll past the cross-roads towards Fair Anchor. The coast was clear. So, wondering a little at the farmer's delay, he wended his way back to Culvercoombe. To his amazement, in the hall he ran against Butts carrying a portmanteau, and at the same moment Miss Sally issued from the yellow drawing-room with a Bradshaw in her hand.

"Where are the children?" she asked.

"Nowhere in sight."

"That's odd. Tossell's punctual in everything as a rule—rent included. Well, I must leave you to keep an eye on them. . . . Do you know anything about Bursfield? The best hotel there, for instance? I see there are two advertised here, The Imperial—everything's Imperial nowadays—with a night-porter and a lift—I detest lifts—never use 'em—and the Grand Central, family and commercial, electric light. I abominate commercials, but they know how to feed. Why the deuce can't these people advertise something worth knowing? Electric light—who wants to eat overdone steaks by electricity?"

"But, my dear lady, why this sudden curiosity about Bursfield and its hotels?"

"Because, my dear man, I'm going there, to-night; by the 7.12. Butts has just carried my portmanteau upstairs."

"Your portmanteau?"

"Yes; I don't believe in trunks and dress boxes—my things will bear folding, and Humphreys"—meaning her maid—"is already folding 'em. Man, don't stare. I'm going to have the time of my life at Bursfield in Glasson's absence. You saw Glasson depart? Well, he didn't tell; but you may pack me in another portmanteau if he's not posting off to Monte Carlo."

"Well?"

"Well, he won't find Miles Chandon there. Because why? Because I've written out this telegram, which I'll trouble you to send as soon as the post office opens to-morrow. Nuisance there's no telegraphing in the country on Sundays. I thought of getting a porter to dispatch it for me at Taunton; but it wouldn't reach Monte Carlo until some unearthly hour, and we've plenty of time. Miles Chandon will get it to-morrow, probably just as Glasson is beginning to get on terms with the Channel crossing. He's the very subject for sea-sickness, the brute! . . . And the two will probably pass one another at some time in the middle of the night, while I'm sleeping like a top after a happy day at Bursfield."

"You count on Chandon's coming?"

"Here's the telegram—'*Return Meriton Wednesday at latest. Important. Sally Breward.*'"

"Will that fetch him?"

"Of course it will. Miles Chandon owes me something, as I think I told you, and is a gentleman moreover."

"Oh, very well, I'll send it, and I have only one other question. What precisely is your business at Bursfield?"

Miss Sally grinned.

"Hay-making," she answered, "while the sun shines—that is to say, in Glasson's absence. I propose to make a considerable deal of hay. Something will depend on Mr. Hucks; but from the child's account of him, I build great hopes on Mr. Hucks. . . . There's one thing more. I've sent the barouche to the station. If I drive my own cart over to Fair Anchor, there's nobody but Butts to bring it back, and you know Butts's driving. If I take the brown, the brown'll bolt with him, and if I take the chestnut filly he'll let her down. So I must commandeer you and Archdeacon."

Accordingly Parson Chichester drove Miss Sally over to the station, and bestowed her comfortably in the 7.12 up train. She was in the highest spirits. Having dispatched her and watched the train out of sight, the parson lit his lamps, climbed into his dog-cart again, and headed Archdeacon back for home.

He had struck the Inistow road, when his ear caught the beat of hoofs approaching at a gallop through the darkness. He quartered and cried hullo! as the rider drew close. On the moors it was unusual to meet a rider at night; nobody rode so hard unless for a doctor, and no doctor dwelt in this direction.

"Hullo, friend!"

"Hullo!"

The rider reined up, and by the light of his lamps Parson Chichester recognised the young giant Roger.

"What's your errand, my friend?"

"To Culvercoombe. The children—"

"Miss Sally has left by the night train. I drove her over to Fair Anchor myself. What of the children? We were expecting them all the afternoon."

"They are gone—lost! Last night, as we reckon, they took the boat and made a bolt for it. All this day we've been searching, and an hour agone word comes from the coast-guard that the boat has driven ashore, empty, on Clatworthy beach."

CHAPTER XXV.

MISS SALLY BREAKS THE DOORS.

"*And to shew Thy pity upon all prisoners and captives.*"—THE LITANY

Mr. Hucks sat in his counting-house, counting out his money—or so much of it as he had collected from his tenantry on his Saturday rounds. It amounted to 12 pounds 2 shillings and 9 pence in cash; but to this must be added a caged bullfinch, a pair of dumb-bells, a down mattress and an ophicleide. He had coveted the ophicleide for weeks; but he knew how to wait, and in the end it had fallen to his hand—if the simile may be permitted—like a ripe peach.

The clock at the Great Brewery struck ten, the hour at which the banks opened. Mr. Hucks whistled to himself softly, but out of tune—sure sign that he was in a good humour—as he closed the neck of his money-bag and tied the string with a neat knot. Just as he was reaching, however, for coat and walking-stick, someone knocked at the door.

"Come in!" he called, and resumed his seat as a lady entered—a stranger to him. At first glance he guessed she might be the wife of some impecunious musician, come to plead for restitution of an instrument. Such things happened now and again on Monday mornings; nor was the mistake without excuse in Miss Sally's attire. When travelling without her maid she had a way of putting on anything handy, and in the order more or less as it came to hand. Without specifying, it may be said that two or three articles usually ranked as underclothing had this morning partially worked their way up to the top stratum, and that by consequence her person presented more than one example of what geologists call a "fault"—though it is actually rather a misfortune. As for her hat, she had started by putting it on sideways, and then, since it would not "sit," and she had mislaid her hat-pins, had bound it boldly in place with a grey woollen comforter, and knotted the ends under her chin. What gave Mr. Hucks pause was, first, the brusqueness of her entry, and next, the high clear tone of her accost.

"Mr. Christopher Hucks?"

"At your service, ma'am."

"I hope so, because I want your help."

"As for that, ma'am, I don't know who sent you; but it ain't generally reckoned in my line."

Miss Sally glanced round the counting-house.

"You have the materials for doing quite a lot of miscellaneous good in the world. But I'm not come to borrow money, if that makes you easier—"

"It do, ma'am."

"—and I don't know a note of music."

"Me either," murmured Mr. Hucks regretfully.

"That being so, we'll come to business. May I take a seat?"

"Where you—" He was going to say "please," but substituted "choose"

"Thank you. My name's Breward—Sally Breward, and I live at a place called Culvercoombe, on the Devon and Somerset border. My business is that I'm interested in a couple of children, about whom you know something. They broke out, some days ago, from an Orphanage kept here by one Glasson; and I gather that you gave them a helping hand."

"Whoever told you that—" began Mr. Hucks.

"Nobody told me. I said that I gathered it. The girl never gave you away for a moment. We will agree, if you prefer it, that I put two and two together. But look here: you can be open with me or not, as you please; I'm going to be open with you. And first let me say that the boy is pretty certainly the son of a neighbour of mine, and heir to considerable estates."

Mr. Hucks whistled softly to himself.

"As for the girl who helped him to escape, she's probably just what she says—a show-child who, happening to be laid up lame in hospital, chanced on this scent, and has held to it—to make an addition of my own—with the pluck of a terrier."

Mr. Hucks nodded, but would not commit himself.

"Where are they now?" he asked. "In your keepin'?"

"That's just the trouble." Miss Sally unfolded a scrap of pinkish-coloured paper. "I left them in good keeping with an honest farmer and his wife—tenants of mine; I had a telegram sent to the boy's father, who is abroad; and I posted up here by night mail to satisfy myself by a few inquiries."

"You've seen Glasson, then?" Mr. Hucks interrupted.

"I have; but not in any way you suspect. I haven't called, for instance, at the Orphanage—though I intend to. Glasson's not at home. He was down in my neighbourhood yesterday afternoon, nosing around for information."

"Then he knows the children are thereabouts?"

"No, he does not. But has been pushing researches. He has learnt who is the boy's probable father, and where he lives—at a place called Meriton. He came to Meriton to get the father's foreign address, and when the butler refused it, he called on me."

"I see." Mr. Hucks nodded. "And you refused it too?"

"I did better. I gave it to him—"

"Eh?"

"—at the same time taking care that the father—his name is Chandon, by the way, and he's a baronet—should get a wire from me to come home by the first train he can catch. By this means, you see, I not only get Glasson out of the neighbourhood, where he might have run against the children, or picked up news of them, but I send him all the way to the South of France expressly to find his bird flown. It's cruel, I grant you; but I've no tenderness for blackmailers—especially when they keep Orphanages."

"You're right there. You've no call to waste any pity on Glasson. But the question is, Will he come? The father, I mean."

"Certainly, since I tell him," Miss Sally answered with composure.

"And him a bart—a bloomin' bart—what the Tichborne chap used to call a bart of the B.K.!"

Mr. Hucks stared at his visitor with rounded eyes, drew a long breath, puffed out his cheeks and emitted it, and wound up by removing his hat and laying it on the ledge of the desk.

"Well," said he, "you've done it clever. You've done it so mighty clever that I don't see why you come to me to help. *I* can't order barts about."

"No," said Miss Sally; "in this part of the business I fear you cannot help. Read *that*, please."

She spread open the telegraph form which she had been holding all this while, and laid it on the desk before him.

"Breward, Grand Central Hotel, Bursfield."
"'Regret to say children missing. Supposed left Inistow Cove Tossell's boat Saturday night. Boat found ashore Clatworthy Beach. Search parties along coast. Will report any news.—Chichester.'"

"When did you get this, ma'am, making so bold?"

"At nine this morning. If you look, you will see the telegram was handed in at 8.37, and received here at 8.50—is it not? The sender is a Mr. Chichester, a clergyman and a friend of mine."

"Aye," said Mr. Hucks, after slowly examining the telegram and the office stamp. He raised his formidable grey eyes and fixed them full on Miss Sally.

"Oh," she said after awhile, but without blanching, "I see what's in your mind."

"No you don't," he answered abruptly. "It *did* cross my mind, but it's not there any longer. You're straight. And you're quality—though maybe your kind don't answer to the pictcher-books. . . . Well, about this wire now. . . . What's your opinion?"

"Why, that the children are lost."

"Meanin' by that drowned—or just missing?"

"From that message what must one conclude?"

"Well," said Mr. Hucks slowly, after another perusal of the telegram, "I don't conclude much from it; but from my knowledge of the gal-child, I jolly well conclude that they're no more drowned than you or me. They've just made another bolt for it, and the shipwrecked boat's no more than a blind."

"They were comfortable enough at Inistow Farm. Why should they want to bolt?" Miss Sally urged.

"Because, ma'am, that gal has a business conscience developed to a degree I never struck yet in man or woman. You've dealt open with me, and I'll deal open with you. I *did* help that pair to give Glasson the slip; not from any kindheartedness, I'd have you to know, if you're thinkin' to accuse me of it; but as a kind of by-speculation. For I saw that dirty thief Glasson was mad to get the boy back, and it seemed to me there was likely some money in it. I gave 'em their chance, yes; because it happened so, and I couldn't see no other way. Now, observe me—that gal knew all the time I wasn't doing it for my health, as you might say; she knew well enough I was just as hard as Glasson, though maybe in a different way. She knew this, and as things turned out, she might have run off with the boy and snapped her fingers at me. But does she? Nothing o' the sort. She freezes to her bargain, same as if she'd all a lawyer's knowledge and none of his conscience. First, she clears me back every penny I've invested in Mortimer, and with interest; and I'm the first man that ever invested on that scamp and saw his money again. When that's paid she strikes out on a trail of her own—but not to lose herself and the boy: not she. At every halt she reports herself and him; and by her last I was to write to her at a place called Holmness, which I posted a letter there yesterday."

"Holmness!" ejaculated Miss Sally. "Holmness, did you say?"

"That's so. Might it be anywhere in your parts?"

"Of course it is. But Holmness, my good sir, is an island."

"She mentioned that, now I come to think of it. Island or not, she'll get there, if she bursts; and I won't believe other till I hear from the Dead Letter Office."

"You addressed a letter to Holmness? . . . But it's too absurd; the place is a mere barren rock, three good miles from the mainland. Nothing there but rabbits, and in summer a few sheep."

"Mayhap she didn't know it when she gave the address. But," persisted Mr. Hucks doggedly, "she's there if she's alive. You go back and try."

[He gave Tilda, as the reader knows, more credit than she deserved; but from this may be deduced a sound moral—that the value of probity, as an asset in dealing, is quite incalculable.]

Miss Sally considered for a full minute—for two minutes, Mr. Hucks watching her face from under his shaggy eyebrows.

"It is barely possible," she owned at length. "But supposing they have reached Holmness, it can only be to starve. Good Lord! they may be starving to death there at this moment!"

Mr. Hucks kept his composure.

"It's plain to me you haven't measured that gal," he said slowly. "Is this Holmness in sight from the farm—whatever you call it—where they were missed?"

"Right opposite the coast there."

"And not more than three miles away? Then you may take it she won't have started without provisions. It wouldn't be her way."

[Again, the reader perceives, he gave Tilda undeserved credit; but always in this world the Arthur Miles's will be left out of account by men of business, to upset again and again their calculations.]

"So," he continued, "there's no need for you to be running and sending telegrams to folks there to chivvy 'em. Take the next train home and pick up the credit yourself."

"Mr. Hucks," said Miss Sally after a pause, "you are a remarkable man. I am half inclined to believe you; and if you should prove to be right, I shall not know how to repay you."

"Well," said Mr. Hucks, "it seems likely I've helped, after all. I'm not pressing for payment; though, as between persons of business, I'm glad you mention it."

"If these children are recovered, you shall name any price in reason. But there is another matter in which you can help me, I hope. I want admission to Glasson's Orphanage."

"The 'Oly Innocents? It goes by nomination, and I'm not a subscriber," said Mr. Hucks with a grin, which Miss Sally ignored.

"Will it be enough if I call and ask to be shown over the institution?"

"Quite enough—to get the door slammed in your face."

"Well, I mean to have a look inside, even though I get you to put me in a sack and lower me into the coal-cellar."

"That's an idea, though," said Mr. Hucks rising.

He went to the door and, stepping into the yard, emitted a loud roar like the bellow of a bull. Apparently it was his method of telephoning to his employees. After a moment a distant voice called back, "Aye, aye, boss!"

"Where's Sam Bossom?"

"In the stables."

"Then send him along here, and tell him to look sharp. He's the man for our job," explained Mr. Hucks, returning to the counting-house; "and maybe you'll like to make his acquaintance, too, after what you've 'eard."

"Before he comes I should like even better to hear your plan of campaign; for it seems that you have one."

"I have; but it being what you might call a trifle 'igh-'anded, I wasn't proposin' to drag a lady into it—leastways, not to make her an accomplice before the fac'."

"I'll risk that," she assured him.

"Well, you see, Glasson owes me for coal; thirteen ten on the last lot delivered, and six pounds owin' before that—total nineteen ten. I warned him he'd got the last lot out o' me by a trick; an' I'm goin' to send Sam to see if there's a chance to recover it. That'll be by the back way—same as the children got out. Eh? Here's the man," he wound up as Sam Bossom's honest face appeared in the doorway.

"Good morning, Mr. Bossom." Miss Sally held out a hand. "I'm proud to make your acquaintance."

"Thank ye, ma'am." Sam looked at the hand, but rubbed his own up and down the seat of his trousers. "What for, if it's not makin' too bold?"

"The lady here," explained Mr. Hucks, "is a friend of two children that broke out of 'Oly Innocents t'other day—as it maybe you'll remember. What's more, she 's brought news o' them."

"Oh!" said Sam, his face clearing. "Doin' pretty well, I 'ope?"

"They were quite well when I left them, two days ago. Come, shake hands and tell me. How is everyone at the 'Four Alls'?"

"If it 'adn't been for them children—" blurted Sam, and came to a full stop.

Miss Sally nodded.

"They are wonders, those Babes in the Wood; and the funniest thing about 'em is, while they went along asking their way, they were all the time teaching it to others."

"Well," struck in Mr. Hucks, while Sam scratched his head over this, "I suggest the conspiracy may just as well get going at once. Sam, I want you to step along to 'Oly Innocents with us, and on the road I'll fix up *your* modest hopper'andy."

Of this *modus operandi* the opening move was made as the trio reached the confines of the Orphanage premises. Here, by the angle of the red brick wall, Mr. Bossom halted to strike a match for his pipe. He struck it upon the iron cover of the manhole, and thus made opportunity to assure himself that the cover was still removable. Satisfied of this, he lit his pipe and stood for a minute puffing at it, and staring, now at the stagnant canal water, now after the retreating figures of Miss Sally and Mr. Hucks, as without a backward look they passed down the towpath to the Iron Bridge.

At the bridge they turned, as Tilda had turned, to the left, and came, as Tilda had come, to the Orphanage gate with its box labelled, "For Voluntary Donations."

Mr. Hucks rang the bell; and after a minute or so Mrs. Huggins, slatternly as ever, opened the front door and came shuffling down the pathway.

"Eh?" said she, halting within the gate, a pilaster of which hid Miss Sally from her. "Mr. 'Ucks? And what might *you* be wantin', Mr. 'Ucks?"

"Nineteen pound ten," Mr. Hucks answered tersely.

"Then you can't 'ave it."

"That's a pity." He appeared to ruminate for a second or two. "And I can't offer to take it out in orphans, neither. Very well, then, I must see Glasson."

"You can't; 'e's not at 'ome."

"That's a worse pity. Hist, now!" he went on with a sudden change of tone, "it's about the runaways. I've news of 'em."

He said it at the top of his voice.

"For the Lord's sake—" entreated the woman, glancing nervously across his shoulder at the traffic in the street. "The Doctor don't want it discussed for all the town to 'ear."

"No, I bet he don't. But it's your own fault, missus. This side o' the gate a man can't scarcely hear hisself speak."

"Come in, then, if you've brought news. The Doctor'll be glad enough when 'e comes back."

"Will he?" Mr. Hucks, as she opened, planted his bulk against the gate, pushing it back and at the same time making way for Miss Sally to follow him. "Yes, I got news; but here's a lady can tell it better than me— 'avin' come acrost them right away down in Somerset."

Mrs. Huggins stepped forward, but too late. "I don't want no crowd in 'ere," she muttered, falling back a pace, however, as Miss Sally confronted her.

"You'll have one in two two's if you make any disturbance," Miss Sally promised her, with half a glance back at the street. "Show me into the house, if you please."

"Shan't."

The woman placed herself in the pathway, with arms akimbo, barring her passage.

"You behave very foolishly in denying me," said Miss Sally.

"Maybe; but I got my orders. *You* never took no orders from a man, I should say—not by the looks o' yer."

"You are right there."

Miss Sally regarded her with a smile of conscious strength, stern but good-natured. Her gaze wandered past the woman's shoulder, and the smile broadened. Mrs. Huggins saw it broaden, and cast a look behind her, towards the house—to see Mr. Bossom, coal-grimed but cheerful, grinning down on her from the front door-step.

"It's a trap!" she gasped, shooting a venomous look at Mr. Hucks.

"It *looks* like one," said Miss Sally, stepping past her; "and I shall be curious to know, by and by, who baited it."

"Where shall I take ye, ma'am?" asked Sam Bossom.

"Show me the children first, if you please."

He walked before her down the unsavoury passage. He was unacquainted with the interior, and knew only that the way through the kitchens, by which he had come, led to the kitchen garden and missed the children's quarters. Avoiding this, and opening a door at random—a door on his right—he stepped into the bare drawing-room. Miss Sally followed, and Mrs. Huggins at her heels, protesting. Mr. Hucks brought up the rear. Finding himself in an apartment which apparently led nowhither, Sam would have turned and shepherded the party back into the corridor; but Miss Sally strode past him, attempted to fling up the window-sash, but in vain, and looking over it, beheld what Tilda had beheld—the gravelled yard, the children walking listlessly to and fro, the groups passing and repassing with scarce a lift of the eyes, the boys walking with the boys and the girls with the girls.

"But it is horrible—horrible!" cried Miss Sally. "Mr. Hucks, lend me your stick, if you please. This window won't open."

He passed his stick to her, supposing that she meant in some way to prise the window open. But she took it and deliberately smashed a pane—two panes—all the six panes with their coloured transparencies of the Prodigal Son. And the worst was, that the children in the yard, as the glass broke and fell, scarcely betrayed surprise. One or two glanced furtively towards the window. It seemed that they dared do no more.

"Save us!" exclaimed Miss Sally. "They're starving; that's what's the matter!"

"They are not, ma'am!" still protested Mrs. Huggins.

"Tut, woman, don't talk to *me*. I've bred cattle, and I know. Fetch me a list of the pious persons that have lent their names to this swindle. You, Mr. Hucks, take me upstairs; I'll explore this den from garret to basement, though it cost my stomach all that by the smell I judge it will. And you, Sam Bossom—here's a five-pound note: take it to the nearest pastry-cook's and buy up the stock. Fetch it here in cabs; hire every cab you meet on the way; and when you've brought 'em, tell 'em to wait!"

An hour later a procession of fifteen cabs drove up to the Grand Central Hotel, Bursfield, to the frank dismay of hall-porters and manager; a dismay which Miss Sally accepted with the lordliest indifference.

"You see that they're stowed," she advised Mr. Hucks shortly, as they helped the dazed children to alight. "And if there's any difficulty, send the manager to me. He'll find me in the telegraph office." She consulted a prospectus of the Holy Innocents, extorted from Mrs. Huggins. "I shall be there for an hour at least. There are two dozen patrons on this list—besides a score of executive committee, and I'm going—bless you, Mr. Hucks—to give those philanthropists the dry grins."

"A telegram for you, ma'am," said the hall-porter, advancing with a nervous eye on the children congregated, and still congregating, in the hall.

Miss Sally took it and read:—

"Coming Fair Anchor, 4.30 Tuesday. Chandon."

She knit her brows and examined the telegraph form carefully. The message was forwarded from Fair Anchor. It had been handed in at the Monte Carlo post office on Sunday night, addressed to Culvercoombe, but at what hour she could not decipher. The Fair Anchor office was closed on Sunday, and opened on Monday at eight o'clock. The telegram had been received there at 8.12; had been taken to Culvercoombe, and apparently re-transmitted at 12.15. All this was unimportant. But how on earth had her telegram, to which this was evidently a reply, reached Monte Carlo on Sunday evening—last evening?

She considered awhile, and hit on the explanation. Parson Chichester last evening, calling on the coast-guard in his search, must have used their telephone and got the message through by some office open on Sundays.

CHAPTER XXVI.

THE RESCUE

"*O, who lives on the Island,*
  Betwix' the sea an' the sky?
—I think it must be a lady, a lady,
I think it must be a genuwine lady,
  She carries her head so high."—OLD BALLAD.

In the moonlit garden of the Casino at Monte Carlo Miles Chandon smoked a cigar pensively, leaning against the low wall that overlooks the pigeon-shooters' enclosure, the railway station and the foreshore. He was alone, as always. That a man who, since the great folly of his life, had obstinately cultivated solitude should make holiday in Monte Carlo, of all places, is paradoxical enough; but in truth the crowd around the tables, the diners at the hotel, the pigeon-shooters, the whole cosmopolitan gathering of idle rich and predatory poor, were a Spectacle to him and no more. If once or twice a day he staked a few napoleons on black or red in the inner room of the Casino, it was as a man, finding himself at Homburg or Marienbad, might take a drink of the waters from curiosity and to fill up the time. He made no friends in the throng. He found no pleasure in it. But when he grew weary at home in his laboratory, or when his doctor advised that confinement and too much poring over chemicals were telling on his health, he packed up and made for Monte Carlo, or some other expensive place popularly supposed to be a "pleasure-resort." As a matter of fact, he did not understand pleasure, or what it means.

Finding him in this pensive attitude in the moonlit garden by the sea, you might guess that he was sentimentalising over his past. He was doing nothing of the sort. He was watching a small greyish-white object the moon revealed on the roof of the railway station below, just within the parapet. He knew it to be a pigeon that had escaped, wounded, from the sportsmen in the enclosure. Late that afternoon he had seen the poor creature fluttering. He wondered that the officials (at Monte Carlo they clean up everything) had not seen it before and removed it. He watched it, curious to know if it were still alive. He had a fancy at the back of his head—that if the small body fluttered again he would go back to his rooms, fetch a revolver, and give the *coup de grace*. And he smiled as he played with the fancy, foreseeing the rush of agitated officials that a revolver-shot in the gardens would instantly bring upon him. It would be great fun, explaining; but the offence no doubt would be punishable. By what? Banishment, probably.

He turned for a moment at the sound of a footstep, and was aware of his man Louis.

"A telegram, sir."

"Eh? Now who in the world—Matters hasn't burnt down Meriton, I hope?"

He opened the telegram and walked with it to the nearest of the electric lamps; read it, and stood pondering.

"Louis, when does the new night-express leave for Paris?"

"In twenty-five minutes, sir."

"Then I've a mind to catch it. Put up a travelling-suit in my bag. I can get out of these clothes in the train. You had better pack the rest, pay the bill, and follow to-morrow."

"If you wish it, sir. But if I may suggest—"

"Yes?"

"In twenty minutes I can do all that easily, and book the sleeping-berths too. I suggest, sir, you will find it more comfortable, having me on the train."

"Admirable man—hurry up, then!"

The admirable man saluted respectfully and retired "hurt," as they say in the cricket reports. He never hurried; it was part of the secret by which he was always punctual. At the station he even found time to suggest that his master might wish to send a telegram, and to dispatch it.

This was on Sunday. They reached London late on Monday evening, and there—Louis having telegraphed from Paris—Sir Miles found his favourite room ready for him at Claridge's. Next morning, as his hansom drew up a few minutes after eleven o'clock by the entrance to Paddington Station, he observed that the porter who stepped forward from the rank to attend on him, did so with a preoccupied air. The man was grinning, and kept glancing along the pavement to his right.

"Luggage on the cab just behind," said Sir Miles, alighting.
"Never mind me; my man will take the tickets and get me a seat. But what's the excitement here?"

"Lady along there, sir—offering to fight her cabby. Says he can't drive for nuts—"

"Hullo!"

Sir Miles looked, recognised Miss Sally, and walked briskly towards her. She caught sight of him and nodded.

"Thought you would come. Excuse me a moment."

She lifted her voice and addressed the cabby again—

"Oh, you can talk. They taught you that at the Board School, no doubt. But drive you cannot; and talk you would not, if you knew the respect due to a mouth—your own or your horse's."

With this parting shot she turned to Sir Miles again, and held out her hand.

"Tell your man he needn't trouble about a seat for you. I've engaged a compartment where we can talk."

"Well?" he asked, ten minutes later, lowering his newspaper as the train drew out of the station.

"Well, in the first place, it's very good of you to come."

"Oh, as for that . . . You know that if I can ever do you any service—"

"But you can't. It was for your own sake I telegraphed."

"Mine? Is Meriton really burnt to the ground, then? But even that news wouldn't gravely afflict me."

"It isn't—and it would. At any rate, it might now, I hope," said Miss Sally enigmatically.

He waited for her to continue.

"Your wife's dead!" she said.

She heard him draw a quick breath.

"Indeed?" he asked indifferently.

"But your son isn't—at least, I hope not."

He looked up and met her eyes.

"But I had word," he said slowly, "word from her, and in her own handwriting. A boy was born, and died six or seven weeks later—as I remember, the letter said within a week after his christening."

Miss Sally nodded.

"That settles it," she said; "being untrue, as I happen to know. The child was alive and hearty a year after the christening, when they left Cawsand and moved to the East coast. The fact is, my friend, you had run up—if not in your wife, then in the coastguardsman Ned Commins—against a pride as stubborn as your own. They wrote you a lie—that's certain; and I'm as hard as most upon liars; but, considering all, I don't blame 'em. They weren't mercenary, anyway. They only wanted to have no more truck with you."

"Have you seen the boy?"

Again Miss Sally nodded.

"Yes, and there's no doubting the parentage. I never saw that cross-hatched under-lip in any but a Chandon, though you *do* hide it with a beard: let alone that he carries the four lozenges tattooed on his shoulder. Ned Commins did that. There was a moment, belike, when they weakened—either he or the woman. But you had best hear the story, and then you can judge the evidence for yourself."

She told it. He listened with set face, interposing here and there to ask a question, or to weigh one detail of her narrative against another.

"If the children should be lost—which God forbid!" she wound up, "—and if I never did another good day's work in my life, I'll remember that they started me to clear that infernal Orphanage. It's by the interposition of Heaven that you didn't find me on Paddington platform with three-and-twenty children under my wing. 'Interposition of Heaven,' did I say? You may call it, if you will, the constant and consistent foolishness of my brother Elphinstone. In every tight corner of my life I've learnt to trust in Elphinstone for a fool, and he has never betrayed me yet. There I was in the hotel with these twenty-three derelicts, all underfed, and all more or less mentally defective through Glasson's ill-treatment. Two or three were actually crying, in a feeble way, to be 'taken home,' as they called it. They were afraid—afraid of their kind, afraid of strange faces, afraid of everything but to be starved and whipped. I was forced to send out and buy new clothes for some, there and then; and their backs, when I stripped 'em, were criss-crossed with weals—not quite fresh, you understand, for Glasson had been kept busy of late, and the woman Huggins hadn't his arm. Well, there I was, stranded, with these creatures on my hands, all of 'em, as you may say, looking up at me in a dumb way, and wanting to know why I couldn't have let 'em alone—and if ever I smash up another Orphanage you may call me a Turk, and put me in a harem—when all of a sudden it occurred to me to look up the names of the benevolent parties backing the institution. The woman had given me a copy of the prospectus, intending to impress me. I promised myself I'd rattle these philanthropists as they 'd never been rattled before in their lives. And then—why had I ever doubted him?—half-way down the list I lit on Elphinstone's name. . . . His place is at Henley-in-Arden, you see, and not far from Bursfield. . . . So I rattled the others (I spent three-quarters of an hour in the telegraph office, and before eleven last night I had thirty-two answers. They are all in my bag, and you shall look 'em over by and by, if you want to be tickled), but I sent Elphinstone what the girl Tilda would call a cough-drop. It ran to five sheets or thereabouts, and cost four-and-eightpence; and I wound up by telling him I meant every word I'd said. He's in Bursfield at this moment, you may bet, carting those orphans around into temporary quarters. And Elphinstone is a kind-hearted man, but orphans are not exactly his line—not what he'd call congenial to him."

"But these two? You seem to me pretty sure about finding them on Holmness: too sure, I suggest. Either you've forgotten to say why you're certain, or I may have missed—"

"You are getting keen, I see. No, I have no right to be sure, except that I rely on the girl—and on Hucks. (You ought to know Hucks, by the way; he is a warrior.) But I *am* sure: so sure that I have wired for a steam-launch to be ready by Clatworthy pier. . . . Will you come?"

"I propose to see this affair through," he said deliberately.

Miss Sally gave him a sharp look, and once again nodded approval.

"And, moreover, so sure," she went on, "that I have not wired to send Chichester in search. That's worrying me, I confess; for although Hucks is positive the girl would not start for Holmness without provisions— and on my reading of her, he's right—this is Tuesday, and they have been missing ever since Saturday night, or Sunday morning at latest."

"If that is worrying you," said Chandon, "it may ease your mind to know that there is food and drink on the Island. I built a cottage there two years ago, with a laboratory; I spent six weeks in it this summer; and— well, ships have been wrecked On Holmness, and, as an old naval officer, I've provided for that sort of thing."

Miss Sally slapped her knee. (Her gestures were always unconventional.)

"We shall find 'em there!" she announced. "I'm willing to lay you five to one in what you like."

They changed at Taunton for Fair Anchor. At Fair Anchor Station Sir Miles's motor awaited them. It had been ordered by Parson Chichester, instructed by telegram from Taunton.

The parson himself stood on the platform, but he could give no news of the missing ones.

"We'll have 'em before nightfall," promised Miss Sally. "Come with us, if you will."

So all three climbed into the motor, and were whirled across the moor, and down the steep descent into Clatworthy village, and by Clatworthy pier a launch lay ready for them with a full head of steam.

During the passage few words were said; and indeed the eager throb of the launch's engine discouraged conversation. Chandon steered, with his eyes fixed on the Island. Miss Sally, too, gazed ahead for the most part; but from time to time she contrived a glance at his weary face— grey even in the sunset towards which they were speeding.

Sunset lay broad and level across the Severn Sea, lighting its milky flood with splashes of purple, of lilac, of gold. The sun itself, as they approached the Island, dropped behind its crags, silhouetting them against a sky of palest blue.

They drove into its chill shadow, and landed on the very beach from which the children had watched the stag swim out to meet his death. They climbed up by a pathway winding between thorn and gorse, and on the ridge met the flaming sunlight again.

Miss Sally shielded her eyes.

"They will be here, if anywhere," said Sir Miles, and led the way down the long saddle-back to the entrance of the gully.

"Hullo!" exclaimed he, coming to a halt as the chimneys of the bungalow rose into view above the gorse bushes. From one of them a steady stream of smoke was curling.

"It's a hundred to one!" gasped Miss Sally triumphantly.

They hurried down—to use her own expression—like a pack in full cry. It was Parson Chichester who claimed afterwards that he won by a short length, and lifting the latch, pushed the door open. And this was the scene he opened on, so far as it has since been reconstructed:—

Tilda stood with her back to the doorway and a couple of paces from it, surveying a table laid—so far as Sir Miles's stock of glass and cutlery allowed—for a dinner-party of eight. She was draped from the waist down in a crimson window-curtain, which spread behind her in a full-flowing train. In her hand she held her recovered book—the *Lady's Vade-Mecum*; and she read from it, addressing Arthur Miles, who stood and enacted butler by the side-table, in a posture of studied subservience—

"Dinner bein' announced, the 'ostess will dismiss all care, or at least appear to do so: and, 'avin' marshalled 'er guests in order of precedence (see page 67 supra) will take the arm of the gentleman favoured to conduct 'er. Some light and playful remark will 'ere be not out of place, such as—"

"Well, I'm d——d, if you'll excuse me," ejaculated Miss Sally.

Late that night, in his smoking-room at Meriton, Sir Miles Chandon knocked out the ashes of his pipe against the bars of the grate, rose, stretched himself, and looked about him. Matters had left a bedroom candle ready to hand on a side-table, as his custom was. But Sir Miles took up the lamp instead.

Lamp in hand, he went up the great staircase, and along the unlit fifty yards of corridor to the room where his son lay. In all the great house he could hear no sound, scarcely even the tread of his own foot on the thick carpeting.

He opened the door almost noiselessly and stood by the bed, holding the lamp high.

But noiselessly though Sir Miles had come, the boy was awake. Nor was it in his nature, being awake, to feign sleep. He looked up, blinking a little, but with no fear in his gentle eyes.

His father had not counted on this. He felt an absurd bashfulness tying his tongue. At length he struggled to say—

"'Thought I'd make sure you were comfortable. That's all."

"Oh, yes—thank you. Comfortable and—and—only just thinking a bit."

"We'll have a long talk to-morrow. That girl—she's a good sort, eh?"

"Tilda? . . . Why, of course, she did it *all*. She's the best in the world!"

EPILOGUE

The time is seven years later—seven years and a half, rather; the season, spring; the hour, eight in the morning; and the place, a corner of Culvercoombe, where Miss Sally's terraced garden slopes to meet the wild woodland through an old orchard billowy overhead with pink and white blossom and sheeted underfoot with blue-bells. At the foot of the orchard, and on the very edge of the woodland, lies a small enclosure, where from the head of the slope you catch sight, between the apple trees, of a number of white stones glimmering; but your eyes rest rather on the figure of a girl who has just left the enclosure, and is mounting the slope with a spade on her shoulder.

You watch her, yourself invisible, while she approaches. You might gaze until she has passed, and yet not recognise her for Tilda. She wears a coat and skirt of grey homespun, fashioned for country wear yet faultless in cut, the skirt short enough to reveal a pair of trim ankles cased in shooting-gaiters. Beneath her grey shooting-cap, also of homespun, her hair falls in two broad bands over the brows, and is gathered up at the back of the head in a plain Grecian knot. By the brows, if you had remarked them in days gone by, when neither you nor she gave a second thought to her looks, you might know her again; or perhaps by the poise of the chin, and a touch of decision in the eyes. In all else the child has vanished, and given place to this good-looking girl, with a spring in her gait and a glow on her cheek that tell of clean country nurture.

At the head of the path above the orchard grows an old ash tree, and so leans that its boughs, now bursting into leaf, droop pendent almost as a weeping willow. Between them you catch a glimpse of the Bristol Channel, blue-grey beyond a notch of the distant hills. She pauses here for a look. The moors that stretch for miles on all sides of Culvercoombe are very silent this sunny morning. It is the season when the sportsman pauses and takes breath for a while, and neither gun nor horn is abroad. The birds are nesting; the stag more than a month since has "hung his old head on the pale," and hides while his new antlers are growing amid the young green bracken that would seem to imitate them in its manner of growth; the hinds have dropped their calves, and fare with them unmolested. It is the moors' halcyon time, and the weather to-day well befits it.

Tilda's face is grave, however, as she stands there in the morning sunshine. She is looking back upon the enclosure where the white stones overtop the bluebells. They are headstones, and mark the cemetery where Miss Sally, not ordinarily given to sentiment, has a fancy for interring her favourite dogs.

You guess now why Tilda carries a spade, and what has happened, but may care to know how it happened.

Sir Elphinstone is paying a visit just now to Culvercoombe. He regards Tilda with mixed feelings, and Tilda knows it. The knowledge nettles her a little and amuses her a good deal. Just now Miss Sally and he are improving their appetites for breakfast by an early canter over the moor, and no doubt are discussing her by the way.

Last night, with the express purpose of teasing him, Miss Sally had asked Tilda to take up a book and read to her for a while. The three were seated in the drawing-room after dinner, and Sir Elphinstone beginning to grow impatient for his game of piquet. On the hearth-rug before the fire were stretched Godolphus and three of Miss Sally's prize setters; but Godolphus had the warmest corner, and dozed there stertorously.

The book chanced to be Gautier's *Emaux et Camees*, and Tilda to open it at the *Carnaval de Venise*—

"Il est un vieil air populaire
 Par tous les violons racle,
 Aux abois de chiens en colere
 Par tous les orgues nasille."

She read the first verse with a pure clear accent and paused, with a glance first at the hearth-rug, then at Sir Elphinstone in his chair. Perhaps the sight of him stirred a small flame of defiance. At any rate she closed the book, went straight to the piano, and recklessly rattled out the old tune, at once so silly and haunting. Had she not heard it a thousand times in the old circus days?

Her eyes were on the keyboard. Hardly daring to lift them, she followed up the air with a wild variation and dropped back upon it again—not upon the air pure and simple, but upon the air as it might be rendered by a two-thirds-intoxicated coachful of circus bandsmen. The first half-a-dozen bars tickled Miss Sally in the midriff, so that she laughed aloud. But the laugh ended upon a sharp exclamation, and Tilda, still jangling, looked up as Sir Elphinstone chimed in with a "What the devil!" and started from his chair.

'Dolph was the cause of it. 'Dolph at the first notes had lifted his head, unobserved. Then slowly raising himself on his rheumatic fore-legs, the old dog heaved erect and waddled towards the piano. Even so no one paid any heed to him until, halting a foot or so from the hem of Tilda's skirt, he abased his head to the carpet while his hind-legs strained in a grotesque effort to pitch his body over in a somersault.

It was at this that Sir Elphinstone had exclaimed. Tilda, glancing down sideways across her shoulder, saw and checked a laugh. She understood. She let her fingers rest on a crashing chord, and rose from the music-stool as the dog rolled over on his flank.

"'Dolph! My poor old darling!"

She knelt to him, stretching out her arms. The candlelight fell on them, and on the sheen of her evening frock, and on the small dark curls clustering on the nape of her bowed neck; and by the same light 'Dolph lifted his head and gazed up at her. That look endured for five seconds, perhaps; but in it shone more than she could remember, and more than she could ever forget—a life's devotion compressed into one last leap of the flame, to expire only with life itself. As her hands went swiftly down to him, his tongue strove to lick them; but his head fell back, and his spirit went out into whatever darkness the spirits of dead dogs possess.

You know now why Tilda is not riding this morning, why she carries a spade on her shoulder, and why her face on this sunny morning wears a pensive shadow as she gazes back through the orchard trees. But 'Dolph, the circus mongrel, sleeps among hounds of nobler breed, and shall have a stone as honourable as any.

Now, if you were to look more closely, you might perceive a small stain of green on the front of the homespun skirt otherwise so trim, and might jump to the erroneous conclusion that before leaving the enclosure she had knelt to say a prayer over the snapping of this last tie with her old disreputable life. It is not precisely Christian, perhaps, to pray over a dog's grave; but I am pretty sure that Parson Chichester, who has made some tentative openings towards preparing Tilda for Confirmation, would overlook the irregularity, and even welcome it as a foreshadowing of grace. But Parson Chichester is a discerning man, as well as an honest; and for some reason, although Tilda has long passed the normal age to be prepared for that rite, he has forborne to press her as yet even to be baptised. It will all come in time, he hopes; but he has a queer soul to deal with.

—A queer soul, and (as he perceives) a self-respecting one. If she come to it, she will come in her own time. So let it be confessed, as a secret she would be extremely annoyed to hear revealed, that she did indeed kneel five minutes since, but with no thought of religion; to try rather, over 'Dolph's grave, if she could bend her body back in the old acrobatic trick.

She could not, of course. She had known that she could not even as— with a glance around her to make sure she was unobserved—she had made the effort. Time had taken away the old Tilda with the old 'Dolph. She was a girl grown, a girl with limbs firmed by outdoor sports and country living. And she had learnt much—so much, that to have learnt it she had necessarily forgotten much. You or I, meeting her this morning for the first time, had made no doubt of her being a young lady of rather exceptional breeding.

She looked back to the spot where 'Dolph rested among dogs of loftiest race. She knew that Sir Elphinstone and Miss Sally were discussing her while they rode, and she could hear two words Sir Elphinstone let fall. She repeated them to herself—"Nobody's child."

She did not remember that she had once thanked her gods for it.

The rural postman carried a brass cowhorn, and made a practice of sounding it as he mounted the road leading to Culvercoombe. Its note, sounding through the clear morning air, aroused Tilda from her brown study, and she ran lightly up the slope to catch him on the upper terrace.

He handed her the day's mail—a dozen letters or more, and among them one addressed to her. In the whole world was but one handwriting that ever came for her; recognisable always, though with each post it grew firmer in character.

The envelope bore an Italian stamp and a Neapolitan postmark. Arthur Miles was a midshipman now, soon to be a second-lieutenant; his ship, the *Indomitable*, attached to the Mediterranean fleet. She broke the seal. . . . The letter was a boyish one, full of naval slang, impersonal, the sort of letter growing boys write to their mothers. But Arthur Miles had no mother; and if he wrote to his father, Tilda knew that he wrote more formally.

"We were sent up here," the letter said, "on getting word that Vesuvius meant to erupt badly, and that we might be useful. But the show seems to be hanging fire, and we may be ordered back to Malta at any moment. Half a dozen of us made up a picnic yesterday, to have a look at the crater at close quarters. We cooked some eggs on it, to show our unconcern, and while we were cooking them up came an American, who had pitched camp in the foolhardiest spot. Guess why—to paint it! Guess who he was—why, Jessup! Do you remember Jessup? He introduced himself, and I knew him at once; but he did not know me, and I did not enlighten him. He said that the Art of the Future must depend on the development of wireless telegraphy, and that in the meanwhile he was just marking time with earthquakes."

Tilda, having read thus far, looks up at the sound of horses' hoofs. Miss Sally and Sir Elphinstone are returning from their ride.

"And, after all, why not?" Miss Sally is saying.

"The very mistake his father made!"

"Homoeopathy is one of my fads, remember."

"A nobody's child!"

"True; and so would *he* have been, but for her."

Milton Keynes UK
Ingram Content Group UK Ltd.
UKHW031258251024
450245UK00004B/458